Good Boys, Bad Hombres

T0390644

GOOD BOYS, BAD HOMBRES

The Racial Politics of Mentoring Latino Boys in Schools

MICHAEL V. SINGH

University of Minnesota Press
Minneapolis
London

A portion of chapter 5 was previously published as "Seven Justice-Oriented Principles for Men of Color Working with Boys of Color," *Project MALES Practice Brief* 1 (September 2021): 1–10; available at https://diversity.utexas.edu/projectmales/. A different version of portions of chapter 5 was published in "Resisting the Neoliberal Role Model: Latino Male Mentors' Perspectives on the Intersectional Politics of Role Modeling," *American Educational Research Journal* 58, no. 2 (April 2021): 283–314.

Published by the University of Minnesota Press
111 Third Avenue South, Suite 290
Minneapolis, MN 55401-2520
http://www.upress.umn.edu

ISBN 978-1-5179-1297-0 (hc)
ISBN 978-1-5179-1298-7 (pb)

Library of Congress record available at https://lccn.loc.gov/2024000282

Printed on acid-free paper

The University of Minnesota is an equal-opportunity educator and employer.

CONTENTS

SUPPORTING LATINO BOYS IN THE ERA OF NEOLIBERAL MULTICULTURALISM

On a warm spring evening in 2018, I attended a dinner celebration at a local country club. Under a vast white tent perched on the edge of the golf course, Latinx families mingled with one another while helping themselves to a buffet-style dinner. Music played softly in the background, covering popular songs in genres like cumbia, merengue, and traditional Mexican rancheras. The host of this celebration was Pueblo Unido, a large, nonprofit community development corporation in the California city of Arroyo Seco.[1] The night's festivities were in celebration of the boys and families of Latino Male Success (LMS), Pueblo Unido's Latino male mentorship program that partners with ten middle and high schools in Arroyo Seco Unified School District (ASUSD). LMS serves roughly 225 boys in ASUSD by offering each school a school-day LMS course, run by a single mentor, who instructs students on good academic practices, teaches lessons on Chicano/Latino manhood, and serves as a positive male role model in the boys' lives. This celebration, described as a ceremonia (ceremony) on the flyer, represented a rite of passage into an "honorable manhood" for boys who had completed a full year in the program.

I had spent the last ten months volunteering and conducting research with LMS, and the ceremonia marked the end of my first school year with the organization. It was the first of two school years I would spend volunteering with LMS. That evening, after reaching the reception area, I took an open seat and introduced myself to some of the families sitting at my table. Although this event did not mark an academic promotion for the boys who had participated in the program, the energy surrounding the dinner felt similar to a graduation. Some parents and students wore semi-formal attire appropriate for a wedding, while others appeared to have come straight from their jobs to attend the event.

As I mingled with the families, I was happy to meet the parents and siblings of several of the boys I had worked with throughout the year. One mother raved about Mr. Iván, a high school mentor I had been shadowing twice a week. She felt he had successfully kept her tenth grade son out of trouble by providing strong but caring discipline. Like her son, Mr. Iván had grown up in North Arroyo Seco, and she made it clear that she saw Mr. Iván as a wonderful role model for boys from the neighborhood, "un buen ejemplo" (a good example). She only wished that her other son could have had a role model like Mr. Iván when he was in high school. Another parent, the father of a middle school boy I did not know, remarked that he had admittedly thought LMS was simply a class at school and had not realized it was such a big deal. "¿Un gran honor, no?" he remarked, gesturing to the grandeur of the country club.

As the ceremony began, the 10 mentors of the LMS program gathered the students from their respective schools into small groups near the front of the banquet tent near a microphone. Following a brief welcome statement by two LMS and Pueblo Unido administrators, the mic was passed to a student leader from each group. Speaking to the crowd of beaming parents, the boys expressed their gratitude to LMS for giving them the opportunity to be in the program and thanked their mentors for putting them on track to become hombres de palabra (men of honor)—a term commonly used in program literature and curriculum. As one boy put it, his mentor truly believed in the man he "could become." Following the boys' words, the LMS program director proceeded to introduce the evening's keynote speaker, Refugio Pérez.

"¡Hola familia! ¿Cómo están?" shouted Pérez as he took the mic.

Refugio Pérez is a young entrepreneur and motivational speaker. Throughout his short but productive career he has worked for several of "the world's largest corporations" including "Tesla, Apple, Salesforce, Uber, and General Motors" (as advertised on the LMS ceremonia flyer). Pérez is the author of motivational books, and his Amazon book page describes him as "the epitome of the American Dream" and "the truest definition of a bootstrapper." His most popular book, *The Parenthood Guide*, is a guide for parents to "help their children overcome adversity through an entrepreneur mindset." His speech presented a vision of Latino male achievement that mirrored the values of the LMS program, one they hoped the boys and families would carry with them into the future.

A charismatic speaker, Pérez addressed the crowd primarily in Spanish, but he also switched to English sometimes to reiterate an important point or to specifically address the students. The speech began with a dramatic interactive activity with the crowd. Pulling out a crisp $100 bill, Pérez proceeded to discuss the importance of perseverance and a winning mindset. He then asked abruptly, "¿Quién lo quiere? [Who wants it?]," and thrust the bill in the air. There was no answer. "¿Quién lo quiere?" repeated Pérez, this time louder. "Yo [Me]," responded a few voices in the crowd. "¿Quién lo quiere?" shouted Pérez, this time even louder. "¡Yo!" boomed the response. Pérez repeated the question several more times as the crowd's energy began to grow.

"¿Quiere que subamos y le quitemos el dinero? [Does he want us to go up and take the money?]," asked a student's father.

From the name tag on his oil-stained mechanic's shirt, I could see the man's name was Martín. He looked curious and captivated by the waving money.

"No sé [I'm not sure]," I responded.

Finally, a young girl, presumably the younger sister of one of the students, ran up to the stage with the encouragement of her mother and snatched the $100 bill. The crowd roared.

"As you can see, we are not messing around here," joked Pérez in English.

Pérez continued his speech by sharing his own life story as motivation to the boys. He came to the United States at the age of 14 after growing up in rural Guatemala, where he had tended to cows and cultivated beans and corn. When he arrived he spoke no English and was left alone as a teen to work and go to school. He faced adversity and tragedy, yet this did not stop him from "trabajando por unas de las corporaciones más grandes del mundo [working for some of the largest corporations in the world]." He then spoke in English to address the boys specifically:

> So jóvenes [young people], if you sometimes use the excuse that my parents are not around and that's why I can't make it, just know, if Refugio can make it without his father, then I can make it, too; if Refugio made it without his mother, I can make it, too. If he learned English with three girlfriends, I'm going to get six!

This last line sparked laughter in the crowd. Two boys in the background gave one another a small handshake. Pérez had referenced his earlier joke that when he was advised to get an English-speaking girlfriend to learn the language, he had decided to pursue three girls instead.

Pérez's speech lasted roughly thirty minutes and reiterated themes of individual perseverance, hard work, and a steadfast belief in the American dream. Beyond the content of the speech, however, there was a performative element to the keynote intended to signal how an entrepreneurial mindset could ignite a physical transformation. As Pérez's speech reached its final minutes, he began to slowly unbutton his casual shirt, revealing a clean and pressed dress shirt underneath. While continuing to deliver his message, he retrieved a bag from behind the stage and removed a necktie. He skillfully tied the necktie while maintaining eye contact with the crowd. He then removed a sport coat from his bag and put it on to complete his businessman ensemble. The crowd stood up and applauded what had been an exciting keynote speech. From across the hall, I made eye contact with Mr. Javier, a middle school mentor I had been shadowing throughout the school year. I knew him to be among the most politicized mentors, frequently teaching extracurricular lessons on racism and inequality. He shook his head softly, signaling his discomfort with the speech. As we passed by one another later in the ceremony, he stopped me for a moment: "We gotta talk about the speech later, yeah? You know I'm not with that message."

Despite the motivational message and drama of Pérez's speech, behind the scenes of the ceremonia that evening there was a deeper ideological dispute embedded in LMS's mentoring program. This tension, which Mr. Javier's reaction to the speech gestured at, is connected to larger debates surrounding the politics of supporting young people of color in schools. In the context of LMS, this tension arose from contrasting rationales behind the imagined purpose of the LMS program and more complicated questions surrounding *why* and *how* Latino men are asked to be mentors and role models for Latino boys in schools in the first place. In Pérez's keynote speech, entrepreneurialism and respectability were presented as foundational to the narrative of Latino male success. In his own story, Pérez described how he overcame adversity through hard work and a no-excuses attitude. While his story demonstrates a classic version of the American dream, Pérez offered a slight revision by focusing less on the opportunities given by the state and more on the global corporations for whom he had worked. These companies, which he and others named many times throughout the ceremony, marked a new terrain in which young Latino men might find acceptance and economic opportunity. Through Pérez's example and the story of his transformation, the boys and families of LMS witnessed the power of the program to change the trajectory of the students—as well as the students themselves—*if* they shed bad habits, avoided excuses, and invested in their human capital and potential productivity.

Despite being presented in the keynote speech that evening, this perspective was not held by all the mentors at LMS. While some in the program strongly supported this goal, others harbored mixed feelings. The latter questioned if this was the type of social justice work they had hoped to accomplish as youth workers. Others, like Mr. Javier, were outwardly critical of the goals of LMS and its funders. These subversive mentors challenged the principles of LMS by teaching extracurricular lessons on racism and rejecting the idea that they represented this archetypical "good role model" that LMS promoted in its literature.

Far from neutral, school-based mentorship programs for Latino boys like LMS bring to their projects an array of assumptions and values surrounding the root causes of the problems facing Latino boys, as well as the most ideal solutions to these problems. An enduring belief that threatens to overtake the goals of school-based mentorship (particularly in disenfranchised communities of color) is that individuals themselves are the primary sources of their own economic marginalization through poor choices and self-harming behavior. This belief, commonly known as the "culture of poverty," asserts that social mobility can be obtained only when individuals take responsibility for changing the way they act. Yet this focus on individual habits and character excludes and denies the root causes of inequality in the United States: unequal opportunities, histories of racial exclusion, mass incarceration, systemic disenfranchisement along the lines of race, class, gender, and immigration status, and free-market economies that produce wealth for a few and poverty for many (Dávila 2004; Gándara and Contreras 2009; Gilmore 2007; Kohl-Arenas 2015). Although "culture of poverty" arguments have long been condemned as racist (Yosso 2005), a number of critical race scholars in education have pointed to a resurgence in deficit-oriented youth programming that focuses intensely on the character and actions of individual students (Baldridge 2019; Love 2019), as well as the ability of educators of color to correct these "problematic" behaviors (Brockenbrough 2015; Endo 2019; M. V. Singh 2018). These interventions can advance "culture of poverty" arguments *even* while seeking to be culturally relevant and authentic to the targeted community. At LMS this was manifest in the way the program stressed personal responsibility and a no-excuses attitude among students. For LMS, success would be achieved through improving the character of its students and helping them adopt respectable and responsible life practices. Latino male respectability was to be modeled by LMS mentors, and often intersected with the ability to perform dominant and heteropatriarchal images of manhood.[2]

In this book I document how LMS—a large, multi-school mentoring program for Latino boys—reproduced a deficit-oriented vision of Latino boys by centering an archetypical "positive Latino male role model" as the imagined solution to their educational struggles. However, this model, which helped shape a commonsense idea among students about how boys should perform Latino manhood, drew directly on visions of a hegemonic and heteropatriarchal masculinity and encouraged students to internalize personal struggles that were imposed on them by systemic racism. Throughout this book I describe the role model as a figure, image, or archetype. This framing challenges the notion that there are inherent or universal qualities conducive to a good role model (Martino and Rezai-Rashti 2012). Instead, the image of this positive Latino male role model—and its presentation as a good example for Latino boys in LMS—was directly shaped by racial power. Intersecting discourses of race, gender, class, and sexuality (among others) converged within the notion of the role model and influenced how proper and productive ways of being for Latino boys were (re)imagined. This reconfiguration of Latino manhood, as I discuss in this book, is one of the consequences of the way LMS, like many other urban education programs, increasingly integrate neoliberal multiculturalist ideologies into their programming, while following racial and heteropatriarchal logics that undergird the perceived need for this kind of "good" example.

At LMS, the mentors were presented to students as embodying an idea of success that drew on characteristics of personal accountability and hegemonic masculinity in the face of racism and structural inequality. These characteristics comprised a broader framing that positioned mentors to be dominant patriarchs who were "successful against the odds," even if some did not see themselves that way at all. As I discuss throughout this book, this tension led the mentors themselves to struggle to understand their position as good role models, and in some cases to reject it. But this inability or lack of interest on the part of the mentors to embody this ideal is also tightly connected to the broader context in which this "good male role model" for Latino boys has emerged—specifically, the historical marginalization that Latino boys in the United States face in schools. Ultimately, the story of LMS highlights how ideological shifts in urban education influence how we make sense of the marginalization of Latino boys, and how successful lives for these boys are imagined.

The 1990s and early 2000s saw an emergence of scholarship documenting the punishment and marginalization experienced by Latino boys in U.S. schools (Gándara and Contreras 2009; Huber et al. 2006; N. Lopez 2002; Saenz and Ponjuan 2009). In his research, sociologist Victor Rios has described how Latino boys regularly experience surveillance, microaggressions, and outright disdain on school campuses. Rios finds schools functioning as a key component of a larger youth control complex in which Latino boys' lives become defined by punishment and pushout.[3] Rios's work joins a large corpus of literature describing the effects of the discipline and punishment experienced by Latino boys, Black boys, and boys of color in school (Huerta 2018; N. Lopez 2002; Malagon 2010; Nolan 2011; Rios 2017). Much of this literature describes the disciplinary processes in which schools and society (re)produce the racist image of what Ann Arnett Ferguson (2001) has described as the *bad boy*.

In contrast to the literature on punishment, however, *Good Boys, Bad Hombres* tells a slightly different and untold story of youth control in schools by focusing on the politics of empowerment and inclusion. In the following pages, I hope to shed light on the way affirmative racial discourses converge in youth empowerment programs to reimagine the problems facing Latino boys, as well as what empowerment should look like. In LMS, I found that Latino boyhoods are shaped less by traditional forms of punishment than through an *invitation* to a respectable and productive masculinity. This invitation to a positive Latino manhood was framed as authentic and culturally rooted in Latinx tradition.

In this context, the archetype of the positive male role model, the "good example" that the mentors at LMS were framed as embodying, represented a unique blending of Latinx cultural signifiers with qualities conducive to a proper neoliberal subjectivity. This was posed in contrast to the notion of the "bad boy" that circulates in the boys' lives through social media, popular culture, and day-to-day interactions in their community and schools. The notion of the bad boy—a racialized figure of dark boyhood that is prone to delinquency and disinterested in education—served to warn against the deviant practices often associated with Latino men and boys, as well as Blackness.[4] In Arroyo Seco, bad boys were at risk of becoming bad hombres.

Despite being framed as new and positive, however, I argue that the figure of the good LMS mentor, who was positioned as an archetype of respectable Latino manhood, was also built atop similar deficit-based ideologies. This paternalistic expression of empowerment functioned as a mechanism of control and conditioning. Here, male empowerment not only constructed Latino boys as potentially problematic but also obscured the role of racism in the boys' educational struggles by imposing ideologies of personal accountability and developing empowerment strategies that, in some cases, drew on problematic dialectics of racial competition and anti-Blackness. *Good Boys, Bad Hombres* is a story that reveals a broader lesson about the way race and masculinity are woven into neoliberalism[5] and how Latino boys and their families are affected by the concrete expression of that ideology in their schools. Through an ethnographic investigation into the framing and practice of a school-based mentorship program for Latino boys, this book shows how neoliberal multiculturalism and the turn to empower boys of color constructs a unique and contested vision for Latino manhood in schools and beyond.

LMS IN ARROYO SECO: RESPONDING TO A CRISIS IN THE SCHOOL DISTRICT

Arroyo Seco is a large West Coast city known for its racial diversity and rich cultural expression. Although sensationalized in the media for crime and poverty, Arroyo Seco is the prideful homeplace for sizable Black, Latinx, Asian, and American Indian communities. Its many neighborhoods are vibrant hubs of cultural exchange, and political artwork and murals are sprinkled throughout the city. In North Arroyo Seco, the region located north of the downtown area, the city's demographics are primarily African American and Latinx. Among the diverse Latinx community, Mexicans and Mexican Americans are the largest demographic. They are joined by a sizable and growing population of Central Americans, primarily from El Salvador, Honduras, and Guatemala, many of whom are Indigenous Maya. Like many urban centers in the United States, Arroyo Seco is presently undergoing rapid renovations to its previously deteriorated urban infrastructure to attract capital and investment. This revitalization has primarily benefited (and facilitated) the recent influx of middle- and high-income residents, overly represented by white newcomers. The boom of local industries and reinvestment in the city has sparked rapid gentrification. U.S. Census data for Arroyo Seco reports a steady decline of particularly Black residents since the early 2000s, and a recent surge of new, higher-income whites.

Despite the massive accumulation of capital in Arroyo Seco, as well as neighboring cities in the region, Arroyo Seco's public schools have remained impoverished and in severe debt. The schools continue to serve an overwhelming majority of students of color. The district is led by a diverse and predominantly nonwhite school board and superintendent's office. In the past decades, the district has been a battleground of neoliberal school reform. This has led to widespread community school closures, a sharp rise in charter schools, and fierce clashes between district leadership, corporate philanthropists, and the teachers' union.

Latino Male Success was founded in 2010, and, as a school-based mentorship program for Latino boys, it has evolved within the context of Arroyo Seco's larger economic, demographic, and ideological changes. It was founded and is currently managed by Pueblo Unido, a local nonprofit 501(c)(3) community development corporation whose mission is to improve the quality of life of Arroyo Seco residents, with a focus on its predominantly Latinx neighborhoods on the north side of the city. The LMS program is a relatively small representation of Pueblo Unido's overall efforts in the community, which include job training, annual community cultural events, housing development, and microfinance. Although it is under the jurisdiction of Pueblo Unido, LMS receives a small portion of its budget from Arroyo Seco Unified School District and is frequently portrayed in the media as a district program. The program was established in 2010 through a partnership between Pueblo Unido and ASUSD. When it was founded, LMS originally served just four schools. However, in recent years it has expanded to ten middle and high schools, serving students ages twelve to twenty years old. Each school site was staffed with one full-time LMS mentor. Part of my research for this book included shadowing the mentors of three different LMS schools over the course of two school years (2017–18 and 2018–19).

ASUSD's decentralized structure can be categorized as a portfolio model of district governance, in which the district manages its community schools as well as a range of contracts with charter schools, and school-based services run by external organizations such as foundations and nonprofits (Bulkley, Henig, and Levin 2010). Pueblo Unido's LMS is one such external program partnering with ASUSD to offer school-day services. The Arroyo Seco district selected the schools in which LMS now operates based on those schools' low academic performance as well as high numbers of Latinx students. Consequently, all the schools in which LMS operates are located on the north side of Arroyo Seco, home to the largest Latinx communities in the city. All schools partnering with LMS were ASUSD public schools with Latinx populations ranging from 32 percent to 71 percent of the student body.[6] LMS class sizes ranged from roughly 15 to 30 students. This allowed about 6 percent of Latino boys in the overall school district to access the mentorship program. LMS mentors run period-long classes during the regular school day as either an advisory course or a Chicano studies class.[7]

In addition to running their one class period a day (or two if mentors separated certain grade levels), the broad and at times ambiguous duties of the mentors included maintaining contact with parents, conducting regular check-ins with students, and advocating for students among teachers and administration in academic and disciplinary matters. Mentors ranged from twenty-three to thirty years old, and all but one held a bachelor's degree. All mentors self-identified as Latino men, and the vast majority were Mexican American. Being a Latino man played a key factor in their being hired in the first place, and it was through this status that they were seen as viable models of a respectable and successful Latino manhood. Despite such similarities, the mentors were an eclectic bunch. Their mentoring styles, approaches to professionalism, and politics greatly varied. As a Latino man who was in his late twenties during the time of this ethnography, I believe my identity also played a large role in my invitation to join LMS as a researcher and unofficial mentor.[8]

During my two years with LMS, I regularly observed two middle school classrooms, run by Mr. Javier and Mr. Antonio, and one high school classroom, run by Mr. Iván. At the end of my first year, Mr. Antonio left LMS, and Mr. Sergio was hired to run his middle school group.[9] While their roles in the schools varied, the most important duty in the eyes of the LMS administrators (and many mentors themselves) was to build genuine connections with the boys and serve as a positive Latino male role model in their lives. But as this book outlines, this ideal male role model at LMS, even as it was constructed around an idea of love and care, came filled with contradictions.

AGAINST THE ODDS: EMPOWERING BOYS OF COLOR

The recent emergence of boy-oriented racial/ethnic empowerment programs like LMS intersects with a number of specific ideological and economic trends in the United States. I argue that at the core of this turn to empower boys has been the widespread framing of Latino boys as a societal problem that must be fixed.

In popular culture, Latino boys are often depicted as in crisis. As the narrative goes, Latino boys navigate dangerous communities and dilapidated schools in which violence is ubiquitous and success is nonexistent. Criminal temptation is everywhere. These portrayals capitalize on racist stereotypes associated with Latinx communities, often uncritically sensationalizing issues of poverty, gang violence, and social abandonment (Yosso and García 2010). Despite these dramatized representations, it must be acknowledged that Latino boys do regularly experience very real inequality and pushout in schools. However, defining these experiences through a narrative of crisis suggests that the problem is recent and temporary rather than chronic and perpetual (Noguera 1996), and many scholars who study the experiences of Latino boys have argued for the importance of avoiding this kind of narrative—even as the academic and educational marketplace remains eager to consume stories of damage and crisis (Tuck 2009). Despite these concerns, among a large segment of public and private school administrators, nonprofit organizations, and corporate funders, the language of "crisis," "peril," "at-risk," and "endangered" has come to define how Latino boys are understood in schools.

In response to this crisis, the past twenty years have seen an explosion of educational intervention strategies aimed at addressing and empowering Latino boys, Black boys, and the popular grouping *boys of color*[10] (Brockenbrough 2018; Brooms, Clark, and Smith 2018;

Cervantes, Burmicky, Martinez 2022; Harper 2015; Huerta, Howard, and Haro 2020; Sáenz, Ponjuán, and Figueroa 2016; Villavicencio 2021; Watson, Sealey-Ruiz, and Jackson 2016). This emerging industry has widely been facilitated through private enterprise or public–private partnerships and represents an ideological blending of community interests and corporate philanthropic values (Baldridge 2019; Dumas 2016a). While programming for boys of color manifests in a variety of ways, the strategy of providing boys with mentors and role models has become a widespread and popular approach (Endo 2019; Hall 2006; Martino 2015; Odih 2002). As an early advocate of these programs, educational leader Pedro Noguera (2003) described the power of these programs in their ability to "affirm the identities" of boys of color as well as provide access to "positive role models and social support" that can "buffer young people from the pressures within their schools and communities" (451).

The mentorship program and partnership between LMS and the ASUSD serves as a prime example of this kind of program targeting boys and young men of color. These programs span a wide range of educational settings, including K–12 school-day programs, after-school programs, undergraduate university programs, and mentoring programs at the graduate and professional level. On the national stage, former president Barack Obama's My Brother's Keeper (MBK) program is an exemplar of this trend. MBK was a 2014 White House initiative that sought to create opportunities and improve life outcomes for boys and young men of color. Following its presidential establishment, the program transitioned into the private sector, becoming a primary initiative of the Obama Foundation. These programs seek to establish homeplaces on school campuses where students may increase their sense of belonging, build camaraderie, affirm their identities, and activate the sociocultural wealth they bring to their education (Brooms 2016; Brooms, Clark, and Smith 2018; Kugiya, Burmicky, and Sáenz 2020; Sáenz et al. 2015). Crucial components of these programs are loving and caring men of color who serve as mentors, role models, and guides that help students navigate institutional spaces never created with their success in mind (Hall 2006).

While these initiatives have begun to chip away at what continues to be immense academic inequalities, it is important to acknowledge that challenges facing boys, men, and entire communities of color are material and structural. The Latinx communities from Arroyo Seco, for example, face the same kinds of injustices as other communities of color across the country: food insecurity, unequal access to healthcare, labor exploitation, police terror, environmental racism, housing discrimination, and poorly resourced schools. In many ways, these issues intersect and influence one another. Although the role model/mentor approach offers a widely accepted and commonsense solution to increasing student achievement (i.e., academically successful men of color can help guide boys of color to be successful), this book reveals the ways this recent wave of mentorship programs for boys and men of color have reproduced harmful narratives surrounding boys of color by drawing on problematic racial and gender discourses as well as notions of anti-Blackness.

As neoliberal ideas regarding entrepreneurship and personal responsibility have become increasingly integrated into American public education—directly mixing with both old and new racial discourses surrounding Latino manhood—other, more structural strategies for political struggle and the right for public education have been abandoned as primary objectives of mainstream social justice movements. Instead, foundations and the private sector lead (and fund) the charge for educational equality and racial inclusion through promises of diversity, technocratic fixes, and innovative expertise (Spence 2016). But this approach, which draws from what critical race scholars refer to as *neoliberal multiculturalism* (Melamed 2011), has a profound impact on how racism is understood and addressed, turning structural racial discrimination into an individual problem, absolving the state of its responsibility for racial violence against communities of color, and diverting financial resources from more comprehensive forms of racial justice. The archetype of Latino manhood that the mentors at LMS were expected to represent and impart in their work with Latino boys illustrates this broader shift. LMS sought to offer a new and successful future for (some) Latino boys in Arroyo Seco by developing their character, maximizing their human capital, and improving their grades. The figure of the mentor—framed as embodying an adult male Latino role model who had conquered and escaped the risks that Latino boys supposedly face to become a contributing member of society—played a central part in that empowerment project.

For many of the boys, having a Latino male mentor (an expert from the private sector) had a positive impact on their academic performance and behavior in school. For others, however, there was little improvement or even a declining academic performance over the course of the two years I was with the program. However, my primary focus in this book is not what makes Latino male mentoring programs successful. Latino boys, like all students, respond positively to caring educators, rigorous and culturally sustaining curriculum, and a safe and well-resourced learning and living environment. Instead, *Good Boys, Bad Hombres* explores the ways contemporary racial discourse informs how a successful manhood is understood for programs targeting Latino boys and asks how the figure of the positive Latino male role model is constructed.

As this book outlines, I found neoliberal multiculturalism functioning as a form of governmentality in LMS. The notion of governmentality describes the ways a unique knowledge of race and Latino maleness shapes how Latino men and boys are (self-)defined and understood.[11] In LMS, a deficit orientation to Latino male mentorship framed students as in danger of adopting a problematic or deviant masculinity. Administrators, funders, and LMS implicitly or explicitly framed Latino boys as unmotivated, prone to violence, and lacking traditional heteropatriarchal values. The program and funders presented this failure of proper manhood—and its absence in the Latinx community—as a primary source of underachievement among Latino boys. To address this, the program was explicitly designed around "character development"— focusing on the attitudes, values, and behaviors—of a proper Latino maleness. This framing of the racial achievement gap, however, obscured structural racism in Arroyo Seco and reified racial stereotypes associated with Latino boys. The iconic image of the "bad boy" served as a guiding principle that justified the need for this character development, and the figure of the "positive Latino male role model" was often framed as a solution to the bad boy—the former's potential for productivity and success justified the policing and disinvestment of the latter.

Although there were instances where mentors and students welcomed the values that LMS sought to impress on them, at other times both mentors and students identified contradictions in the goals of the program and sought to subvert these ideals. Some students, for example, challenged the notion that Latino boys needed strict rules and discipline, and repudiated pushes for respectability; instead, they discussed the need for more prioritization of joy, pleasure, and critical race education. Some mentors also resisted these kinds of deficit-framing techniques (particularly Mr. Javier and Mr. Agustín, who were tremendously critical of the politics of their organization and whose work is discussed in detail in chapters 5 and 6). These mentors resisted LMS's deficit approach through critical mentoring practices, engagements with anti-Black framings of Latinx education, and queering representations of Latino manhood. Overall, the story of LMS describes the ways the racial politics of neoliberalism come to define the goals and practices of Latino male empowerment. While these values were at times accepted and normalized, mentors, students, and community members also challenged the rationale and goals of the program, reimagining what intersectional racial justice might look like beyond neoliberal multiculturalism and questioning how Latino men and boys could be warriors, allies, or co-conspirators in this vision.

LIBERAL RACE DISCOURSES IN THE UNITED STATES

The story of LMS is a story about the ways shifting discourse of race and racism frame how we understand racial inequality in schools. Although racism and white supremacy have been key organizing principles of the United States since its inception, race is a discourse constantly in flux (Hall 1996). As time passes and social norms change, so do forms of racial knowledge. The ability of racism to establish itself as rational and legitimate in a given era has made it insidious and durable, and racial inequalities maintain their legitimacy as new racial discourse emerges to justify these inequalities (Omi and Winant 2014). Nikhil Singh (2004) offers an understanding of racialization that posits race as a value-making discourse independent from essentialist notions of a white/nonwhite binary:

> We need to recognize the technology of race as something more than skin color or biophysical essence, but precisely as those historic repertoires and cultural and signifying systems that stigmatize and depreciate one form of humanity for the purpose of another's health, development, safety, profit, and pleasure. (223)

This flexible definition of race is useful in tracing the changing nature of racial discourse across time and space.

Following the end of World War II, critical race theorists identified white supremacy as entering a phase of permanent crisis, spurred by racial contradictions revealed in the war (Winant 2002). Widespread condemnation of Nazism and the Jewish Holocaust highlighted racial contradictions among the Allied powers, in which white supremacy had also been foundational in social and economic relations. In the United States, the civil rights movement emerged to condemn Jim Crow segregation and the continued acceptance of stark, racial prejudice and policy around the country. Around the globe, anticolonial movements took hold, exposing the hypocrisies of colonialism, politicizing race, and demanding an end to white supremacy as a world order. Howard Winant (2002) describes this moment as a "racial break," stating the post–World War II period represents a moment in which these contradictory sociopolitical forces combined to "discredit and finally undo the old world racial system" (141). Colonialism and its corresponding capitalist relationships had relied on white supremacy as an organizing principle of race, geopolitics, and capitalism. As the United States rose to global preeminence, it was forced to manage the racial contradictions and antagonisms of racial capitalism by rearticulating the relationship between capitalism and racial ideology. Following the racial break, white-supremacist ideologies have subsided, as race has become rearticulated through liberal symbolic frameworks (e.g., equality, market individualism, civil liberties). Jodi Melamed (2006, 2011) offers a genealogy of "liberal" racial discourse that has defined how race is understood in the United States in the post–World War II era. I will take a moment to overview these shifts to better frame how a unique understanding of race and racism—one focused on individual empowerment and even antiracism—influences the goals and practices of a program like LMS today.

Racial Liberalism

By the 1940s, racial liberalism had begun to displace explicit forms of white supremacy as the dominant racial discourse in the United States. Racial liberalism challenged the notion that race was rooted in innate, biological human differences and popularized the belief that discrimination and political disenfranchisement of nonwhite people should be unlawful in a liberal democracy. Although this transition was not immediate, the civil rights movement pushed the United States to redefine itself as a nation formally against racism. While many still believed (and continue to believe) in traditional forms of white supremacy, the rise of racial liberalism re-signified expressions of racism such as slavery, housing and school segregation, formal discrimination, and racial lynching/murder as counter to American ideals (Melamed 2011).

Although official and state-sponsored antiracism in the United

States, first articulated through racial liberalism, established racial equality as a national imperative, it narrowed and defined the scope of antiracist thinking. As opposed to reparations or a dismantling of racialized capitalist relations in the United States and around the globe (Marable 1999; Robinson 2000), racial liberalism defined legitimate antiracism as the inclusion of nonwhite people as full and protected citizens in the U.S. capitalist liberal democracy. This extension of civil rights, social integration, and legal equality to African Americans and other people of color was premised on the notion that racial minorities would become equals to whites when given the full benefits of citizenship. When this did not occur, racial liberalism (re)coded race through cultural explanations as to why racial minorities continued to be economically and socially marginalized. Melamed (2006) contends:

> Racial liberalism's model of race as culture normed by an idealized American national culture also made it possible to ascribe stigma to segments of African American society without the act of ascription appearing to be an act of racial power. Instead, it appeared as fair, expected, and right. It did so by differentiating between "healthy" African American cultural formations (those aligned with idealized American cultural norms and nationalist sentiment) and "pathological" ones. Racial liberalism then explained Black cultural "pathology" to be both the effect of racism (that is, cultural maladaptation to social prejudice) and the cause of Black inequality, in effect deploying liberal antiracism to renew racial stigma and to disavow structural racism. (8)

By granting liberal freedoms and re-signifying Americanism as racially inclusive, racial liberalism served as a new and legitimate racial discourse in the United States. Although the global capitalist economy continued to extract surplus values from people of color (both at home and around the world), this new language depoliticized the link between race and economic relations.

Liberal Multiculturalism

The legal victories of the civil rights era would immediately demonstrate their inability to resolve racial inequality in the United States as Black people and other racial minorities continued to live in impoverished and (less-explicitly) segregated neighborhoods. Radical antiracist movements in the late 1960s and 1970s (such as the American Indian

Movement, Black Power Movement, and Chicano Movement) emerged to challenge the continued racism terrorizing communities of color. To manage this racial upheaval, Melamed (2011) explains, U.S. racial discourse absorbed a culture of multiculturalism. While these radical antiracist movements challenged core tenets of the capitalist U.S. state (including the validity of its very existence on stolen land), liberal multiculturalism sought to include racial diversity into the meaning of Americanism.[12] If racial liberalism reconstructed white supremacy as un-American, liberal multiculturalism sought to construct the United States as an openly multicultural, diverse, and liberal nation-state.

Like racial liberalism, liberal multiculturalism reconstituted how racial inequality was understood and addressed. On one hand, it celebrated cultural diversity (e.g., diversity in television, literature, music, and school curriculum) and multicultural political representation (e.g., the Congressional Black and Hispanic Caucuses; established in 1971 and 1976, respectively). On the other hand, material and targeted forms of antiracism actually became taboo. To single out one race, even to redress racial inequality, was viewed as unfair or even "reverse racist." According to Melamed (2011):

> Liberal multiculturalism socialized whites to see themselves as good antiracists by virtue of their antiracist feeling and desire for diversity, even as whites continued to accrue unearned benefits from material and social arrangements that favored them. At the same time, the cultural pluralism as the base of liberal-multicultural orders made any rebalancing of the free market or individual rights toward more even racial outcomes appear as an affront against basic fairness. (37)

In short, liberal multiculturalism set the conditions for color-blind racism (Bonilla-Silva 2009) as the U.S. embraced its multicultural society while condemning explicit efforts of racial reparation as "reverse racism." Although I describe neoliberal multiculturalism as the dominant contemporary racial discourse, liberal multicultural tenets and values continue to circulate and manifest in today's racial landscape.

Neoliberal Multiculturalism

Beginning in the early 2000s and continuing into the present, neoliberal multiculturalism is the third and most recent phase of liberal race hegemony. Melamed (2006) describes neoliberal multiculturalism as a racial discourse in which "multicultural reference masks the centrality of race and racism to neoliberalism" (1). Like the other liberal race discourses, neoliberal multiculturalism abandons white superiority rhetoric rooted in innate racial difference and instead engenders new racial subjects by inviting people of color to embody a respectable and productive neoliberal subjectivity in a multicultural and market-driven society. Through the extension of multiculturalism in the global market, neoliberal multiculturalism reconciles the extreme racial inequality created through neoliberalism by distinguishing between the proper multicultural subjects and the culturally stagnant racial other. While multicultural subjects are lauded as prime examples of multicultural world citizens, those dispossessed by neoliberalism are framed as unwilling or unable to take advantage of inclusion and opportunity and thus deserving of the increased poverty, war, incarceration, and early death brought on by racial neoliberal politics (Gilmore 2007; Wacquant 2009).

Despite the centrality of race and racism within neoliberal economic and social policy, Melamed (2006) argues that as a racial discourse, neoliberalism adopts a multicultural rhetoric that frames communities of color not as politically, socially, and economically disenfranchised, but rather as not fully integrated into the benevolence of the free market. The notions of diversity, fair competition, consumer choice, and entrepreneurialism are seen as leading to racial equality in a fair and unprejudiced system of capital. Here, the market and private sector are not viewed as perpetuating and profiting from racism and poverty; rather, these are innovative champions of diversity and inclusion. The centrality of race in contemporary forms of racial violence (e.g., housing insecurity, poverty wages, defunded social welfare, increased funding of policing and war industry) is juxtaposed against the private sector's newfound zest for "diverse" leadership and philanthropic endeavors in communities undergoing policing, gentrification, and exploitation.

By presenting wealthy elites, foundations, and multinational corporations as champions of diversity, the neoliberal multicultural era has normalized a color-blind acceptance of wealth disparities along shifting, and more fluid, racial boundaries. Melamed (2011) asserts:

> Neoliberal-multicultural racialization has made this disparity appear fair by ascribing racialized privilege to neoliberalism's beneficiaries and racialized stigma to its dispossessed. In particular, it has

valued its beneficiaries as multicultural, reasonable, law-abiding, and good global citizens and devalued the dispossessed as monocultural, backward, weak, and irrational—unfit for global citizenship because they lack the proper neoliberal subjectivity. (44)

Rather than constructing strict racial boundaries based on innate white superiority, neoliberal multiculturalism distinguishes between the *respectable* multicultural subject and the culturally stagnant racial other. The notion of respectability, commonly referred to as "the politics of respectability," first began as a description of Black leaders' attempts to reject racist tropes assigned to African Americans by embracing middle-class values (Collins 2005). These controlling stereotypes were often gendered and weaponized against Black women in particular (Higginbotham 1994). However, respectability politics has since evolved into a dangerous common sense about racial inequality, as well as other forms of marginalization (Harris 2013), in which elite and upwardly mobile members of marginalized groups are believed to gain success because their social values and ways of being are compatible with dominant societal values. By contrast, those who are marginalized are deemed to be "stuck" in deplorable and unrespectable behaviors, which then contribute to their marginalization. Although respectability politics is not a new phenomenon, neoliberal multiculturalism's intense focus on the individual and human capital obscures structural barriers facing the racially marginalized.

These neoliberal respectability politics intersect with notions of gender and sexuality to align proper and productive racial subjectivities with heteronormative ideals. Critical ethnic studies scholar Grace Kyungwon Hong (2015) argues that for communities of color, "gendered and sexual respectability becomes the dividing line between those who are rendered deviant, immoral, and thus precarious in opposition to those whose value to capital has been secured through a variety of norms" (57). Considering the affirmative and biopolitical attributes of neoliberal power, Hong notes that documents and policies, such as the now infamous Moynihan Report,[13] sparked a new wave of neoliberal governance through framing impoverished communities of color as requiring cultural intervention, help, and care. Undergirding these interventions was a merging of racial pathologies with perceived gendered and sexual deviancies. Citing the "failure" to maintain proper heteropatriarchal family structures, the invitation to respectability serves to regulate and punish those populations existing outside of the conditioning power of neoliberalism. Hong argues that respectability in this context is increasingly defined by "the attainment of monogamous couplehood, normative reproductivity, and consumerist subjectivity" that serves to determine "those who are worthy of capital investment and thus protected and those who are not and thus precarious" (60).[14] A new generation of education race scholars have explored how neoliberal politics of respectability serve to empower some young people of color while pathologizing others (Baldridge 2019; Clay 2019; Dumas 2016a; Oeur 2018).

NEOLIBERAL MULTICULTURALISM AND THE EMPOWERMENT OF LATINO BOYS

This brief genealogy of evolving U.S. racial discourses demonstrates the malleability of race and racism in the United States. Although white supremacy is an economic and political system that has unwaveringly benefited those people racialized as white, while devaluing and exploiting to the point of death those people racialized as not white (and particularly those racialized as Black), *as a racial discourse* white supremacy lost its dominance during the post–World War II racial break (López 1996; Winant 2002). By tracing the new racial discourses of racial liberalism, liberal multiculturalism, and neoliberal multiculturalism, we understand two important aspects of race and racism. First, as new racial discourses emerge, newly accepted and disguised forms of race-making occur to legitimize racial dispossession and violence. Second, in constructing a new discourse that defines race and racism, hegemonic racial discourses control what counts as valid and useful forms of racial justice work. Both points are key for this study in analyzing how the problem of race was understood in LMS, as well as the imagined proper intervention to promote racial equality for Latino boys.

The notion of governmentality is useful in understanding how neoliberal multiculturalism, as a form of knowledge and rationality, produces new racial subjects as it constructs a discourse surrounding the problems and solutions these groups face. As Lester Spence (2012) states, under neoliberal governmentality the racial problems of people of color "have been taken outside of the realm of the political by rendering them *technical* and *actionable*" (140; emphasis in original) through market principles. In education, the fact that students of color continue to experience a massive achievement gap and pushout rates (i.e., racism) becomes a matter of incentivizing student and school competition through testing and marketable skill-building programs. Within communities of color, neoliberal multiculturalism's hegemonic status obscures the political and structural nature of racism and instead calls for market logics and inclusion into an existing system of inequality, rather than political struggle (Dumas 2013; Pedroni and Apple 2005). In many cases, neoliberal discourse even adopts the rhetoric of past eras of antiracist struggle, marketing charter schools and school voucher systems as a freedom struggle for the right to choose one's school (Leonardo 2007; Scott 2013).

In the United States, these trends have ignited a wave of privatization in the field of education and greatly weakened the notion of "public" in public schooling (Apple 2006; Lipman 2011; Weiner and Compton 2008). Large urban school districts like Arroyo Seco have adopted portfolio management models of governance, in which central district offices oversee a portfolio of schools (traditional public schools, private organizations, and charter schools) as well as an array of independent educational service providers that partner with district schools (Bulkley, Henig, and Levin 2010). This form of governance disperses the power of public education to philanthropists, foundations, and nonprofit organizations whose schools, charter networks, and educational programs compete in an educational market. Pueblo Unido, the nonprofit of which LMS is a part, is funded directly through this kind of privatized model. It is a model that encourages investment and donations from businesses and other private funders by celebrating key neoliberal values such as personal accountability, rags-to-riches stories of wealth, and troubled youth overcoming adversity while pointedly obscuring the role of those market institutions in the maintenance of the inequalities that students of color are facing.

CHALLENGING OR REPRODUCING DEFICIT NARRATIVES IN YOUTH WORK

Research has long documented that boys of color experience extreme educational disparities in comparison to other groups (Fergus, Noguera, and Martin 2014; N. Lopez 2002; Noguera 2009; Schott 2010). To make sense of these disparities, national political discourse and popular media representations espouse deficit narratives for boys and young men of color in schools (A. L. Brown and Donnor 2011; Harper 2015). In these narratives, boys of color are seen as inherent problems who lack positive cultural traits and represent a national crisis. Naomi Klein (2008) has described how the notion of crisis serves as a key justification for neoliberal interventions of privatization and punishment. Although boys of color (and all people of color) have constantly been marginalized and seen as threats throughout U.S. history, in the last several decades young men of color have come to be understood as a national crisis. On one hand, this crisis has relied upon punishment and policing. For example, as 1970s neoliberal economic policies cut government services and social welfare programs in California, the state experienced a massive prison boom to respond to a perceived crisis of crime among Black and Latino men (Gilmore 2007). This perceived criminal crisis also gave rise to the use of policing technologies in schools (Nolan 2011) and the well-documented school-to-prison pipeline (Kim, Losen, and Hewitt 2010). To justify these racial practices, this era has drawn on the archetypes of the "bad boy," the "superpredator," and the "bad hombre."

However, on the other end of this crisis response has been a booming nonprofit-industrial complex which has widely targeted "at-risk" youth (INCITE! 2017). Soo Ah Kwon (2013) argues that nonprofit youth organizations charged with "improving the life chances of 'at-risk' youth of color" are "directly linked to the modern state and the reconfiguration of civil society as a technology of neoliberal citizenship" (9). For boys of color, and Latino boys in particular, this book is interested in how this affirmative neoliberal governmentality governs and shapes Latino boys amid this crisis. In the past decades the crisis of boys of color has led to the creation of an astounding number of educational programs targeting boys and young men of color in hopes of saving them from lives of social deviance. By operating under neoliberal multicultural logics, youth empowerment is defined by the ability of young people to shed cultural pathologies and maximize their human capital to compete in a global, multicultural market.

Despite the pervasiveness of deficit-oriented youth programming, out-of-school educational spaces remain places of both hope and resistance. Educational researcher of race and youth work Bianca Baldridge offers the notion of the *youthwork paradox* to help describe the frequently contradictory goals of community-based educational spaces (CBES). Baldridge (2020b) describes the youthwork paradox as "a conflict in which CBES have the potential to both disrupt and reify racism and deficit narratives in education" (619). Here, Baldridge maintains, those working in youth programming navigate the contradictory terrain of supporting young people amid a pressure to simply discipline or fix them. The notion of the youthwork paradox highlights the complexity of community-based educational spaces and offers an alternative to dichotomous framings of these spaces as either critical and liberatory or deficit-oriented and problematic.

In my work with LMS, I found that the idea that youth programming can be both repressive and liberating was descriptive of what I witnessed and learned from the students and mentors of the program. On one hand, it was clear that the program, which was formerly characterized as "character development" for potentially troublesome Latino boys, brought a deficit orientation to youth work. As a result, students and mentors in LMS readily adopted the language and practices of redeeming and fixing a population demeaned failing or in crisis. On the other hand, students and mentors both subtly and outwardly resisted the notion that Latino boys were at fault for their own marginalization. They also found ways to take advantage of the joy and happiness students felt in bonding with friends and mentors. In the coming chapters, I attempt to highlight the words and stories of the Latino men and boys in LMS to better make sense of these contradictions. In particular, chapter 5 highlights the stories of two subversive mentors, Mr. Javier and Mr. Agustín, as they intentionally and strategically resisted deficit-oriented notions of role modeling.

BRINGING INTERSECTIONALITY AND QUEER-OF-COLOR CRITIQUE TO THE STUDY OF LATINO BOYS

For some mentors in LMS, resistance to deficit-oriented approaches to Latino male mentoring pushed beyond critiquing the racist undertones of character development and emphasized the need to trace the ways gender and sexuality also intersect with the image of the positive Latino male role model. Women-of-color feminists have long pointed to the need to attend to intersectionality. For research on boys and men of color, this means recognizing not just the multiplicity of identity but also that these identities exist with a matrix of interlocking systems of oppression. This necessitates research to not just acknowledge intersections—such as acknowledging that students are both Latinx (race/ethnicity) and boys (gender)—but also to attend to racism, sexism, and heteropatriarchy (Cabrera et al. 2022; Patrón and Burmicky 2023).

Black feminist and intersectional theorist Kimberlé Crenshaw has been an outspoken critic of the ways boy-of-color programming can serve as an intersectional failure by failing to address patriarchal visions of racial justice and normalizing hegemonic notions of gender. In a scathing opinion piece in the *New York Times*, Crenshaw (2014) criticizes then president Obama for offering what she describes as a "patriarchy enhancement" approach to racial justice. In this framing, programs like MBK and former New York City mayor Michael Bloomberg's 2011 Young Men's Initiative focus intensely on the struggles facing boys and men of color. This targeted approach invisibilizes women, girls, and gender-nonbinary people of color who are similarly affected by poverty, underfunded schools, income disparities, mass incarceration, and housing and job discrimination. Rather than addressing the root causes of these issues (and then attending to subgroups' unique locations within a matrix of inequality), programs like MBK target one group as a form of collective justice, leading Crenshaw (2016) to later deem the program an "intersectional failure." She argues that, in contrast to an intersectional approach to justice, MBK views racial inequality in terms of *patriarchal absences*—meaning "the problems of communities of color, are problems because men are not appropriately socialized to be the type of men that are responsible for families and for communities." This long-standing belief posits traditional family structures and the restoration of fallen patriarchs as pivotal in addressing racial inequality.

Alma García (1989) locates the rise of Chicana feminism as, in part, a challenge to this framing and a critique of intersecting discourses of nationalism, family, and sexism that emerged within the Chicano Movement. Chicana feminists rejected the patriarchal nationalism touted by activist men in the movement as the true Chicano culture. This brand of cultural nationalism had aimed to restore and reproduce "traditional" gender roles as a source of pride in the Chicano community. Building upon this legacy of critique, Richard T. Rodríguez (2009) utilizes a queer-of-color lens to challenge the ways heteropatriarchal imaginations of la familia police the ways Chicanx identity and kinship are articulated in popular and "empowering" texts of the Chicano Movement. Through a queer-of-color analysis (Brockenbrough 2013; R. Ferguson 2003), Rodríguez decenters normative familial relationships in Chicanx cultural expressions to offer a fluid and unbounded conceptualization of being and becoming. This perspective makes space for the epistemologies and existence of queer Chicanx subjects while simultaneously challenging the systems that render them unproductive, abject, and without value.

Bringing a queer-of-color lens to the study of Latino male mentorship necessitates an interrogation of the ways intersecting discourses of race, gender, sexuality, and capital assign normalcy and value to a unique Latino male subjectivity while rendering others improper and deviant. Scholars of race, gender, and sexuality have criticized the notion of the positive male role model for its grounding in "reductionist and essentialist notions of racial and gender affiliation" (Rezai-Rashti and Martino 2010, 38; also see Hutchings 2023). In this critique, the performative act of defining a positive male role model is inextricably linked to the ways colonial and capitalist systems of value construct cisgender and heteropatriarchal manhood as most valuable and ideal (Britzman 1993; Martino 2015). Research documents the ways Black and Latino men teachers are frequently asked to embody hypermasculine roles in the lives of boys of color (Lara and Fránquiz 2015; M. V. Singh 2019). This includes positioning men of color teachers to be the disciplinarians of unruly boys of color (Bristol and Mentor 2018; Brockenbrough 2015; M. V. Singh 2018) as well as framing these teachers as the positive paternal figures who are presumed to be absent in many boys' lives (Brockenbrough 2018).

In a study with Black men teacher candidates, Ashley Woodson and Amber Pabon (2016) describe a dire need to create room for diverse expressions of racial, gendered, and sexual identities among Black men teachers. Through interviews with Black men preservice teachers, they found that "heteropatriarchal assumptions" dictated what types of Black men would be ideal teachers and role models for Black children. These assumptions discouraged gay and trans Black men from entering the teaching profession. As one research participant stated, "If cisgender male identity is what Black males need in role models, then I am not an appropriate mentor or teacher. Everyone seems to want a Black male teacher, but they really want a Black cisgender male teacher" (57). While popular efforts to position men-of-color educators and youth workers as role models continue to lack a substantive engagement with issues of intersectional justice, a growing literature seeks to add nuance and criticality to the discussion (A. L. Brown 2012; Warren 2020).

INTENT OF STUDY

This book brings a critical and intersectional lens to the study of school-based Latino male mentorship. I describe how interlocking neoliberal discourses of gender, class, and sexuality seek to engender new racial subjectivities for Latino men and boys by defining proper and productive ways of being. This configuration is embodied by the figure of the positive Latino male role model. The goal of this research is to examine how the neoliberal multicultural turn in urban education influences the ways an ideal Latino maleness is envisioned by youth programming for Latino boys. The recent proliferation of educational programs targeting Latino men and boys represents a key moment in which intersecting discourses of race, gender, class, and sexuality shape how we understand the barriers facing Latino men and boys, as well as solutions. Structured as an ethnographic case study, this project explores the discourses that outline the figure of the role model in LMS and examines how this positive Latino manhood was practiced, embodied, or resisted. In the spirit of critical ethnic studies, my goal is to examine the ways oppressive discourses reproduce themselves as well as to highlight critical voices that disrupt this reproduction for justice-centered approaches to education. Guiding research questions include: How does neoliberal multiculturalism influence the goals and practices of LMS? How is Latino manhood in the program understood and constructed? In what ways are neoliberal politics disrupted through justice-oriented framings and practices of Latinx education and/or Latino masculinity?

BOOK ORGANIZATION

Chapter 1 explores the background and history of LMS and the roots of the emergence of neoliberal ideology in educational youth programs. It discusses how the neoliberal ideologies integrated into LMS's program design has its roots in a discourse of "crisis" that emerged in the 1980s surrounding boys and men of color in the United States. I argue that the neoliberal state sought to manage this problem through parallel systems of punishment (mass incarceration) and care (youth programming). I demonstrate the ways the discourse of the "good boy" and "bad boy" influences the work of LMS. This was evident through narratives of redemption from risky behavior that were popular in fundraisers and funding efforts. The program also took a deficit-oriented approach to youth work that saw students in need of "character development" as a means to improve their lives and social standing.

In chapter 2, I explore the ways financial incentives and other market-oriented approaches to youth work instill neoliberal ideas of increasing one's "human capital" and individual responsibility. Ethnographic accounts of lessons and classroom practices describe the ways students were taught to embrace neoliberal subjectivities as a form of empowerment. This invitation to accountability and respectability also intersected with the ways students learned to understand and perform manhood. I offer the term *benevolent heteropatriarchy* to describe the ways manhood training in the program urged boys to reject popular manifestations of toxic masculinity but remained rooted in traditional heteropatriarchal gender roles. Through detailed ethnographic vignettes, this chapter brings the reader into the classroom as students naturalize a unique blending of traditional Latino masculine characteristics and neoliberal multicultural values.

Chapter 3 discusses how LMS mentors understand and experience deficit- and damage-centered rhetoric associated with Latino boys as well as the superhero-like narratives ascribed to Latino male educators who can save them. I highlight mentors' deep appreciation for the bonds and intimacy built with students amid a school environment that is often unwelcoming to Latino men and boys. However, despite this love and appreciation for their students, mentors primarily used the popular language of damage and deficit to describe their value in the lives of their students. Most believed that they fulfilled much-needed representations of discipline and masculine respectability. This chapter emphasizes the ways discourses of love and deficit intermingle and coexist. Rather than framing educators in a binary of good or bad, neoliberal or not neoliberal, I make the case for supporting educators in their desire to build critical and justice-centered approaches to mentoring.

In chapter 4, I examine how LMS students experience and feel narratives of damage and brokenness associated with Latino men and boys in schools and society. Through students' own analysis of the purpose of LMS as well as their experiences in it, I describe the ways students navigate being the target of Latino male empowerment. While some students adopt the damage-centered belief that Latino boys are broken and need to be fixed, others challenge the merits of tough love and question punitive practices in the program. The chapter concludes by examining the students' critiques to suggest new ways to frame mentoring Latino boys that emphasize love and joy rather than tough love and discipline.

Chapter 5 discusses the work of Mr. Javier and Mr. Agustín, two LMS mentors who actively and explicitly resisted deficit orientations of mentorship and instead implemented critical mentoring strategies. While both incorporated critical race and gender lessons into their mentoring, I also argue that their strategic "failure" to perform the role of a positive Latino male role model was a powerful act of resistance. Furthermore, as the only gay mentor in LMS, Mr. Agustín describes using his own "bad example" to help illuminate the assumed straightness of the LMS mentors and students and to queer the image of the positive Latino male role model. This challenge served as a form of dis-identification that illuminates and disrupts heteropatriarchal narratives of Latino male success. Overall, this chapter underscores the important role of both discursive and embodied politics in enacting critical and intersectional approaches to mentoring Latino boys.

Chapter 6 uses a relational race framework to examine the impact that Blackness and anti-Blackness had on LMS's mission and vision of a positive Latino manhood. I argue that anti-Blackness has largely gone unacknowledged in conversations surrounding boys and men of color. For LMS, a rejection of urban Blackness and "negative" Black male role models revealed the ways articulations of a positive Latino manhood were defined, in part, by its distance from Blackness. This chapter also interrogates a clear tension between LMS and Black Males Rising, a Black male mentorship program in Arroyo Seco. Despite these tensions, the chapter also spotlights the ways some mentors addressed anti-Blackness in their teaching and sought to build solidarity with Black men and boys.

The conclusion discusses what the contradictions I witnessed in LMS mean for the larger conversation surrounding boys and men of color in schools. The discourse of damage and deficit continues to rationalize targeted programming for boys of color. However, this approach to empowerment, as this book shows, is framed and practiced in ways that uphold neoliberal and heteropatriarchal values. The conclusion asks, Are these programs the educational justice we are searching for? Ruminating on the growing abolitionist movement in the field of education, I contemplate if male empowerment programs, in their most common form, are worthy of reform. Taking my cue from the prison abolitionist movement, I argue that new narratives and practices, beyond patriarchal redemption, are necessary for the abolitionist project.

MANAGING THE "CRISIS" OF LATINO MEN AND BOYS

When it was first piloted in 2010, LMS served just one middle school by providing a school-based mentor to help connect Latino boys to health services and build healthy life practices. The program was a response to research conducted by the Arroyo Seco County Public Health Department and California Endowment which showed that Latino men and boys in Arroyo Seco, similar to Black men and boys, were experiencing a health crisis surrounding violence, substance abuse, and poverty. Because of its long-standing connection to the Latinx community (although not in youth development), Pueblo Unido was approached by the California Endowment with seed money to house the newly emerging mentorship program. As Pueblo Unido helped to grow LMS to eventually serve ten schools, opportunities for fundraising in both the public and private sectors increasingly favored job readiness, academic excellence, and all-around character development. By the time Refugio Pérez gave his speech at the ceremonia in 2018, discussed in the introduction, the program was no longer funded as a public health project and had fully focused its mission on mentoring students toward better grades, better character, and better job prospects—simply put, better young men. Held up by the school district as a model support program, LMS was financed through Pueblo Unido's fundraising, and the program's language of personal responsibility, self-improvement, and creating "good" Latino boys paralleled what can be categorized as a *neoliberal* approach to educational support for boys of color, which was growing in popularity across the country at this time. In its mission and focus, LMS exemplified this growing trend as it sought to change the character and outcomes of individual boys through educational intervention. It is emblematic of a unique form of racial justice politics reliant on private-sector intervention and an emphasis on individual empowerment.

On February 27, 2014, nearly four years after LMS's establishment, President Barack Obama made waves by introducing My Brother's Keeper (MBK), his landmark racial justice project and perhaps the most prominent example of a neoliberal racial justice intervention aimed at supporting boys and young men of color. "Now, just to be clear—My Brother's Keeper is not some big, new government program" (Obama 2014b), the president quickly clarified. After reminding the crowd gathered in the East Room of his recent State of the Union address, in which he laid out plans for growing the national economy—"government programs that we think are good for all Americans" (Obama 2014a)—the president emphasized MBK's different approach. MBK would be a collaboration between government, the private sector, and philanthropic organizations, and its wide range of local initiatives and support programs would not be funded by the federal government. In the effort to uplift boys and young men of color, maintained the president, government must have a limited role.

> In this effort, government cannot play the only, or even the primary role. We can help give every child access to quality preschool and help them start learning from an early age, but we can't replace the power of a parent who's reading to that child. We can reform our criminal justice system to ensure that it's not infected with bias, but nothing keeps a young man out of trouble like a father who takes an active role in his son's life.

"Parents," he reminded the audience, "will have to parent—and turn off the television, and help with homework." He continued by naming corporations, philanthropists, teachers, religious leaders, families, and of course the individual boys themselves as the primary actors in this struggle. "So we all have a job to do," argued the president. He continued:

> So often, the issues facing boys and young men of color get caught up in long-running ideological arguments about race and class, and crime and poverty, the role of government, partisan politics. We've all heard those arguments before. But the urgency of the situation requires us to move past some of those old arguments and focus on getting something done and focusing on what works.

Obama's formulation repackages a common narrative regarding boys of color: there is a crisis underway, and the seriousness of that crisis requires immediate actions that (seemingly) look beyond ideological debates to get something done.

However, as critical theorist of education and anti-Blackness Michael Dumas (2016a) has pointed out, far from being nonideological, the announcement of MBK "laid out the very ideological argument for a government retreat from racial redress, and provided the justification for a shift to private corporate-sector" (95) leadership—while being presented as racial justice work. In introducing MBK, the president sought to dismiss the "ideological" goals of radical racial justice movements, and perhaps more particularly the Black radical tradition (Kelley 2003), to offer a neoliberal solution to the problem of racial inequality. In this way, MBK abandons a political and structural approach to understanding and addressing racism, and the existing system is left without scrutiny. Instead, boys and young men of color become the primary targets of innovative, technocratic solutions to be managed by public–private partnerships. It is the boys who are seen as broken, lacking, and in need of repair (Dumas 2016a).

Since its inception as a White House initiative, and later under the Obama Foundation, MBK has raised more than one billion dollars from public and private foundations, corporations, and state and local entities and has partnered with hundreds of programs supporting boys and young men of color around the country (Huerta, Howard, and Haro 2020). To be clear, my critique here is not of the many programs and individuals utilizing the resources of MBK to do transformative work in the lives of young people. In fact, research shows that even while being positioned as "saviors" or "fixers," justice-oriented educators find creative ways to teach critical lessons, subvert deficit-oriented practices, and build solidarity with their students (Baldridge 2014; Clay 2019; M. V. Singh 2019). Nevertheless, it is important to recognize the ways MBK functions as part of a larger ideological transition in the United States that locates the problem of racial inequality within the bodies of boys and young men of color, while undermining more fundamental challenges to racial capitalism. MBK is not unique in this regard. Rather, it is part of a recent history of public–private partnerships and neoliberal solutions to the problem often generalized as *boys of color*, or even, simply, *urban youth*.

Although MBK and the many smaller programs in its network perform the commonsense work of supporting "boys and young men of color who are having a particularly tough time," as the president put it, this chapter explains how the youth programming at LMS and similar nonprofits functions as a form of governmentality and containment for students of color. Despite its framing as a social justice invention, many aspects of LMS, which is now an affiliate of MBK, use empowerment as a technology to manage and contain. This is emblematic of a larger youth-control apparatus in which the booming industries of youth punishment and youth empowerment remove or condition "problematic" populations of young people. Concretely, at LMS, the integrated uses of empowerment as containment are evident in the way the language of damage and deficit guides the goals and structure of the program and in the way the program is designed around the idea of managing "at-risk" youth from perpetrating risky behavior such as crime, violence, and sex. Indeed, LMS was founded alongside sweeping gang injunctions in Arroyo Seco and was sometimes referred to as the lighter and more progressive way to manage boys of color in the city.

While I do not aim to paint these processes as the same—and I adamantly believe we must protect young people from imprisonment at all costs—this chapter looks at the ways neoliberal youth empowerment, as opposed to more radical forms of empowerment, serves the carceral state by functioning as a form of social containment. Consequently, as this chapter discusses in detail below, the programming strategies at LMS become a technology of management for a seemingly problematic population in Arroyo Seco: Latino boys. Couched in the rhetoric of care is the hope of transformation through conditioning boys to adopt acceptable principles of personal responsibility and self-blame when confronting their disenfranchisement and marginalization. Since these logics often presume racial, gender, and sexual deficits in Latino boys, they ultimately serve to reify racist stereotypes while constructing an idealized Latino masculinity—or a good boy—that is traditionally heteropatriarchal, entrepreneurial, and economically productive.

THE POLITICS OF MANAGING A YOUTH "CRISIS"

In August 2017, I visited the Pueblo Unido headquarters to meet the LMS staff for the first time. The Pueblo Unido central office is located in the heart of the Mariposa District, commonly known as the economic hub of North Arroyo Seco. There, the dirty but vibrant streets are lined with an assortment of taquerías, community service providers, athletic stores, and small groceries displaying colorful fruits and selling jugos verdes out of side windows. Large pickup trucks pass by blaring brass-

filled banda music from northern Mexico, their rear windows displaying tributes to states like Michoacán, Guanajuato, and Jalisco. On the
sidewalks, Black and Latinx professionals intermix with morning shop-
pers. Some of the young mothers wear colorful Maya blouses and speak
K'iche' or Mam to their small children, who steady themselves by holding on to bare manikins standing outside discount fashion shops.

The Pueblo Unido office stands several buildings down from one
of the main intersections of the district. The three-story building is
painted an earthy yellow, and the Pueblo Unido logo, emblazoned with
its name and a large Mesoamerican pyramid, marks the front of the
building. As I walked into the main lobby of the small office building,
a security guard blocked my path to the elevator. After he discovered
that my name was not on the list of attendees for morning meetings, I
was asked to wait until a call upstairs could confirm my appointment.
Despite the security checkpoint—something the LMS mentors and students would later complain to me about and describe as divisive—the
office space on the other side of the security line maintained a similarly
vibrant Latinx aesthetic of the community, but within the context of a
professional office space. There was a smattering of cultural art on the
walls, colorful posters from past events, and papier-mâché calaveras
from Arroyo Seco's annual Día de los Muertos celebration. The office
inhabitants were mostly Latinx, and Spanish and Spanglish were openly
spoken. However, the space was also a professional and contemporary-
looking office. It was one large and communal workspace, with a row of
desk-like, low-rising cubicles, several all-glass conference rooms on the
outsides of the large room, and couches in a break area. Pan dulce was
set out on a coffee table.

The office's major art piece was a beautiful print in the central convening space, overlooking a communal break area. I recognized this
artwork from the Pueblo Unido website. It was a timeline mural com-
memorating the long history of Pueblo Unido's efforts in supporting the
Latinx community of Arroyo Seco. The mural begins in the mid-1960s
under the title "The Latino Civil Rights Movement" and marks the establishment of Pueblo Unido (then a grassroots organization under a
slightly different name) as part of this movement. The founding year
is surrounded by a collage of brown fists, rebellious demonstrators,
and slogans reading "CHICANO POWER!" As the mural progresses,
we see fewer images of political critique and more representations of
professionalism and development. By the time the mural reaches the

end of the 1960s, we see the time mark "Incorporated as Non-profit Community Dev. Corp. [Development Corporation] 501(c)(3)." In the mid-1970s, three large dollar signs are featured next to a Ford Foundation arrow to indicate a steady funding stream. As the years progress the artwork highlights key partnerships with transnational corporations and massive banks such as Wells Fargo and JP Morgan Chase. By 2010, a picture of a group of well-dressed Latino boys marks the beginning of the Latino Male Success program. The mural culminates with a celebration of the now massive nonprofit's cumulative "100-million dollar investment" in "community assets." Of these investments, the most notable was the organization of a housing and commercial development project in North Arroyo Seco. Although the project seeks to open affordable housing units in the Mariposa District, it continues to spark controversy and serves as a symbol of the ongoing gentrification of the neighborhood for many housing-rights activists in Arroyo Seco.

I open this section with a description of the Pueblo Unido headquarters to give both the physical community context wherein Pueblo Unido is located and the historical contexts and transitions that the once grassroots organization, now 501(c)(3) nonprofit community development corporation occupies. In many ways, the mural serves as an ideological illustration of the gradual shift from Chicano Movement-era politics to Pueblo Unido's current business orientation. In the shadow of a beautiful quetzal soaring above the mural, neoliberalism, perhaps like all hegemonic discourses, enjoys a level of anonymity by hiding and ruling in plain sight. Masked in colors and imagery meant to signal Mesoamerican authenticity, we see a gradual transition to a new value system and politics permeating Pueblo Unido. If an earlier era of Latinx activism was characterized by criticism of structural inequalities in the United States, calls for a redistribution of wealth, and at times the abolition of the racist, capitalist, nation-state itself (L. V. Márquez 2020; C. Muñoz 2007), Pueblo Unido now looks to support the Latinx community and its neighborhood through market inclusion and investment in individuals. This has included job training workshops, microfinance lending, the active development of neighborhood real estate for commercial use, and bringing in large corporate sponsors interested in investing in community development.

The mural illustrates a gradual rebranding of Chicanx/Latinx politics to adhere to neoliberal values of capital accumulation and investment and describes the ways this shift was central to how Pueblo Unido and its financial backers envisioned their educational intervention with Latino boys. As the subject of this new ideological intervention, Chicanx/Latinx identity is drained of radical political meaning developed in earlier political movements and instead is discursively constructed through the neoliberal and dualist language of the "good boy" and "bad boy." This framing of Latino youth—where good Latino boys are marked by their entrepreneurialism, merit, and conventional heteropatriarchalism and the "bad boys" are marked as socially deviant—has permeated U.S. culture today, particularly in education in ways that directly intersect with mentoring programs like LMS. It is a contemporary story, however, that goes beyond just programs like LMS or Obama's MBK, and one that has roots in a history of radical youth resistance and state power.

RADICAL YOUTH RESISTANCE

In the 1960s there was a wave of militant upheaval across the globe as third-world and Indigenous peoples sought to radically challenge the colonial capitalist world system (Blackwell 2011; Rosales and Rosales 1997; Takaki 2008). In the United States, California was at the forefront of this movement as students and young people used schools and educational spaces to incite resistance to racial capitalism and settler colonialism. In Los Angeles, the 1968 East Los Angeles Walkouts, also known as the Chicano Blowouts, saw thousands of high school students walk out of East and South Los Angeles schools to protest the conditions and pushout rates of Chicanx/Latinx students in the district (Delgado Bernal 1998; López 2004). Later that year, under the banner of the Third World Liberation Front (TWLF), Black, Native American, Latinx, and Asian American students at San Francisco State University and UC Berkeley mounted what was among the longest, most militant student strikes in U.S. history. Student strikers demanded the creation of Third World colleges that taught a curriculum that centered antiracism, anti-imperialism, and the liberation of communities of color (Okihiro 2016). In 1969 Indigenous and allied community members, many of whom were ethnic studies students in Bay Area universities, launched a nineteen-month reclamation of Alcatraz Island in the name of Indigenous rematriation of land and life in the U.S. settler state (Shiekh 1999). And in 1966 Bobby Seale and Huey Newton, two Merritt College students in Oakland, founded the Black Panther Party.

Within several years the organization would have chapters throughout the country and around the world (Bloom and Martin 2016).

Led by youth and young adults, these movements rejected the liberal racial politics of past generations and constructed new, subversive political identities. For young people of color, newly formed or redefined identities such as Black, Indian, Asian American, and Chicano emerged as political identities that challenged the limitations of inclusionary racial politics and demanded community autonomy, reparations, and a world radically different from the United States' white-supremacist, capitalist system (Okihiro 2016). Here, a hegemonic notion of "goodness" was disrupted, as the new ideal role models for a radicalizing youth were university student activists, community radicals like the Brown Berets or Black Panthers, and subversive educators like Garfield High School teacher and walkout organizer Sal Castro. These role models were rabble-rousers and offered examples of resistance to, rather than inclusion into, dominant U.S. society. These new and subversive identities being created by young people were cultivated in grassroots efforts and popular education spaces in direct opposition to capitalist inequalities and the racist state (Buelna 2019). Here, youth empowerment in communities of color posed a threat to existing racial order and power structures.

Repression of these youth-led movements would be swift and violent. At UC Berkeley, California governor Ronald Reagan declared a state of emergency in February 1969 and deployed National Guard troops to drive student protesters off campus (Shiekh 1999). At UCLA, the on-campus murder of Black Panther Party members and UCLA students John Huggins and Bunchy Carter (in no small way incited by FBI intervention) would gravely disrupt the Black Student Union's political organizing for years to come (Bloom and Martin 2016). At a nationwide level, state reaction to the movements of the 1960s was the invention, refinement, and systematic deployment of new and repressive policing technologies to manage these growing movements. The now infamous Counterintelligence Program (COINTELPRO) run by the FBI under J. Edgar Hoover stands as one of the most prominent examples of undeclared warfare on antiracist liberation movements. COINTELPRO was used to surveil, discredit, and infiltrate domestic political organizations. Its abuses of state power, unwavering use of strategic and deadly force, and development of complex forms of surveillance were not unique or episodic. COINTELPRO's violent repression represented an emerging era of policing and control sparked by white fears of radical, antiracist politics in the United States (D. Rodríguez 2017). While the emerging era of widespread criminalization and mass incarceration was a clear act of state power to control communities of color, a parallel apparatus of youth programming sought to manage communities of color by conditioning and regulating the ways young people responded to racial marginalization.

MANAGING YOUNG PEOPLE: PUNISHMENT AND CONTAINED EMPOWERMENT

In an elegant glass conference room at the Pueblo Unido central office, CEO Gerald Espinoza and I met to discuss LMS. Although in the past I had scheduled meetings with him through Consuelo, his secretary, she had called to push back our meeting several times to accommodate his busy schedule. Espinoza was a handsome man in his mid-fifties. He wore a sharp suit, spoke with casual confidence, and had a strong smile. I could understand why multiple LMS mentors had described his personality as smooth and politician-like. This was always said with a negative connotation. As we talked, Espinoza offered his account of why Pueblo Unido had helped establish LMS. Similar to the larger goals of Pueblo Unido, he declared, "we saw a community need, and we responded." He elaborated:

> When you looked out into the community, the biggest issues in Arroyo Seco were always around young Black men and Brown boys, right? Those are the biggest issues, right? It was violence, it was gangs, you know, education, all of that, all the biggest problems out there were these young Black and Brown kids. . . . Pueblo Unido had to do something . . . we had to help.[1]

Espinoza offered me what felt like a well-rehearsed pitch for the program and its importance. In his narrative, potentially good kids were swallowed up by the darkness of North Arroyo Seco and emerged as threats to the community. He emphasized that gang violence, drugs, crime, and teen pregnancy all contributed to this *problem*—Black and Latino males in Arroyo Seco. "We are on the front lines here," he added. "We are in the community offering the boys a new path. . . . There's more than the stereotype for them. . . . They have a choice."

Espinoza's framing of LMS as "on the front lines" in this battle and presenting boys with a better "choice" was fitting. The same year that

LMS was piloted, the city of Arroyo Seco filed a lawsuit for a targeted gang injunction against a Latinx street gang in a North Arroyo Seco neighborhood. When officially issued, the injunction created a geographic zone in North Arroyo Seco in which known gang members' rights were limited—including a strict curfew and the prohibition of associating with one another or suspected gang members. The injunction criminalized Latinx young people in Arroyo Seco and was heavily resisted by community activists. It was just the latest in a long string of laws and policies criminalizing young people of color throughout the country. While the apolitical Pueblo Unido did not participate in the community organizing against the injunction, its simultaneous support of LMS did offer boys an "alternative choice," as Espinoza put it. While the booming *prison-industrial complex* (PIC) sought to remove and incarcerate boys and young men of color, Pueblo Unido joined the many nonprofits and youth empowerment programs to manage this problem through care and inclusion.

Much of the language and deficit-oriented approaches of LMS and other educational programs targeting young people of color—including the racialized and gendered discourse of the "bad boy"—are directly influenced by the way the neoliberal state responds to populations seen as problematic. In the aftermath of the mass movements of the late 1960s and early 1970s, state power undertook a massive restructuring of the ways difference, particularly racial difference, was managed and suppressed. This restructuring would have a profound impact on subsequent generations, and particularly boys of color, as the state managed what was framed as problematic populations. Key to this management has been the role of policing and imprisonment (Alexander 2012) as well as youth empowerment and care (Kwon 2013). Although this book primarily focuses on empowerment and care in the context of a specific educational support program for Latino boys, this rise of the era of punishment toward young people of color has played an important role in the way such educational programs have emerged.

One important source for the rise of this discourse of punishment and care in schools is the widespread fear of crime and deviancy that emerged in the United States in the late 1970s and 1980s. A number of scholars and activists have highlighted the notion of the *prison-industrial complex* as a way to describe the rise of mass incarceration in the United States, and especially the role racism and neoliberalism play in the recent prison boom (A. Y. Davis 2000). The notion of the

PIC pushes against the popular belief that recent increases in incarceration rates and prisoner populations correlate with increases in individual acts of crime. Instead, the PIC points out that the proliferation of prisons and prisoners is intimately linked to larger political-economic structures and racial ideologies. Angela Davis (2003), for example, has described the PIC as a material structure supported by racial discourse and a socially constructed need for policing and punishment. Other scholars have supported this idea, arguing that central to the perceived need for mass amounts of policing and punishment has been fear of and contempt for boys and young men of color (Kwon 2013; Nolan 2011; Rios 2011). This fear and contempt, however, is not just isolated to prisons and policing; its influence extends to all areas of life in the United States, including education, where pathways to adulthood, social prestige, and power are wrapped tightly with broader social and racial structures.

The framing of young people through the lens of "good" and "bad," along with the need for management through threats and punishment, is particularly visible in the political arena, where state legislators from both dominant political parties competed for the title of the "tough on crime candidate" by showing their "concern" for public safety by creating new laws and new crimes for prosecution. This discourse has direct consequences on the ideologies that underpin decisions on educational policy and funding. A number of laws in California enacted over the last forty years, for instance, highlight this "tough on crime" approach and underscore the consequences they have for young people. In 1984, for example, the California legislature commissioned the State Task Force on Youth Gang Violence, which ultimately led to the 1988 Street Terrorism Enforcement and Prevention (STEP) Act. Among many notable outcomes of this law, the STEP Act mandated local law enforcement to identify gang members and submit their names to a statewide database, as well as enhance prison sentences for gang-related crimes (Gilmore 2007). Moreover, in 2000, just ten years before LMS was founded, voters overwhelmingly passed California Proposition 21 (Treatment of Juvenile Offenders). These two laws together heavily increased gang surveillance, mandated enhanced prison time for gang-related crimes, and prevented probation departments from using discretion when incarcerating or releasing juveniles who had been arrested for a variety of specific infractions. Prop 21 also freed prosecutors to file charges against children as young as fourteen years of age in adult court for a range of serious offenses. These California laws from the 1980s marked the beginning of an era in which young people of color were widely vilified, scapegoated, and considered public threats. As Ruth Wilson Gilmore (2007) put it: "Politicians of all races and ethnicities merged gang membership, drug use, and habitual criminal activity into a single social scourge, which was then used to explain everything from unruly youth to inner-city homicides to the need for more prisons to isolate wrongdoers" (109). This social scourge became a high-priority problem to be addressed and managed (Kwon 2013; Offutt-Chaney 2023).

The rise of punitive control during these years would have a direct impact on federal and state educational policy priorities and the way schools treated children of color. In 1983 Los Angeles Unified School District (LAUSD) and Los Angeles Police Department (LAPD) partnered to create the program Drug Abuse Resistance Education, more commonly known as DARE. Basing its headquarters in Inglewood, California, DARE was quickly implemented nationwide. The program brought police officers to schools to preach about the dangers of drug use and gang membership[2] (Sojoyner 2016). It became common sense that schools in areas suspected of having gang activity should have multiple campus police officers and in many cases use metal detectors on students entering school (Nolan 2011). Furthermore, Damien Sojoyner (2016) connects white demands of harsher truancy policies in Southern California to LAUSD's student busing practices with white fears of truant Black and Latinx students roaming the suburbs. The STEP Act made it easier to create legal amendments that disproportionately affected Black and Latinx students, now making truancy a criminal act having legal consequences for parents and students.

While this wave of laws, policies, and programs sought to address the imagined threat of primarily boys of color through punishment and control, a similar apparatus of care and empowerment was also forming to help manage this population. Running parallel to the massive increase in state punishment of young people of color has been an expanding infrastructure of youth intervention programs largely run by nonprofit organizations. Many of these nonprofit programs, however, simply repackage the need for containment through a paternalistic discourse of care, in which boys are saved from the streets and from themselves through interventions. Frequently, the programming at LMS, its mentoring strategies, and its broader fundraising tactics embodied this discourse.

These narratives perform complementary functions in the era of neoliberal multiculturalism. In this framing, good multicultural subjects (those defined by their entrepreneurialism, individualism, and capacity to maximize human capital and earning potential) are positioned as antithetical to the socially deviant bad racial subject. Dylan Rodríguez (2017) draws a direct correlation between the rise of the prison-industrial complex and what is now commonly known as the nonprofit industrial complex (NPIC). He argues that while the PIC violently represses dissent in impoverished, racially segregated communities, the NPIC manages and dictates the boundaries of dissent by integrating community resistance into the state apparatus.[3] While foundations and white philanthropy have long been a part of the U.S. educational landscape (see Watkins 2001), the last several decades have seen foundations pouring large amounts of their money and political/moral values into educational research, charter school expansion, and educational nonprofits working with young people during and after school (Scott 2009). Although it is worth noting many nonprofits operate under what might be considered a white savior complex, this book is focused on the ways communities of color also function within the nonprofit structure to respond to and protect our young people from the perceived risks of the streets, allowing them to lead productive and happy lives.

FRAMING THE INTERVENTION: MANAGING LATINO BOYS IN ARROYO SECO

LMS was founded in 2010. In the beginning, the organization was not specifically focused on academic improvement and job readiness. As Robert Rivera, one of LMS's founders and a former director, described: "We started as primarily a heath-based program for Latino boys, most people don't realize that. . . . That's how we were seen and funded." Long dedicated to helping Latino boys, Rivera spent his whole professional life working as a community organizer, art educator, performer, and director of youth development programs. "That was my program," he told me with a bitter smile on the day we met. "I essentially started it."

Rivera is in his early fifties. Although no longer directly overseeing youth development programs, he continues to work with young people as an arts educator, poet, and occasional adjunct professor. Despite his salt-and-pepper hair, his gritty artist persona gives him an energetic and youthful demeanor that no doubt allows him to connect with young people. Although no longer affiliated with the program, he nevertheless has strong feelings about how it evolved over the years. The organization was founded based on what Rivera and his colleagues viewed as an overlooked need: "forgotten" Latino males. After heading a research project supported by the California Endowment and the county public health department, Rivera was allowed to pilot one Latino boy support group at a North Arroyo Seco middle school.

This first group comprised less than twenty students and would meet every day for one period during the school day. It was focused on health, and Rivera would conduct workshops about healthy life practices, invite health practitioners to present, and connect them to health-based resources on and off campus. Most important for Rivera was the healing aspect of the pilot program. Dialogue circles, referred to simply as circulo (circle), were at the center of everything. Latino boys would share their trials and tribulations with one another, and through these intimate conversations, led by a loving Latino male mentor, the boys would develop into healthy young men—men who could resolve their problems without violence, substance abuse, and other actions detrimental to their well-being. Rivera, as well as several other veteran mentors, described the early role of the mentor as that of an informal social worker and therapist, and the notion of healing was at the center of LMS's vision.[4]

The pilot was a hit. Students and parents gave rave reviews of the program, and the district quickly agreed to expand the program, now called Latino Male Success, to four schools. Each additional school would come with a new Latino male mentor to manage the LMS group at the school site. By 2015 the program employed ten mentors, each assigned to a different school site. LMS also appeared to be a welcomed Latino male counterpart to the larger Black Males Rising (BMR) program, a Black male empowerment program begun by the district shortly before LMS. As LMS moved beyond its pilot year, however, it remained independent of the district and was firmly housed in the large Latinx nonprofit Pueblo Unido.

As seed money began to wane, Pueblo Unido helped to maintain and expand LMS by seeking outside funding and grants. Sometimes grants and funds came with conditions. Tutoring became an official service of LMS, and workforce training workshops became required to satisfy the requirements of a new grant. Students would also be encouraged to partner with other job-readiness programs being developed by Pueblo Unido. This put a strain on the relationship between Pueblo Unido and LMS. "As we got bigger, Pueblo Unido saw us as a money-maker," and "that's where the integrity of the program changed," explained Rivera. For him, the pressure to expand and fund the program had driven Pueblo Unido to make LMS marketable to new funding sources. Framing LMS as job-readiness training opened the program to partnerships with local giants in the tech sector, who valued the optics of offering workshops and internships to Latino boys in North Arroyo Seco. Rivera described how tension emerged around this time regarding professionalism. Pueblo Unido began reminding LMS staff of the professional dress code and began requiring LMS mentors to spend more time in the Pueblo Unido central office. He pointed out how some of LMS's early community partners like the California Endowment had envisioned the students becoming "politically active" but that Pueblo Unido had rejected this. "They were like, 'Naw, we are not going to make a bunch of little Cesar Chavezes.' . . . So there was conflict." Rivera suggested that, as the new fundraising initiatives became prioritized, Pueblo Unido began to monitor and control the staff at LMS more. "I finally left," he said.

In our conversation, Rivera described the struggle to define the goals and purpose of LMS as well as the role of funding and corporate partnerships in dictating a vision for Latino boyhoods in Arroyo Seco. Rivera describes the early years of LMS as the program shifted from a focus on health and critical cultural awareness toward its current focus on academic excellence and workforce training. This struggle to dictate the goals and mission of LMS was a common theme I witnessed during my research. I encountered a variety of descriptions of the mission, and different parties described the problem that LMS sought to address differently. While some individuals pointed to racism and framed the problem as structural and political, it was clear to me that this was a counternarrative to the prevailing mission of LMS. Through an examination of the curriculum, official mission statements, program documents, the LMS motto, and qualitative data gathered with administrators and funders, it was clear the problem was the boys themselves. And LMS was meant to address this problem.

Scholars of neoliberalism have often noted that the notion of crisis often justifies the need for private-sector intervention (Klein 2008). Through the promise of innovation and expertise, something seen as desperately needed in the early 2000s, LMS was able to secure a partnership with ASUSD under a renewing memorandum of understanding (MOU). Under the agreement, ASUSD would offer a small amount of funds to support LMS (a fraction of the LMS budget), but more importantly, offer space on public school campuses as well as access to the students themselves during the school day. In the MOU, ASUSD highlighted the need for this agreement based on the growing number of Latinx students in the district (although Arroyo Seco has had a large Latinx population for many decades), the need to support this population in a culturally relevant way (and Pueblo Unido's expertise in doing so), as well as the perceived success of the district's existing Black Males Rising program. Among the primary services stated in the MOU are "male-oriented wellness," "workforce development," and "character development."

CREATING GOOD BOYS THROUGH CHARACTER DEVELOPMENT

Today, LMS is primarily known as a character development program that leads to improved academic performance and job readiness. This is made clear in numerous ways. Its website highlights a narrative of personal journey and masculine growth as boys learn to become "men of their word" under the guidance of strong, adult male Latino mentors. Fundraising literature suggests donations will help "improve outcomes in health, education, behavior, family interaction, and career planning" by "reaching young men and boys to help them choose and stay on a path in life." Administrators consistently described the program as a place where boys develop habits to become good men with good values. Moreover, the program's curriculum and values are clearly directed at this objective, and the curriculum the mentors use prioritizes this ideal. Each LMS mentor is provided a six-week curriculum to teach during the school year. While mentors had a considerable amount of flexibility and autonomy to make their own lesson plans during their class time, the curriculum was a defining aspect of the program and greatly contributed to the ethos of LMS.

The curriculum, titled Muchachos Virtuosos, came from a regional network of Latino male programming partners whose goal was to promote a healthy and culturally rooted Latino manhood. LMS's use of a curriculum specifically defined as "character development" is indicative of the ways neoliberal interventions in urban education discursively construct the intersectional deficits of boys of color. Stated differently, the necessity of a character development curriculum is supported by the image of the bad boy. This curriculum promotes the development of a traditional heteropatriarchal manhood for boys of color and propagates the notion that a failed masculinity is central to the disenfranchisement of boys and men of color.

Although on most days mentors created their own lessons, the Muchachos Virtuosos curriculum was central to the overall program values and vision of LMS. It was not uncommon for school staff or community members to mistakenly refer to LMS as Muchachos Virtuosos rather than Latino Male Success or LMS. Muchachos Virtuosos was composed of a variety of lessons tailored to improving the character of Latino boys. The opening lesson of the curriculum is a discussion surrounding a short story. In the story, a mother struggles to find a man to guide her son across the "man's bridge" to adulthood. Unlike the women's bridge, which is full of mutual support, the man's bridge is blocked by untrustworthy, violent, and disrespectful drunkards. The moral of the story is that men must find a way to break the mold and achieve an honorable manhood that has been lost. This primary lesson sets the tone for the rest of the curriculum, which focuses on avoiding drugs and teen pregnancy and cultivating respect for one's family. The second lesson of Muchachos Virtuosos is titled "Credible Word/Palabra" and centers around having students become honest, noble, and trustworthy young men. This is a good representation of the six-week curriculum for struggling Latino boys.

The defining ethos of LMS also drew from the cuatro valores (four values) in the Muchachos Virtuosos curriculum. These cuatro valores served as a motto and mantra of the program. They are visible in all LMS classrooms and present on program sweatshirts, and students are required to memorize them:

1. Keep your word
2. Don't bring harm to others
3. Take responsibility for your actions
4. Be a positive example to others

Having these values at the core of LMS's school-based intervention with Latino boys served to frame Latino males through their potential to lack these four qualities, questioning their character and positioning the students as at risk of being dishonest, violent, irresponsible, and negative influences in their community. Scholars have pointed out the shortsightedness and inherent racism coded in the persistent focus on the character of structurally marginalized students. For example, abolitionist educator Bettina Love (2019) has described how the notion of character development is indicative of the private sector's "obsession" with testing and measuring "the character of dark and poor children" (76) in an effort to package and sell a beating-the-odds product. As Love states, this type of educational "*Hunger Games* propaganda leads educators to believe that the key to 'success' for dark children lies in improving their grit and zest 'levels'" (73). This focus on character reframes students of color from being marginalized by the racist structures of schooling and society to instead embody moral deviancy that results in untapped potential, value, and grit. Although the values of these core tenets are not innately problematic, the lack of a political or structural referent at best gives them little meaning, and at worst normalizes the notion that Latino boys need to develop a virtuous character that is presumably absent. For Latino boys, being the target population of a program founded in character development reaffirmed their positionality as deviant yet potentially productive racial subjects.

PATHOLOGIZING LATINO BOYS AND THE "RIGHT PATH" DISCOURSE

From its very beginning, LMS's internal and public documents, such as web pages, media clips, fundraiser events, and curriculum, all discursively present the problem of Latino boys as primarily their own pathological behaviors and potential fate of succumbing to the violence and crime that was so prevalent in North Arroyo Seco. This framing was also consistently present in the way LMS administrators described the program during interviews. These problems were framed through "culture of poverty" arguments (see Lewis 2011), which focus on the cultural behavior of individuals and pay little attention to the political and structural issues that contribute to racial inequalities.

In all administrator interviews and official mission statements of LMS, race or racism was never mentioned. Instead, popular in LMS administrator interviews, fundraisers, and program documents was what I describe as the *right path discourse*. Based on document analysis and interviews with administrators and funders, I define right path discourse as the language of individualized responsibility and possibility for "at-risk" youth who, if properly self-disciplined and not tempted by cultural vices, may become productive investments and exemplify the American dream. From this perspective, one steadily increases one's human capital and earning potential by following the right path. In this sense, the right path in education is not necessarily a path to critical race consciousness and revolutionary activism (perhaps unlike the educational goals of the 1960s and 1970s grassroots community groups), but rather a means of accumulating résumé-building skills and accomplishments that maximize the student's competitiveness on the job market and capacity to earn.

At LMS, for example, part of manhood building involved intimate discussions about representations of Latino manhood that students saw in the media, their home, and their community. Mentors were expected to help identify the primary role models in the lives of their students and help students differentiate between positive and negative examples. One mentor, Mr. Javier, offered a critical perspective on this sort of activity. While he acknowledged it was good to unpack what the students saw every day in their community, this could sometimes pathologize "negative examples" who were identified as part of the wrong path. "It can feel like [we're saying], 'Don't be like them. They're bad. Throw them out,'" he shared on the topic of differentiating what types of Latino men were on the "wrong path." This made it tricky for him to navigate this sort of lesson in LMS. If mentors were taught to help boys "break the cycle"—as several mentors put it—of negative Latino male behavior, it had to be acknowledged that many Latino men and boys, past and present, were guilty of this behavior.

Although this "right path" approach is framed through care and empowerment, it relies on a discourse that obfuscates structural racism and systematic racial inequality in U.S. schools and instead promotes the notion that there is a clear avenue to educational success. Frequently, when mass numbers of students of color are systematically pushed out of schools, the problem is individualized (Fine 1991), faulting the student who becomes disinterested in academics, stops attending classes, and departs from the imagined right path to success. Through this framing of the problems facing Latino boys, the Latino male mentor/role model becomes an obvious and popular solution for directing boys, giving them a clear example to follow on the pathway to success (M. V. Singh 2018). For example, the LMS director shared this framing of the central goal of LMS:

> I think our biggest goal here is to keep boys on the right path . . . show them they have options. Arroyo Seco is a rough place for a Latino male. Drugs, violence, gangs, you know how it is, especially in the North. People don't get out. Our boys, they don't get exposed to anything else, they don't know there's more out there for them, other options [like] college, success, a career . . . that's where our mentors come in.

Here, the program director caringly states what LMS mentors can give to the boys: a clear vision of success outside of the chaos of their own community. While this statement is rooted in genuine concern for the boys, it also does the discursive work of articulating an idealized Latino manhood by naming the devalued and perverse characteristics that make up the bad boy. This failed Latino male identity is characterized by cultural stagnation, perceived self-inflicted violence, and the social death that individuals can experience if they join a gang. Realizing the multiple "options" at hand and making the correct choice could lead the boys out of North Arroyo Seco and into professional success and a productive identity.

I highlight the program director's words not to criticize him (his passion and commitment to the boys were always apparent to me) but to demonstrate one of the countless ways LMS and Pueblo Unido leadership offered the "right path" discourse as the guiding function of their work with young people. In this interview, we understand the boys as holding potential beyond their socially and economically stagnant community. This community, whose culture of poverty and violence threatened to engulf the boys, now represented a maze to be navigated and, in the end, escaped. Key to aiding in the growth of the boys' human capital were the mentors, a group of college-educated Latino men who, in line with neoliberal shifts in urban education, were outside technicians (perhaps experts) brought into public schools to help solve the district's problems with Latino boys through character development, guidance, mentorship, and modeling an idealized Latino masculinity.

This narrative was particularly useful for fundraising efforts as the boys of LMS became humanized and valued by donors through their potential to earn and produce. In one fundraiser gala, a Latino city councilman from a North Arroyo Seco district shared his journey to the right path as a way to humanize the boys through their potential to be productive, like himself. He stated:

> We all *know* who these boys are and they're not bad kids. . . . I *know* them better than most, you see, I never shy away from saying I am from Arroyo Seco, and I'm proud of it [crowd applause]. . . . I *know* what it's like to grow up on the Northside. I was a little knucklehead myself, a travieso [troublemaker] who needed a big brother to knock me on the head sometimes and keep me on the right path.

Here, the councilman asserts a collective knowledge to the individual and corporate philanthropists of the gala, many of whom are men of color themselves. Although bad kids may exist, *these* boys are not bad kids. In fact, the boys have the potential to succeed if someone can help keep them on the right path. In this way, the philanthropists were able to participate in the neoliberal multicultural practice of problem-solving racial inequality by investing in at-risk Latino boys. These were not the bad kids we have heard of and fear, but rather worthy investments to contribute to diversity and social justice. Invisible in this narrative was the exclusion of low-income communities of color from the massive accumulations of wealth in the region gained by many funders and developers present at the gala. This process had ignited rapid gentrification in Arroyo Seco as well as other surrounding cities and had a profound impact on the boys and their families. However, in this framing it is the boys' own cultural limitation and lack of self-restraint that stand in the way of their own success. This was seen as an individual problem rather than a structural one, and it would be remedied by the mentors who now stood around the fundraising floor. Within this neoliberal solution, the mentors would serve as role models to compound the worth of the boys. As LMS's assistant program director stated in one of the region's prominent newspapers several years before that gala: Latino boys are "resources" that "are not to be wasted."

MENTORING AND THE PERFORMANCE OF THE "BAD BOY" AND THE "GOOD ROLE MODEL"

Problematic friends and delinquent community members were often the first issues mentioned as factors that threatened to knock Latino boys off the right path. This point was made in LMS fundraising literature, speeches by administrators and guests, and even mentors in their conversations with students. LMS administrators, funders, and at times mentors repeatedly cited "hanging out with the 'wrong crowd'" as a detriment to the boys' success. This error in association, they suggested, could lead to drugs, skipped classes, bad attitudes, gang activity, and fights. In one of several LMS fundraisers I attended, I was struck by the comments of a Latina ASUSD board member who represented the Mariposa District, an area that encompassed several LMS schools. Speaking in front of a large crowd, she turned to the mentors and addressed them directly:

> You all, the mentors of Latino Male Success, you are key in this struggle, college-educated young Latino men. Talk to the boys and they will listen to you, you are them, tell them not to make the same mistakes you made, teach them, show them, help them to not fall in with the wrong crowd . . . help them follow your path.

I had heard a version of this advice from this school board member a year earlier at a public forum on Latinx education in Arroyo Seco. I had spoken with her after the earlier event, and upon hearing about my aspiration to study Latino male mentorship she told me of the value in college-educated young Latino men like myself talking to young boys about our paths to success. This could help them avoid making "the same mistakes" that college-educated Latino men had made.

In both encounters with this school board member, I was struck by her use of the phrase "avoid making the same mistakes." Having conducted in-depth interviews with all the mentors at LMS, I knew that with the exception of two or three cases the mentors had, like myself, made few serious "errors" in their academic careers, that they had earned strong to stellar grades in high school, and that they had gone on to a four-year university. Several mentors had attended some of California's most prestigious universities, such as UCLA and UC Berkeley, straight out of high school, with others excelling at other University of California and California State University campuses. And yet the narrative of a once delinquent boy turned productive man who has returned to save the community felt comfortable, commonsense, and, in the context of a fundraiser, sellable.

When the school board member described this same framing of mentors during her speech that afternoon, the crowd's response seemed approving, as if the comment was natural and fitting to the topic of Latino male mentorship. Most of the crowd was serious and nodded their heads in agreement and support. Who better to keep boys from falling in with the wrong crowd than successful young men who had nearly fallen into the wrong crowd themselves? In a 2017 study of Black youth workers in a similar kind of educational nonprofit organization, Bianca Baldridge (2017) described how funders and philanthropists are specifically interested in financially supporting the "charismatic Black male leader." These leaders are asked to sell their personal stories, "marked by damage and struggle" (792), as a means to secure funding for their organization. In the neoliberal context of urban education, the savior narrative continues to use notions of damage and deviancy, while upholding the imagined out-of-control lives of reckless young people who populated the "bad boys" or "wrong crowd."

During the time I spent at LMS, I often wondered who these bad boys were and why it was so important that the mentors work so hard to help their students avoid them. The discourse of the "bad boy" and "wrong crowd" was everywhere in LMS, yet the physical bodies of these boys seemed absent. Who were they? On one hand, the simple answer to this question is that these boys were in fact not absent from the program, at least not entirely. It is true that some young people experience decisive individual acts of punishment and exclusion, such as arrest, incarceration, or school expulsion, which result in their removal from school and thus their ineligibility in a program like LMS. However, for many Latino boys, the difference between being on what was described as the right path and the wrong path was not as simple as many administrators and funders made it out to be. Although a small percentage of LMS students seemed obviously on the path to academic success (indicated by high GPAs and Advanced Placement classes), many boys fell outside of this right path–wrong path binary. Many of the students were seen as both, occupying the role of the bad boy in one classroom and the good boy in another. Others exhibited none of the unruly behavior that seemed to categorize the bad boy, yet still found themselves unlikely to graduate from high school.[5]

Over the course of two years at LMS, I never encountered what might be considered this quintessential, violent urban youth whose image had sparked fear and scorn for decades.[6] Yet the bad boy discourse had created a fear of becoming part of the wrong crowd, constructing a threat that would in many ways call for its discursive opposite as a remedy. This dynamic created space for the performative notion of the good Latino male role model. Language produces our daily lived realities through small and large speech acts that we participate in every day. Renowned poststructural theorist Judith Butler (1990) has written extensively about the way preexisting determinants can inform the way a person performs an identity: "The act that one does, the act that one performs, is, in a sense, an act that has been going on before one arrived on the scene" (272). At LMS, through the repeated praise of mentors as ideal role models for Latino boys, preexisting discourses regarding the problematics of Latino boyhood were reified, and a new, or what I call *neoliberal Latino,* masculinity was constantly present, spoken about, understood, and embodied. This is not to say that any one individual mentor empirically lived the perfect neoliberal life (indeed, this life would be in perpetual redefinition) but that the constant discourse surrounding the importance of the role model built and rebuilt the values contributing to this role model. The boys' voices were also actively displayed as speaking this language. In flyers and other program literature advertising the benefits and triumphs of the program, Pueblo Unido highlights quotations from some of the boys expressing this sentiment.[7] One boy simply states, "I just wanted to get out of trouble." As another says, "I decided to join this program because it was going to help me be a better person." For Latino boys, this "better person" was already known and understood through the language and values assigned to good Latino boys, frequently juxtaposed with who and what was known to be bad. The better person was often embodied through the discursive construction of the ideal role model: the mentor.

When I spoke to the program director in 2018, I asked specifically about this role modeling. His response clearly laid out some of the valued characteristics of Latino masculinity, underscoring the mentor's central role in this performance:

> Yeah, our mentors are definitely role models, and I think that's huge for our boys. You know, they grow up without having positive role models, dudes slingin' [selling drugs] and not doing anything with their lives. . . . Or like no dad at home, right? And so now here's this guy, went to college, wears good clothes, takes care of his family in some of our cases. It feels good for our boys to be around a real man you know? Someone who takes care of business.

In verbalizing an idealized Latino manhood embodied by the mentors, the program director first addresses the perceived problematics of Latino male identity before articulating a reformed manhood conducive to the values of neoliberalism. Here a *real man* is an individual who is meritocratic and takes care of business, no matter what. Moreover, he is allotted value through his college degree and respectable clothing, two attributes that increase his ability to accumulate capital in the formal and legal economy. Beyond the juxtaposition of the violent and unproductive man of color with the virtuous neoliberal Latino man, embedded in this quotation is a direct gesture to the ways neoliberal solutions to racial deviancies intersect with heteronormativity and patriarchy.

FUTURE FAMILY MEN: NEOLIBERAL FRAMINGS OF GENDERED AND SEXUAL DEFICITS

Embedded in the goal of building good boys in LMS was the need to instill a deep appreciation for heteropatriarchal values and traditional familial arrangements. The mission of LMS was often framed as one of masculine recuperation and the need for Latino boys to fulfill traditional heteropatriarchal norms in the Latinx community. Scholars of the racial politics of gender and sexuality point to the ways neoliberalism incites specific racialized gender and sexual formations (Hong and Ferguson 2011). By narrating communities of color as deficient, the neoliberal project incorporates communities of color by constituting them as populations requiring help and care to achieve proper personhood. This care incorporates an invitation into embodying gendered and sexual respectability—inviting communities of color to adopt normative familial and sexual practices as a means of racial uplift. This invitation to respectability serves to regulate and punish those populations existing outside of the conditioning power of neoliberalism—justifying their own dispossession. Respectability in this context is, as Grace Kyungwon Hong (2015) has described it, increasingly defined by "the attainment of monogamous couplehood, normative reproductivity, and consumerist subjectivity" that serves to determine "those who are worthy of capital investment and thus protected and those who are not and thus precarious" (60).[8]

Other scholars have pointed to the way that long-standing racist images of Latino males as embodying a deviant manhood intersects with the gendered and sexual values of neoliberalism—which stress the nuclear family, monogamy, and heteropatriarchal reproduction. Lisa Marie Cacho (2007) argues that in an increasingly multicultural society, the requirements for personhood for devalued racial subjects depend on capitalist and heteropatriarchal measures of worth. The image of the macho has long categorized Latino males as hypersexual, chauvinistic womanizers, and drunkards, who are overbearing, violent, and frequently toxic and failed patriarchs whose behavior is to the detriment of their nuclear family. To achieve social value, Latino males are asked to "perform masculinity in proper, respectable ways" as a means to "redeem, reform, or counter" (148) their perceived social (racialized) deviancy. For LMS and other youth programs that seek to incorporate "at-risk" boys of color into racial respectability, part of reaching young men is purging them of a problematic masculinity and sexual deviancy. To redeem or restore Latino manhood, proper gender and sexuality was required. This shapes the image of the good boy as cisgender, straight, and prepared to one day perform the tasks of a productive (heteropatriarchal) manhood. Thus, youth programming becomes a project of instilling a proper gendered sexual subjectivity (Hutchings 2023).

In LMS, empowering Latino boys intersected with the need to restore a proper heteropatriarchal manhood. Boys were seen as at risk of racialized delinquency but also suspected of eventually failing to perform a heteronormative and patriarchal lifestyle. In interviews with LMS administrators and mentors, as well as conversations with donors and community members, a commonsensical aspect of LMS, although not formally in its mission statement, was that it would help prepare Latino boys for fatherhood in a traditional family. This framed LMS mentors as father-like figures and positioned the boys as potentially lacking these role models in their community. The temptation to adopt a negative or deviant masculinity threatened the heteropatriarchal stability of the Latinx community. Thus, modeling a positive masculinity connected to a positive patriarchal role fulfillment was key. A good boy was implicitly or explicitly heterosexual and a responsible patriarch of his future family and community.

In explaining the importance of LMS's work, the Pueblo Unido CEO connected character development to the needs of the larger Latinx community. "Some of these boys are about to be young fathers. I mean, think about that. That's why character development is huge to us," he shared. This concern for traditional (heteronormative) family values was a running theme in LMS, and throughout the study, differing or queer family arrangements were, except in a handful of cases, never discussed or mentioned. This targeted idealization of the family is what Kimberlé Crenshaw refers to as a "patriarchy enhancement" solution. An outspoken critic of President Obama's MBK initiative, Crenshaw argues that MBK and similar male mentorship programs frame the source of the problem as being that "the men are not appropriately socialized to be the kind of men who are responsible for families and for communities"; she identifies this way of seeing racial inequality as solely in terms of "patriarchal absences" (Crenshaw 2014).

While the goal of the program and curriculum often implicitly intersected with the need to build future (cis-straight) family men in LMS, one lesson in the Muchachos Virtuosos curriculum connects the need for traditionally responsible manhood, in this case sexual restraint, as intersecting with a culturally relevant and innate aspect of Latinx culture. As part of the lesson, boys are asked to read an excerpt of the Florentine Codex.[9] The curriculum introduces the excerpt:

The passage below, addressed to a son, by his father, speaks of the importance of sexual moderation . . .

Do not throw yourself upon women
Like the dog which throws itself upon food.
Be not like the dog
When he is given food or drink,
Giving yourself up to women before the time comes.
Even though you may long for women,
Hold back, hold back with your heart
Until you are a grown man, strong and robust.
Look at the maguey plant.
If it is opened before it has grown
And its liquid is taken out,
It has no substance.
It does not produce liquid, it is useless.
Before it is opened
To withdraw its water
It should be allowed to grow and attain full size.
Then its sweet water is removed
All in good time.
This is how you must act:
Before you know a woman
You must grow and be a complete man.
And then you will be ready for marriage;
You will beget children of good stature,
Healthy, agile, and comely.

In this document, sexual restraint is seen as a rite of passage for a young man. The conditioning of one's sexuality is intertwined with one's ability to successfully marry and father children.

Through its inclusion in a school-based intervention for Latino boys, this curriculum constructs boys as racially deviant but explicitly connects this deviancy to gendered and sexual shortcomings. This lesson explicitly assumes a cis-straight boy who will one day marry and father children, thereby remedying the deviancies of Latino manhood through a sanitized narrative of sexual moderation, marriage, and the masculine responsibilities of human reproduction. The use of a Nahua codex grasps at a seemingly innate cultural connection for Latinx students. In some way, these values are asserted as having *always* been the values of good Latino boys. The lesson is framed as ancient Indigenous wisdom to offer a level of cultural relevancy and empowerment, despite the fact that its employment here is more aligned with conditioning boys to uphold neoliberal and Western, not Indigenous, practices of sexuality and familial reproduction.

The aforementioned lesson also forecloses queer futurities for the children of LMS, who are invited into a neoliberal manhood. A discourse that values patriarchy devalues queer and trans masculinities as insignificant in a solution that assigns importance to the traditional nuclear family. Despite being framed as a social justice–oriented manhood training program, LMS documents lacked any mention of queer or trans masculinity, and nontraditional family arrangements and queer lifestyles were rarely, if at all, mentioned. During my interview with the program director of LMS, I asked about sexuality in the program and how queer students fit in the greater mission of LMS. The director looked taken aback, responding, "We don't have any LGBQ students." However, during my time at LMS, I encountered several students who identified as gay or questioned their presumed heterosexuality. Numerous LMS mentors confirmed that in their years as mentors they had had students who identified as gay. The assertion by the program director demonstrates queer erasure within the Latino manhood cultivated in LMS. The program director then offered an anecdote.

> We've had a student who was a female but kind of like queer. . . .
> They [the school] were saying that she could be part of our group,
> but the way the mentor approached it was like, "Well the kid is going
> to go through a lot of changes that I won't be able to help with.

Or I won't be able to like kind of like have an idea what that change is, because I've never dealt with that." So in that instance, the understanding with the student, the administration, and us was that it would be best served if she was not part of the circle. . . . I think it would be tougher for that youth to be helped because she would feel isolated. . . . We would not know how to serve that youth.

In this account of an instance years before my fieldwork began, we hear of a student interested in LMS, a gendered space not assigned to them at birth, and their denied entry into the program. The needs of the student are presented as beyond the scope and abilities of LMS, further revealing the limited and specific Latino male subject envisioned by the program. Nowhere in the founding documents or on the LMS website were queer or non-cisgender students mentioned. Instead, an affirming discourse around an ideal cisgender and heteronormative Latino male subjectivity helped to shape the gendered and sexual qualities of an imagined LMS student. This universalizing practice rejects nondominant gender performances and queerness by excluding or erasing them in the larger project of Latino male empowerment. This discourse—which was present in language across the program literature and curriculum and was reiterated by the current program administrators—shaped the need, mission, and goals of LMS. It used the figure of the "bad boy"—a deviant (potentially violent, criminal, and queer) Latino manhood—to construct an ideal cisgender and heteronormative Latino male subjectivity to be embraced by students. In this way, LMS's school-based intervention was aimed at constructing good boys—boys who held value as individual workers, productive citizens, and future heteropatriarchs in their families and communities.

CONCLUSION: BAD AND GOOD HOMBRES

During a presidential debate in October 2016, then candidate Donald Trump used the memorable phrase "bad hombres" to describe what he considered the mass amounts of violent Latino men living in the United States without legal status. By characterizing undocumented Latino men as murderous and sexually violent, Trump tapped into preexisting racial fears of Latino men and called for the bolstering of one of the most powerful branches of the PIC, Immigration and Customs Enforcement (ICE). As in years past, images of tattooed and ruthless Latino men were used to spark fear in white (and increasingly nonwhite) Americans, imagining these now international gang members pouring across the southern border from Mexico and Central America (Santa Ana 2002). These violent men and boys were coming through illegal channels to traffic drugs, spill their drug war on U.S. streets, and show little remorse for the rape and murders they commit. In Trump's words, "We have some bad hombres here, and we're going to get them out."

This vision of the bad and good Latino male has become a common framing model in the United States, and it directly intersects with the way educational programs like LMS today approach their work with Latino boys. Racial fears of men and boys of color, and particularly Black men, have always been a central part of white supremacy in the United States (A. L. Brown 2011). These fears helped lay the groundwork for the rise of hyperpolicing and the PIC in the late 1970s, something that in turn became a key moment in the way boys and men of color are imagined in popular culture, politics, and education. This moment began the cultural construction of the deviant Latino male—the radical, the queer, the gangster, the superpredator, and the present-day bad hombre—that has been used to justify the policing and punishment of boys of color inside and outside of schools. However, running parallel to the rise of the PIC is the NPIC, which influences the framing of Latinx young people in educational contexts like LMS—both by-products of the neoliberal era, both bent on managing and controlling difference. Although the PIC and policing represent physical repression and violence, nonprofit youth programming represents a more covert form of repression, or what Michel Foucault (2010) refers to as *biopolitics*. Responding to the image of problematic young people of color, youth programs control, manage, and frame the ways through which young people are "empowered" to lead successful and happy lives (Kwon 2013). In the case of LMS, the threat of having Latino boys grow up to embody the popular image of the violent urban Latino male serves as a guiding force in the ways the mentorship program and many of its supporters understand its goal and mission.

This performative relationship between good and bad hombres was central to the ways LMS understood its existence and value to the Arroyo Seco community. On one hand, this relationship vilifies the "wrong crowd" as hopeless, violent, uncomplicated individuals whose life choices eventually led to academic, economic, and social failure. On the other, good hombres, the type of Latino manhood cultivated by LMS through "character development," was largely defined by neoliberal values. Although the term "good hombres" has not been explicitly used by former president Trump, I use it here to illustrate the ways racist stereotypes and images can determine the manner whereby people of color redefine their own identities to respond to what they are not. This serves to limit their boundaries of expression by confining their language of self-definition to the rationalities and grammars that circumscribe the hegemonic qualities of a good racial subject.

For the program, success is categorized by the boys' self-investment in their future earning potential, indicated by their merit-driven academic success, respectability, and self-discipline. Success is also intertwined with the notion of fulfilling the patriarchal order of a productive, hetero-nuclear family. Here, the boys were imagined to be straight and cisgender, training for a life as family men and financial providers of their family and community. Both instances represent a neoliberal multicultural intervention in racial inequality. If past eras of Latinx education sought to radically challenge white supremacy in the United States through subversive education and activism, the era of neoliberal multiculturalism addresses the problem of race as remedied through preparedness for market inclusion and human capital investment. In LMS, Latino male mentors are outside technicians who enter schools to make cultural interventions with Latino boys.

In this chapter I have focused solely on the ways these interventions were framed from the administrative and curricular level, positioning the program to challenge racial pathological behavior, which for Latino boys included a lack of academic self-discipline and the inability to achieve proper and respectable heteropatriarchal values. In the following chapters I explore the ways neoliberal discourse surrounding the problems and solutions of Latino boys became both animated and challenged in the classroom among the boys and mentors on the everyday level.

CULTIVATING HUMAN CAPITAL

Lessons in Neoliberal Empowerment

> Within neoliberal rationality, human capital is both our "is" and
> our "ought"–what we are said to be, what we should be, and what
> the rationality makes us into through its norms and construction of
> environments.
>
> **—Wendy Brown,** *Undoing the Demos*

On a Monday afternoon, Mr. Antonio's middle school group of LMS students chatted among themselves in a circle as they prepared paints for an art activity. Mr. Antonio's classroom was one of three LMS classes I had been visiting twice a week during my time with LMS. During this kind of lesson, the boys were permitted to talk freely while playing music. As they prepared their paints, several boys took turns connecting their phones to the large speakers behind Mr. Antonio's desk—periodically sneaking back to raise the volume. As they switched from one phone to the next, the music jumped from top-forty hip-hop and local rap artists to corridos and banda music. These abrupt musical transitions uniquely represented this group of boys and caused Mr. Antonio and I to make eye contact and smile to one another.

Today the boys' task was to begin painting the papier-mâché máscaras (masks) that they had created the previous week. This project entailed having boys paint both the front and back sides of their masks. The front symbolized aspects of the boys that people already know or that they choose to let people see. The back represented the emotions and feelings they choose to keep private. The máscara project's goal is to allow students to reflect on what aspects of themselves they present to the world and what feelings and emotions they keep hidden. The project culminates in an oral presentation of the máscara to the rest of the class.

Once the paints were set up and the activity underway, several of the eighth grade boys complained that they were unsure how to begin. "Just paint some Arroyo Seco shit," suggested Kevin as he held up his work. His mask was painted in the colors of a local professional sports team, whose regalia helped to define the region's identity. On the forehead, Kevin had inscribed in graffiti-style lettering "Upper North," the northernmost area of North Arroyo Seco, and a region notorious for its crime and poverty. There was a murmur of approval.

"Good, Kevin, that's a real good idea," announced Mr. Antonio, who walked up to the front of the classroom and prepared for an impromptu lesson, "It reminds me of something I wanted to share with you all. The other night at a fundraiser, guess how much some of those masks sold for." There was a pause with no reply. Mr. Antonio let the silence linger as he smiled and looked around the classroom: "100, 200, even 500 dollars." This statement was met by a chorus of exclamations. Some boys shook their heads in disbelief. "No? Don't believe me? Ask Michael. He was there too." "Yeah, sort of," I replied reluctantly—although I felt it was a bit more complicated.

A week earlier, Mr. Antonio and I had attended an upscale fundraiser for LMS at a local country club. Many of the LMS mentors had been shocked by the wealth of some attendees. The top levels of sponsorship at the fundraiser included the Gold level ($10,000) and Silver level ($5,000). There were also options of an individual or team donation to play golf ($150–$900), a $50 single-dinner ticket (my humble contribution to attend the event), and a live, no-limit auction of donated gifts from business partners. During the auction, attendees—most of whom were Black and Latino businessmen—raised numbered cards to indicate an increased bid to the charismatic auctioneer and CEO of Pueblo Unido, Gerald Espinoza. Higher-end items (such as Southwest Airlines tickets, NFL tickets, and brunch with the mayor) were paired with a student's máscara from the previous year. The masks were colorful and featured a wide range of cultural images and personal symbols painted by past students. They were elegantly situated in wooden display cases that had been acquired for the auction. I had understood the masks to be less of a purchase and more of a gift that accompanied a large donation.[1]

"Something you're going to need to learn how to do is sell your story," continued Mr. Antonio that day in the classroom. "It's worth something; people love to hear it." He looked around at some of the boys' work and continued, "Like Álvaro, you should draw a Salvadoran flag or something like that." Álvaro had made the long journey from El Salvador with his mother and brother just four years earlier. He looked down at his mask and pondered the idea. Another boy, Jesús, raised his máscara, displaying a near-complete Mexican flag he had painted. "Nice, Jesús," responded Mr. Antonio. The painting proceeded as the boys continued to enjoy their music and joke about the potential value of their masks at an imagined fundraiser in the future.

Today, neoliberalism stretches beyond economic structure and into the ways educators like Mr. Antonio and the students in his class understand their lives. In her book *Undoing the Demos: Neoliberalism's Stealth Revolution*, Wendy Brown (2015) explains that neoliberalism "transmogrifies every human domain and endeavor, along with humans themselves, according to a specific image of the economic" (10). In schools, neoliberalism has reinscribed the role of education to be a means of investing in one's human capital and potential to earn, while also creating the student as capital—who is then tasked with leveraging their own competitive position and worth through educational attainment and skills (Apple 2006; Ball and Olmedo 2013).

This was not the first or last time that Mr. Antonio would talk frankly about narrating one's life story into a profitable commodity. He often used his own experiences as an example. Mr. Antonio was also from Arroyo Seco and had shared with the class that in his youth he had done drugs, gotten tattoos, and been expelled from his first high school. However, he eventually graduated and went on to earn a bachelor's degree from a local state college. He knew that this story of resilience was admired in the progressive world, and he used it to his advantage. "I am a Latino male with a college degree. . . . I know that we are in high demand in education and social worky type areas," he explained to me. "It's a sad reality, but it's true. Like, you got to know people love to hear that stuff [one's narrative of struggle]," he continued. "I don't take it to the political level with the masks"—referencing a debate among mentors about the ethics of including the máscaras in the fundraiser—"That's how the world works, and the boys need to know how the game is played." For Mr. Antonio, being an LMS mentor was not about being "political"; it was about preparing young men to be successful. He wanted his students to be able to compete in the real world.

Despite being well intentioned, Mr. Antonio's approach to helping the boys he worked with—an approach that correlated with what was expected of mentors at LMS—points to a larger dilemma in the way young people of color today are framed within educational support programs. Across the United States, programs like LMS that target boys and young men of color act as a form of governmentality as they use their paternalistic embrace to encourage boys to embody a subjectivity that reiterates neoliberal values that make a *good boy*. While many involved in LMS described the program's values and practices as both positive and universal, many of the central values of LMS reinforced problematic ideas about Latino boys. Approaches like Mr. Antonio's— where Latino boys are told to embrace their ability to "sell" the narrative of overcoming this struggle—illustrate a neoliberal subjectivity to be embraced by Latino boys. As critical theorists of education have argued, schools and learning practices are inherently rooted in power and social context (Apple 2004), and LMS was no exception. In the previous chapter I outlined the ways public–private educational interventions, such as the MBK initiative, use familiar racial imaginations to construct boys and young men of color as problems in need of intervention. This chapter enters the classroom to explore the everyday practice of neoliberal empowerment. This form of empowerment departs from previous notions of racial justice work that focus on political activism and a politics of disruption. Instead, empowerment in the neoliberal era has been recalibrated to mean empowerment of the individual. It is the freedom to maximize one's potential to be competitive and create one's own success. In this chapter I shed light on the ways neoliberal formulations of empowerment affected the everyday lessons of LMS and influenced how the boys came to understand their value and place in the world.

PROMOTING MERITOCRACY AND INDIVIDUALISM

Incentivizing Success

A founding principle of liberalism is that free competition among individuals maximizes the productivity and wealth of a collective. Adam Smith, the early theorist of economic liberalism, believed that in the absence of intervention, the "invisible hand" of the market leads individuals to compete with one another as they pursue their own material self-interests. Competition incentivizes individuals to improve their own standing while simultaneously pushing the larger society forward. In the neoliberal era this basic principle has been staunchly adopted in a variety of sectors, including efforts to address issues of low achievement and inequality in public schools in the United States. For example, the No Child Left Behind Act (NCLB) of 2002 required states to develop standardized tests and then compete for resources based on their students' test scores. Since NCLB, school choice efforts have further marketized education, leading schools to compete with one another to attract families, and in turn, leading families to compete with one another for access to the best schools. While these efforts assert that competition will ameliorate racial inequality and improve schools in communities of color, scholars of education have found that these reforms are often motivated by racist understandings of "bad" schools (Leonardo 2007) and that they continue to produce winners and losers instead of equity and collective uplift (Apple 2006; Buras and Apple 2005). Despite a long legacy of scholarship connecting racism with capitalism (Marable 1999; Robinson 2000), programs like NCLB, and educational support programs like LMS that utilize liberal and neoliberal ideologies, continue to garner support as viable tools to combat racial injustice.

In recent years, one example of this trend has been the belief that incentivizing students to perform better in schools through immediate cash rewards and other material incentives will decrease the racial achievement gap. The practice of giving cash for good grades was recently made popular by Roland Fryer, a Harvard economist and MacArthur fellow intimately involved in urban education reform. Fryer is founding director of Harvard's Education Innovation Laboratory (EdLabs), which partners with some of the country's largest school districts. Funded in part by a $6 million grant from the Eli and Edythe Broad Foundation (Denne 2008), EdLabs conducted experiment-based research to test the effects of monetary incentives on student performance. In addition to giving kids money for good grades, Fryer's trials tried a cellphone-based program whereby students could earn a cellphone and additional accessories for high grades. Critics of this practice argue that Fryer's design is emblematic of what Lester Spence (2016) refers to as the neoliberal turn in Black educational politics and is rooted in "neoliberal ideas about human capital and innovation" (95). As Spence notes, this framing of the problem posits students of color as simply underincentivized to succeed in education in comparison to their white counterparts.[2]

While the students of LMS were not part of any large-scale experiments testing the efficacy of monetary incentivization, LMS did use its own reward system to help motivate boys to improve their academic performance. One aspect of this system included awarding a $50 American Express gift card to the student of each LMS class with the highest GPA at the end of each marking period (six marking periods in a year). A $25 gift card was also awarded to the most improved. Most LMS classrooms posted grade reports every week or announced grades every Monday. This allowed students to know their standings in relation to one another and was meant to create a sense of ongoing competition and accountability. The cash reward was a thrilling aspect of LMS for students, especially for high-achieving students who could win multiple gift cards in a year. In all three LMS classrooms I observed, I found that although the terms of the competition were simple and straightforward, students could at any moment raise a question about the $50 award. This made the cash competition an ongoing topic of discussion. *Is the GPA list updated? What day is the money being handed out? But what if Monday is a holiday? What happens if a teacher submits their grades late? What did the last student buy with his money? Does the local corner store accept American Express? Does the taco truck on the corner? Would anyone be willing to trade for cash instead?*

Most LMS mentors also enjoyed the contest.[3] They appreciated being able to pass out cash to their students and believed that the competition helped to raise grades while simultaneously offering a fun game. "The boys love it," Mr. Samuel, a middle school mentor explained to me. "It's really good if I got a few guys who have really high GPAs because then there's some drama, like, who is going to get it?" However, beyond being a source of friendly (and at times not so friendly) competition among the students, I found that using monetary prizes to incentivize students through competition reinforced basic capitalist principles—particularly, the belief that it is fair and normal to accumulate wealth at the expense of others. This could be seen, for example, in an exchange that took place one day after Mr. Antonio awarded a student one of the $50 gift cards. Although it was already known which student would be the winner—a student named Luis—the class quieted down in anticipation of the announcement.

"And of course, the fifty dollars goes to Luis! Let's give it up for him," announced Mr. Antonio as he gave Luis a firm handshake.

The students applauded, some more enthusiastically than others. Mr. Antonio turned to a student named Anthony, who was not clapping. "It looks like Anthony's a little salty because he's not getting that cash money," he joked.

"Naw, he's mad cuz he knows he's gonna be working for me!" interjected Luis. "Flippin' burgers and shit," he then added, while giving the boy next to him a quick handshake.

The class erupted in laughter. Anthony stood up and glared at Luis menacingly. This sparked Mr. Antonio to walk over to Anthony and playfully shake him by the shoulders to deescalate the situation. He joined in the joke, putting a more lighthearted touch on it, "You want to work for Luis? No? I suggest you get to work, Anthony." "Yeah, yeah, I know, I know," Anthony responded as he sat back down.

During this exchange, Mr. Antonio and the students both connected the monetary prize that came from having the highest GPA with potential future socioeconomic hierarchies among the students. Furthermore, their reaction clearly showed how they viewed income as determining the value of a person's labor. This was not the first time the class had referenced working as a fry cook as the epitome of an undesirable job, although some of the students' parents did work in the fast-food industry. Differences in wealth, like differences in grades, appear to be based on individual merit and work ethic. In this way, hard work and high grades become equated with the notion of *deservingness*. If one works hard, one deserves the monetary prize more than others. This rationale presents the boys with a highly decontextualized understanding of academic and wealth inequality in the United States—a country where racial and economic privilege (as opposed to individual merit) profoundly affect one's academic achievement and potential to accumulate wealth (Kozol 2012). Furthermore, this exchange shows how students equated potential economic power (as academic achievement) to masculine dominance held by employers over workers. Displays of potential economic power as masculine power were frequent among the boys, particularly in relationship to the cash grade competition. If one's grade differentiated one above the rest, this was not just an economic achievement but a masculine achievement as well.[4]

While the practice of grade competition for monetary reward provided an affirmative lesson in meritocracy and deservingness for winners, the loss of privileges provided a similar lesson for the lowest-performing students. LMS policy mandated that students with a GPA below 2.5 be excluded from several yearly activities and field trips. This form of punishment included the denial of the coveted program T-shirt,[5] the inability to attend program-wide field trips, and the loss of other opportunities throughout the year. Perhaps the harshest punishment was exclusion from attending the annual field trip to a local sports complex called Xtreme Sports. For this event, students from all ten school sites were permitted to miss most of the school day to enjoy an afternoon of sports and food with their fellow LMS students from across North Arroyo Seco.

This practice naturalized the fairness of meritocracy as common sense and depoliticized as well as obfuscated the social factors that led to the educational disenfranchisement of Latino boys in Arroyo Seco. Not long before a trip to Xtreme Sports, one high-achieving boy in Mr. Iván's high school class, Abraham, offered his assessment of the practice. Abraham was an eighteen-year-old eleventh grader and a multi-year veteran of LMS. He was the de facto leader in Mr. Iván's LMS class, which was mostly composed of ninth and tenth graders. He shared, "My best friend, he can't go on the field trip to Xtreme Sports. And yeah, I'm sad, but I'll be happy because—then he has a mindset, 'All right. I will challenge myself to pass my limit.'" The rationale made sense to Abraham, who genuinely hoped some tough love would push his friend to improve his grades. Despite the obvious incentive, I worried for his friend, a student named Moisés whom I frequently tutored during homework hall or talked with when he was not in the mood for homework. From our conversations, I knew Moisés was frustrated with his home life. He lived with his mother and younger siblings in a small apartment, and his family struggled to make ends meet. It was likely they would move to a nearby city with his aunt's family, perhaps even before the end of the school year. "I don't care that I can't go to Xtreme Sports," Moisés abruptly stated to me several days before the field trip. This declaration was not in the context of an interview but interjected during a casual conversation we were having about the local basketball team. His exclusion from the field trip was clearly on his mind. "Yeah, I can't make it either," I replied, shrugging, and trying to appear uninterested in the field trip. However, truth be told, we both knew it would be a fun day.

Learning the Lesson

Although monetary incentives for good grades continue to be used in some schools to varying degrees, there is still little research that shows it has a statistically significant effect on academic achievement (Fryer 2011).[6] Even so, it is difficult for some to accept that monetary incentives do not lead to improved academic performance, and financial rewards like the gift cards at LMS continue to be used in educational settings. Moreover, these kinds of competitions and incentives often lead to stories of triumphs and letdowns, and the narratives they impart teach the lesson that individual motivation and effort are the key factors to academic excellence. For example, Mr. Jorge, another LMS mentor who, like Mr. Antonio, worked with middle school boys, described how he felt LMS's cash and field trip incentives contributed to a sense of individual responsibility and motivation among his students:

> It [the cash and field trip incentive] definitely keeps them moving. Some of them become part of LMS because of that. That's like one of the things that grabs your attention, "Oh, money for good grades? I'm down for it." But, at least for this marking period, marking period three, there is only one student that had a 3.0. Their overall GPA just keeps dropping and dropping. So sometimes it's good to reward those that did work, but like you wish that everyone was on the same page. But yes, if they have a 2.5 GPA or higher they can go to Xtreme Sports or the college trip we got going. I know of the Xtreme Sports trip we recently had—it was only five of my guys of about thirteen. I was bummed out, but it's about practicing what you preach, keep your word. It's a 2.5 GPA or higher. Like, if you have a 2.49, I'll probably consider, but if it's a 2.4 or 2.3, I'm sorry, man. You were well aware that you were supposed to get 2.5.

I followed up by asking if he felt the lesson was learned by his students. He responded:

> Yes. Even they check themselves. . . . I remember there was a kid that had a 2.35 or something like that. It was higher than others and he's like, "Come on Mr. Jorge, do you think I could go?" And I'm like, "Come on, man. I wish you could go, but rules are rules. I said what I said." And he's like, "You know what? Yes, you're right, Mr. Jorge, nothing's given to you in this world for free, you

have to earn it, you have to work, you have to work for rewards and stuff." And I was like, "Exactly, man, you took the words right out of my mouth, you're well aware of—like there are consequences. And if you do good, there are rewards as well."

As Mr. Jorge points out, many of his students are consistently unable to meet the GPA requirement to attend field trips. However, he believes that the incentive and exclusion of students leads to an important lesson in meritocracy and earning. From this perspective—which was strongly present among LMS mentors like Mr. Jorge and Mr. Antonio—on the pathway to success, young Latino men must work hard to *earn* what is awarded to them. If they do not work hard, there are consequences that they must accept. Mentors throughout the LMS program repeatedly taught this type of lesson of meritocracy and individual responsibility to their students. At times this lesson was learned without much fanfare. At other times, however, it was learned through tears.

One day, for instance, in his middle school classroom, Mr. Antonio made an unexpected announcement: the local NBA team had reached out to Pueblo Unido and offered to donate several tickets to each LMS group for an upcoming game against LeBron James and the Cleveland Cavaliers. This caused a murmur of excitement among the boys. Some squirmed in their seats, their eyes wide open, almost unable to believe the news. However, this moment of excitement was followed by a quiet groan from Diego, who was seated next to me. Diego was a young-looking seventh grader. He had smooth, full cheeks, long hair, and an eclectic style that had led him to struggle to find his place on the middle school campus. However, one thing most did know about Diego was that he adored the local basketball team. I turned to him in surprise. He whispered to me, "I won't be able to go. Watch!" A few seconds later, Mr. Antonio asked which students might be interested in attending. Diego reluctantly put his hand up. "Put your hand down, Diego. You can't have three Fs and expect to go to this game," stated Mr. Antonio, bluntly. Diego's eyes began to water as he put his hand down. He whispered to me again, this time angrily, tears building in his eyes, "What about the people with bad grades? Don't we deserve to get fun things too sometimes?"

Later it would be decided that the fair thing to do was offer the tickets to the two boys currently in the highest standing in the class, Álvaro and Jasiel. Jasiel quickly accepted the ticket, while Álvaro, who knew very little about basketball, only accepted after friends assured him that this was an opportunity not to be passed up. After class, Mr. Antonio approached the visibly upset Diego and apologized for being so direct with his decision to disqualify him from attending the game. However, he explained that based on Diego's GPA, he had been left with few options. Diego accepted the fairness of his exclusion, and Mr. Antonio and Diego's strong bond and closeness remained intact. Nevertheless, Diego's grades would not improve that year.

Instilling Discipline

The underlying lesson that Mr. Antonio hoped to teach Diego by denying him a chance to go to the game was one about meritocracy—that rewards are earned, not handed out. However, this lesson was also a form of discipline. For years, neoliberal notions of teaching discipline and self-control to children of color has been at the forefront of innovative programs and charter schools that were set up with the goal of addressing the racial achievement gap (Duckworth et al. 2011; Golann and Torres 2020). While punishment inflicted against students of color has long existed in schools (A. A. Ferguson 2001), many of the educational programs like LMS and charter schools, which were set up over the last two decades to address the racial achievement gap, utilize similar logics of control to mold students in particular ways—frequently toward a version of an "ideal student" (Baldridge 2019; Kwon 2013). The tactics these schools employ include things like teaching timeliness, order, self-control, and professionalism (Love 2019). Although some charter schools point to improved educational outcomes for some of their students, this strategy draws on deeper neoliberal logics that may help some students but also reinscribe social inequalities (Golann 2015; Golann and Torres 2020).

At LMS, for example, Mr. Antonio's decision to exclude Diego from the chance to go to the basketball game was a form of discipline—teaching the students that low academic standing would justly lead to a lack of reward, and high marks would lead to deserved resources and benefits. The phrase "no excuses" was common among LMS mentors. Most understood their role in the lives of their students as being to help them develop into respectful and responsible young men. No one took this goal more seriously than Mr. Iván, the sole high school mentor whose classroom I shadowed during this research. A five-year veteran mentor, Mr. Iván had been a dedicated mentor who now, at age thirty, was preparing to move on from his position to pursue a master's degree.

In potentially his last year at LMS, he shared with me that he had cherished the ability to work at his old high school and help instill the values of LMS in boys from the community in which he grew up. As a teen, he had been a strong athlete and committed student. After getting his bachelor's degree at a prestigious university, he eagerly returned home to help others follow his path. The best way he knew how to do this was through discipline—something that he felt had worked for him as a teen. He explained to me,

> It's that tough love. My coach in high school gave me that tough love. I'll tell them, "I love you guys. I do this because I care. Everything I do is because I want you to progress. I'm gonna get on your ass until you start doing it. If not me, then who else?" That's how my parents were with me. That's how I am with my guys.

During my time in Mr. Iván's classroom, I saw that he ran a tight ship. A self-described perfectionist, Mr. Iván closely monitored grades and attendance, and he frequently popped into his students' other classes throughout the day to confirm that they were quiet and focused—staying all period to keep watch if need be. In his own classroom, Mr. Iván required disciplined students and enforced a strict no tardy policy. While some boys shared that they had initially thought that having LMS first period would offer some leniency and relief to their struggle with tardiness, they quickly learned it was in fact just the opposite. Students were expected to be seated at 8:05 a.m. when the bell rang. This was a hardline rule, and students were marked tardy whether they were seconds late, or if they had arrived early but were not seated at the sound of the bell. While tardiness affected students' letter grades in the class (some drastically), Mr. Iván believed it was a hard lesson he had to teach. "It's the little things. How can you expect to succeed if you can't get the little things right?" Mr. Iván would reiterate this to his students, usually in moments of frustration or disappointment.

To disobey or not follow through on a commitment with Mr. Iván often led to verbal confrontation, either privately or in front of the class. Mr. Iván's large stature and willingness to raise his voice at students made him an intense figure of authority. These confrontations often centered around instilling a sense of individual responsibility with the boys. One day, for instance, I observed Mr. Iván having a strong but not unusual disciplinary interaction. This time it was with a ninth grader named Alan and occurred during grade check-ins. As on most days, the period began with Mr. Iván going over the class grades individually. The students sat in silence while he went down the list, stating each student's name and GPA and noting if there were any points of concern. As Mr. Iván arrived at Alan's name, he stated, "And next we have Alan who . . . is turned around . . . again." He said this sharply, making Alan jump and turn around in his seat quickly. Although Alan had been smiling and whispering something to his good friend Pedro, who was seated behind him, he now looked nervous and concerned. Mr. Iván continued, "You know I talked to Ms. Jenkins, and she said you haven't been putting in the effort since we had our talk." "I have, though," rebutted Alan, "like I haven't been late this week at all. What day did you talk to her?" "Look, Alan, I'm just tired of this shit. You always have something to say, some little excuse, but every time I look at you, you aren't even looking forward." Mr. Iván had begun shouting, and the class was silent. "And don't look at your friend. He's not tanking English. God, it's like you're not hearing me. When you get your grades, I hope you know whose fault it is. I'm going to bring you a mirror, so you can see whose fault."

Mr. Iván's rant continued and lasted much longer than I expected, leaving a sense of awkwardness in the room that lingered until the end of the period.

I do not share this exchange to paint Mr. Iván as a villainous and uncaring educator. To the contrary, during my time with him I witnessed true dedication and care he felt for his students. Instead, this scene highlights an exchange between mentor and student that seems expected and justified given the goal and vision of LMS. To be "on their ass," to use Mr. Iván's language, was an act of love—the commonsense way Latino men might transform Latino boys into upstanding students. However, similar to no-excuse schools,[7] the LMS program sought to help empower Latino boys through offering discipline and teaching accountability. This often involved conditioning and controlling student bodies. A telling example of this can be seen in the silent study hall that Mr. Iván ran in his classroom on Tuesdays and Thursdays. During this biweekly event, students were to sit silently and complete any pending homework. The expectation of complete silence for the fifty-minute period cannot be underscored enough. If students did not have homework, they were asked to read a book or sit quietly. This was inevitably the case for several students each day, who often laid their heads on their desks for most of the period. Although students periodically pleaded to be able to listen to music or talk quietly with a classmate, Mr. Iván had announced that "learning to sit still and stay quiet" was itself an "important lesson." While this practice was unpopular with students, Abraham, who was mentioned earlier, offered a rare, positive review of the practice. He shared with me, "Guys got to learn how to follow directions, so I think it's good. Sometimes you need to learn to shut your mouth."

The topic of discipline in schools and in programs like LMS is a complicated and difficult issue. Recent studies have indicated that excessive school discipline is among the largest barriers facing Latino boys in schools (Rios 2017). However, scholars have also shown how the use of school punishment is increasingly intertwined with state policing and incarceration, sometimes referred to as the school-to-prison pipeline (Kim, Losen, and Hewitt 2010; Nolan 2011). Many programs like LMS have the specific goal of intervening in this pipeline by directly targeting boys and young men of color. Indeed, at LMS the mentors frequently advocated for their students who might find themselves entangled in the disciplinary mechanisms of the school. A number of mentors also sought to avoid utilizing institutional forms of discipline at their school sites with their students. Instead, discipline was handled within LMS, between the student and the mentor.

Mr. Iván's use of discipline in his classroom is a good illustration of the way Latino men working with young people were expected to use discipline to change the outcomes for Latino boys in school. But this pronounced focus on learning self-discipline placed the focus on individual students—the idea being that they could improve their chances for a better future by changing their own behavior. This vision of empowerment utilized self-control and discipline as means of empowerment. In doing so, it placed the onus of achievement on the boys themselves, while largely forgiving the very racial and economic structures that marginalize students and communities of color in the first place.

ENTREPRENEURIALISM AS EMPOWERMENT

One morning in Mr. Iván's classroom, two women from Pueblo Unido's central office arrived to give a presentation about a summer youth program. The program was created through a partnership between Pueblo Unido and the investment banking company Morgan Stanley and would offer job-readiness training to North Arroyo Seco teens. The training included help with résumé writing, work etiquette, financial planning, and communication skills. The three-week program would culminate in mock job interviews and a youth summit at the local Morgan Stanley headquarters. During the presentation, a ninth grader named Alonzo asked, "What do they do at Morgan Stanley?" The presenters hesitated. "Um, to be honest, I am not sure," replied one of the young women. I would later learn her name was Marisol, a fourth-year college student interning at Pueblo Unido. Her co-facilitator, Yolanda, also looked unsure. She offered, "Something with investing. But all you need to know is they're a big deal—money money money. If you're interested in business this is an amazing opportunity."

Several months later, Pueblo Unido's social media and newsletters blasted photos from the youth summit. In the opening photo, a group of twenty Latinx and Black teens is seen smiling in mixed and matched business attire. They are standing in front of a banner reading "Welcome to Morgan Stanley Pueblo Unido & Youth." In other pictures the teens are seen shaking hands with representatives from Morgan Stanley, Uber, and several Latinx-oriented startups. Some make stern faces while others smile gleefully as they shake hands with their interviewer. The newsletter describes the students as wowed by "inspiring speeches" and elated to "practice their elevator pitches and handshakes." Three LMS mentors who attended the event as chaperones are also dispersed throughout the pictures in business attire. Mr. Iván was not one of them. Although his class had received the presentation about the job-readiness program, none of his students ended up participating. "I was a little disappointed that none of them did it," he shared with me. Even Abraham, the unofficial student leader of Mr. Iván's LMS group, was not able to attend. "We want them to see that you can't let these opportunities pass you by," shared Mr. Iván. "You can't just say 'I'll do it next time.' You need to start taking these opportunities now."

During my time with LMS, I found that part of LMS's mission was to help Latino boys become entrepreneurial young men—to seize opportunities and take risks to help them reach their goals. This approach intersects with the way neoliberal framings of masculinity are integrated into educational programming—what scholars have referred to as "aspirational masculinity"—where programs like LMS directly associate educational success with a student's eventual ability to achieve their patriarchal status and value in society (e.g., the traditional breadwinners) (Stahl, Nelson, and Wallace 2017). This framing, however, placed an enormous amount of pressure on the students, as it creates a binary in which students feel they can either be successful in school or amount to very little in life (Torres 2017). LMS's program design and pedagogical approaches sought to instill an entrepreneurial fervor in the students that would push them to seize opportunities and make smart choices to maximize their success. This meant pushing them to take opportunities like the job-readiness program, or perhaps recognizing how to finesse their own stories to increase their human capital. The ideologies behind this approach of "aspirational masculinity" encourage students to approach education as smart consumers. This was particularly important for LMS middle schoolers getting ready to choose a high school.

One of the most notable areas of the use of market-driven ideas in contemporary education is the notion of school choice. School choice strategies treat schooling as a marketplace where students and their families act as consumers who choose what school to attend according to their personal criteria. It is a market-oriented approach to education that seeks to offer families options and agency in their children's educational journey. It departs from the traditional community school approach, in which children attend their neighborhood public school. School choice options have grown in popularity in recent years, despite protests that school choice shifts the power of schooling into the hands of billionaires and major foundations, whose private and charter school networks compete for students with traditional public schools (Ewing 2018; Lipman 2011). Although advocates of school choice assert that it offers options to struggling families of color, research suggests that increasing school choice does not necessarily increase academic success for Latinx families and other marginalized groups and that it can even exacerbate inequities within a community (Lipman 2011; Morales, Trujillo, and Kissell 2016).

For the middle school mentors at LMS, helping students assess their options for which high school to attend was considered a central part of being a mentor. For middle schoolers in North Arroyo Seco, this usually meant helping students avoid what was commonly referred to as the two "bad" public high schools of the region. Doing what is best for individual LMS students is of course the job of a mentor. However, in the realm of school choice I found this sentiment departed from ongoing efforts to improve the education of all Latinx students in Arroyo Seco. For example, in my time at LMS, I witnessed ASUSD become an ideological battleground between advocates for traditional public schools and the growing power of charter management organizations. As these charter schools expanded, many community schools in North Arroyo Seco had been shut down, while others, including several LMS schools, were at risk of closure. I attended several Latinx community forums hosted by ASUSD, some held at LMS school sites, in which Latinx families and community members began organizing themselves to resist further school closures. As one longtime ASUSD teacher and public school advocate shared with me, "All this charter competition is taking students and resources from our neighborhood school . . . from schools who serve our most vulnerable students."

Although the LMS program mentors did not explicitly seek to advance school choice ideology within this increasingly marketized district, the role of a mentor nevertheless became that of a consultant—to help students and their families navigate the high school marketplace to optimize their potential benefits. This individualized approach inevitably resulted in seeking to create winners in the school choice market and came at the detriment of efforts to collectively uplift all Latinx students in the district and save community schools. Some mentors were quite explicit about their efforts to help the students attend charter schools. Mr. Samuel, a middle school mentor whose school was a natural feeder into Adams High School, one of these community schools, suggested that he used his own social and professional network to help his students avoid the local school. "I have a friend that works at Northside Urban Charter," he said, "so I have a strong relationship with them. A few of my students have gone there and done well, so they tell me, 'Keep sending them our way and we'll see what we can do.'"

When I asked Mr. Samuel about Adams, the community high school located down the block, however, he recommended LMS students avoid that school at all costs. This was despite the fact that LMS had a program at Adams run by a mentor named Oscar.

"So Oscar doesn't mind you diverting students away from Adams?" I asked Mr. Samuel.

"No, no," he replied. "He knows how that school is . . . it's crazy . . . and he wants the best for the boys."

With mentors pushing the charter schools like this, it is not surprising that among the two middle school groups that I observed there was an overrepresentation of students who ended up avoiding Adams. Furthermore, within these two LMS middle school classrooms it appeared that the highest-performing students were the most successful in finding other options. One year, for example, in a group led by Mr. Sergio, who had taken over Mr. Antonio's class when he left LMS, eight of his nine eighth graders avoided attending Adams in the upcoming school year. The only student who would attend Adams was David, a quiet and frequently bullied student whose GPA had remained in "last place" in the classroom for the full school year, under a 1.0.[8]

One day I caught up with Vicente, the highest-achieving eighth grader in Mr. Javier's middle school group, which was the second middle school group that I participated in regularly. I asked if he would be attending Adams High School the following year. "Hell no. I'll be at Northside Urban Charter," he declared, with pride and a sense of accomplishment. Although Adams High School and Northside Urban Charter shared a campus, and both served North Arroyo Seco, Vicente clearly saw a difference in the schools. "I don't have to go to Adams, because I got good grades," he stated confidently. Although urban charter schools have frequently come under attack for selecting the highest-performing students of color and creating new lines of racial divides (see Bell 2009; Buras and Apple 2005; T. M. Davis 2014), I cannot confirm that this was the case for Northside Urban Charter. However, Vicente believed that he would attend Northside Urban Charter, not Adams High, because he had excelled in middle school. "Are you worried about your friends who are going to Adams?" I asked. "Naw, they'll be fine, they just need to work harder, not mess around. Stay away from the drama." In the second year of this study, LMS ended its relationship with Adams High School, dropping LMS's number down to nine school sites. Ending LMS's relationship with Adams High was chalked up to a dwindling LMS budget and a lack of communication and support on the part of Adams High administration.

In addition to charter schools, private schools occupy an important position within the broader marketplace of school choice, and they also compete with public schools for students. During my time with Mr. Antonio, he invited representatives from the local Catholic high school, St. Luke's, to speak to his eighth grade students. St. Luke's had several scholarships and was looking to recruit Latinx students from North Arroyo Seco. The boys welcomed the guest speaker with special focus and attention. Following the presentation, the boys were gifted St. Luke's rubber bracelets that they proudly wore for several weeks after the visit. Although many of the boys seemed intrigued at the thought of attending a private school, some expressed concerns. Several boys spoke about the imagined discipline of private school life while others lamented the possibility of being separated from friends with whom they had attended their local community schools since kindergarten. Mr. Antonio reminded the boys that they were not being required to apply, but that they should know they have options. "At the end of the day you got to do what's best for you," he reminded them, pointing at individual students as he spoke. "If it's a hard school, good. That's good for you." This led to a small debate as students imagined life at both high schools. "I'm just saying you guys got to learn to advocate for yourselves, pick the best high school you can. If you have to go to Adams, fine. But look into your options first."

RESTORING A BENEVOLENT (HETEROPATRIARCHAL) MANHOOD

As a form of biopolitics, neoliberalism produces the political and economic conditions that incite specific racialized gender and sexual formations through a combination of punishment and regulation as well as care and inclusion (Hong and Ferguson 2011). Grace Kyungwon Hong (2015) maintains that by narrating communities of color as deficient and lacking, neoliberal discourse constitutes them as "populations requiring help and care" (57). This care often incorporates an invitation to embody gendered and sexual respectability—inviting communities of color to adopt normative familial gender roles and sexual practices as a means of racial uplift. In popular culture, Latino men have long been depicted as hypermasculine machistas who are failing or abusive spouses and fathers (Mirande 1997; Noguera, Hurtado, and Fergus 2011). As intersectional theorists have pointed out, part of the conditioning power of neoliberal empowerment efforts has been to empower men of color to be *better men*—enhancing their ability to be traditional patriarchs (Crenshaw 2014, 2016). At LMS, this conditioning played out in several ways. One key aspect of developing character centered around rehabilitating a perceived failed Latino manhood into something that was positive and valuable. This focus on benevolent heteropatriarchy, the seemingly positive and non-abusive embodiment of patriarchy within heteronormative gender roles, limited a more substantive engagement with patriarchy and heteronormativity as oppressive forces in LMS.

Creating Traditional Family Men

As one might reasonably expect, LMS openly stood against the notion of sexism. In interviews, everyone from the CEO of Pueblo Unido to the middle school students said that "respecting women" was a strong value of the type of manhood cultivated in the program. Two of LMS's goals were "healthy families" and "character development," areas the program felt overlapped with an agenda of teaching boys to condemn sexism and machismo. In an interview, one high school mentor stated, "Sexism is a problem . . . a big problem that men need to address. . . . A good man, for me, is humble, responsible, and honorable . . . not a mujeriego [womanizer], you know? Be faithful to your wife . . . never hit her." As another mentor stated, "We're building strong but respectful men." A version of this statement was repeated by most mentors and boys when asked how sexism, patriarchy, and gender justice related to the program's vision of manhood.

In the classroom, numerous lessons and activities were dedicated to helping cultivate a better and traditional manhood for students—a Latino manhood beyond toxic machismo. The area that most directly addressed toxic masculinity was sharing circles. Sharing circles occurred several times throughout the year in the three LMS classrooms in which I was a participant, and sometimes they were coupled with related activities. For example, the popular documentary *The Mask You Live In,* a film in which boys and men discuss their struggles with America's narrow definition of manhood, was a popular film that complemented these conversations. In these intimate lessons, boys, mentors, and myself all shared with one another about the pressures of being a Latino man. As a participant in these sharing circles, I want to underscore the power of sharing, and the warmth I felt while connecting with mentors and students. There is something truly healing about opening up and sharing experiences of hardship and struggle in a group of people who have had similar experiences. (Out of respect for the space, I have decided not to share any individual stories from our time in these intimate discussions.)[9] Indeed, how we come to understand the goals of healing work with Latino boys is, in many ways, central to grasping some of the key claims of this book.

In recent years, the topic of addressing toxic masculinity has become popular and widely accepted among educators. However, as this trend gains traction, there has been increasing concern for the disconnection between the practice of healing toxic masculinity and a critical engagement with patriarchy and heterosexism as oppressive systems. As bell hooks (2004) and other feminists of color have pointed out, while the ability to show vulnerability and express emotion is an important entryway into challenging sexism, there must be a critical feminist politics behind manhood work that analyzes and dismantles the cultural and structural aspects of heteropatriarchy. In LMS, I found that, similar to what scholars have found in other educational spaces directed toward boys of color (Lindsay 2018; Oeur 2018), the vision for a healed masculinity often aligned with, rather than deconstructed, dominant forms of heteropatriarchal manhood.

In sharing circles, our guided discussions focused on the violent, toxic, and failing masculinities that students saw in their homes and in their community. In particular, students were asked to unpack machismo in their own families, leading them to reference fathers' or uncles' infidelities, alcoholism, or absences. While these circles created an intimate space where boys were able to bond with one another as boys, a sustained engagement with antisexist and antihomophobic politics was nonexistent. Instead, conversations rarely, if ever, departed from the ways toxic masculinity disrupted traditional notions of fatherhood, family, and proper gender roles for men. Stories of toxic manhood were consistently framed as a detriment to traditional gender roles and heteropatriarchal values, which were constructed as qualities a good boy should emulate. Indeed, the very act of "manhood building" assumes a proper role and location for "men." The question became, how would we be the men our community and our families deserved? One day, at the end of an emotional story surrounding an abusive father, Mr. Antonio offered some words of encouragement in the final moments of class. He stated, "I know you guys will be better fathers to your sons, right? And better husbands to your wives when you grow up?" The class responded yes, in unison.

This was an important moment in that it helped students frame how an awareness of toxic masculinity should be framed—the response *yes*, serving as a call to action to become the fathers and husbands that the community needed. As the students left, I scanned the room and wondered if all wanted to be fathers or husbands, or if those who did not form traditional families in the future would feel unsuccessful. This moment in the classroom, in line with the vision and description of the program, illustrates a clear distinction between a pedagogy to dismantle heteropatriarchy or the process of rehabilitating these concepts into a more benevolent form. I found that without a critical gender perspective, LMS mentors often performed the task of big brothers, guiding their students toward a benevolent yet conventional manhood.

This was one of many instances in which classroom practices helped students align their identities and beliefs with a benevolent form of heteropatriarchal manhood. A number of scholars have documented how men who are educators often serve as key reproducers of heteropatriarchal ideals in the lives of their male students (Martino and Frank 2006). I found this particularly true in LMS, where the role of the mentor was specifically to speak on the performance of manhood. Students enjoyed asking mentors (and me) about our lives outside of the classroom, including dating. Through interviews with mentors as well as classroom observations, I found that many mentors viewed sharing about their monogamous and heterosexual relationships as an important aspect of being a mentor. It helped students "see what a good relationship looks like." One mentor described a skit-like activity he facilitated in which he played the role of a strict father and his students practiced respectfully asking to take his daughter out on a date. Although this was, perhaps, practical for a certain few middle school boys interested in dating, this activity, and many others, presumed that students were heterosexual and reproduced traditional gender roles and heteronormative ideals. Overall, everyday lessons in healing, addressing toxic masculinity, and manhood training were steps toward building a good boy as a heteropatriarchal subject.

The Vision Board: Imagining Successful Futures

In the final days of the school year, Mr. Iván's class began working on vision boards for their final project. The boys were given several days of class to sift through magazine articles and cut out photos, words, and phrases. These clippings were pasted onto poster boards in a way that mapped out their goals and dreams for the future. The activity is intended to help students construct their own goals—creating space for Latino boys to dream of a new reality beyond their present circumstances. The practice of dreaming liberatory futures is a long-standing tradition in education-based social movements (Kelley 2003; Love 2019). Active dreaming allows us to vision (and begin to build) the world we want. In this potential world, for example, perhaps Latino boys excel in and enjoy school, no human being is illegal, and all Black lives truly matter. However, dreams can often be limited by the discursive constraints of the present, making it difficult to imagine beyond hegemonic notions of individual success. While it is my firm belief that Latino boys possess profound dreams of justice, critical pedagogies are often necessary to help guide these aspirations. Critical pedagogies help cultivate realities beyond hegemonic ideologies that frame our present (Freire 2000; hooks 1994).

The boys thoroughly enjoyed the several days allotted to sifting through magazines and listening to music during this fun, end-of-the-year activity. On the day of the presentations, the boys proudly presented their posters, revealing several common themes. For example, many posters included images of the local football team, and several boys mentioned they hoped to one day have season tickets. Other posters featured images of the Great Wall of China and the Eiffel Tower, which represented dreams of travel. However, a striking similarity across all twenty-two posters in the class was the image of a (conventionally beautiful) wife, at least two children, a lavish house, and an expensive sports car or truck. Each of the posters had become an extravagant iteration of a heteronormative American dream. Despite some boys adding unique touches to their work, the homogeneity of the posters was glaring, and it made the presentations feel redundant. Presentation after presentation introduced the boy's wife, children, house, and perhaps an interesting but often vague career that would afford a lavish lifestyle. Toward the end of the presentations, I whispered to Christopher, a tenth grader sitting next to me, to ask if he had noticed the clear trend too. "Yeah, I think everyone took it as, more like, what you want for your own life . . . the kind of life you want to live," he shared, adding, "I liked the way you took your poster, I should have done something like that." During my visit to the classroom earlier in the week, I had quickly made a poster depicting an inverted police car as well as a garden and a hospital. This vision was of a world in which police departments were abolished and communities had access to healthy food and universal healthcare. I hope to play my role as an educator and activist in bringing this world closer into existence in my lifetime. I was happy to see that it resonated with Christopher, who had taken a liking to his ethnic studies course. We continued to discuss what racial justice might look like in our lifetimes.

I share a student's brief interaction with my vision board not just to highlight a missed opportunity of a critical lesson but also to demonstrate the ways the vision board in itself became a lesson in traditional (heteropatriarchal) manhood. Far from neutral, the act of constructing what one boy described as a "perfect life" reinforced dominant narratives of success, rather than helping students deconstruct these narratives and name the ideologies that shape this unique notion of success and the structures that let a few, at the expense of the many, have it. The lesson failed to help students critique the structures of inequality in society, while also reinforcing the notion that wealth was a masculine quality of success, and that this aligned with other areas of masculine success, such as having a wife and family, as well as providing for them. This left students without critical tools to challenge dominant narratives and instead leaned into dominant notions of masculine accomplishment: financial power, material wealth, heterosexual marriage, and fatherhood. But the absence of these critical lessons on gender and sexuality, along with visions of benevolent manhood, often left space for the reproduction of toxic masculine traits and incomplete understandings of gender justice.

The Persistence of Misogynistic and Homophobic Language

On the day of the vision board presentations, the last student to present was Gustavo. Gustavo was a sturdy tenth grader who played football, had an infectious grin, and did not mind pushing Mr. Iván's buttons from time to time. He had missed the previous day of school, and as a result his vision board was sparsely decorated. When the time came for him to present, Gustavo summoned his playful and energetic attitude to push him through his quick presentation. "This is my wife. As you can see, she bad," he started, pointing to an attractive woman near the center of the poster and flashing a sly grin. A few boys chuckled. The presentation took no more than forty seconds as Gustavo quickly described each item on his poster. This included several nice cars, a picture of a Rolex, a New York City penthouse overlooking Central Park, several children, and himself, represented by Robert Downey Jr. portraying Tony Stark in the Marvel film *Iron Man*. Gustavo stated that he hoped to become wealthy in the tech sector. As the presentation neared the end, Mr. Iván interjected, "And who is this?," referring to an image of a woman placed adjacent to his family, but who had not been mentioned. "Oh, that's my side bitch. I mean side chick," Gustavo stated matter-of-factly. He then looked up with a smile. The classroom exploded in laughter. "Gustavo!" shouted Mr. Iván. However, as the classroom began to brace for a confrontation, Mr. Iván's stern face lightened into a smile, and he began to chuckle. "Ay this kid, what are we going to do with you?" he said, shaking his head. He then checked to see if all the boys had presented before beginning to wrap up the period. This would be the last time Gustavo's poster would be mentioned.

I share the example of the vision board activity because it helps reveal two things. First, heteronormative ideals remained a commonsense way of imagining a successful life for the boys of Mr. Iván's high school class. In many ways, the manhood development in LMS reinforced, rather than deconstructed, dominant performances of manhood. While notions of abusive and toxic manhood were condemned, a traditional and heterosexual manhood was implicitly and explicitly framed as ideal. In their vision boards, the boys reflected the values of LMS—representing themselves as financially successful, career-oriented family men. Second, the project demonstrates that when challenging heterosexism and patriarchy is not at the foundation of gender work with boys, misogynistic jokes and beliefs can easily make their way into the classroom—even when "respecting women" is an important aspect of the work. It is essential to note, however, that the persistence of misogynistic beliefs is not unique to Latino male spaces. It should also be noted that, as other scholars have pointed out, hegemonic masculinity is intimately connected to whiteness (Connell 2005).

The persistence of misogynistic, homophobic, and transphobic ideologies in the absence of critical gender education in "all-male" educational spaces has long been a feminist concern (Lindsay 2018). During my time with LMS, the students regularly made homophobic and misogynistic comments and jokes. Mentors at times also made these comments.[10] The way they expressed these attitudes offered a unique insight into how misogynistic language may coexist in a program in which respecting women was so clearly a goal.

Like mentors and administrators, students reiterated themes of opposition to domestic violence, the importance of marital fidelity, and some form of the idea that "a real man respects women" and "takes care of his family." However, in an interview with an eighth grade boy in Mr. Antonio's class, I decided to ask about contradictory behavior that clearly existed in the classroom. Just minutes before the interview, a burst of jokes and gossip about female schoolmates had reached a grotesque extreme. The comments were met with just a light hush from the mentor. In the interview, the boy shook his head in agreement, acknowledging the clear contradiction. After thinking about how to explain, he responded, "Yeah, yeah, that's true, but . . . well, like I wouldn't be saying that stuff when I'm like a dad, and have a family . . . married." He explained that while LMS offered a space for boys to "be themselves," he felt the program pushed boys to step up to be good fathers and husbands in the future.

Scholars of gender and sexuality point to the ways neoliberalism seeks to construct proper and productive subjects—those who will play their role in traditional familial reproduction (Hong and Ferguson 2011). But the construction of these kinds of proper and productive subjects—in the case of LMS, the financially successful, good father and husband of the future—not only limits what is imagined to be proper ways of being but also largely ignores, and in many ways upholds, the oppressive systems that shape gendered oppression (e.g., heteropatriarchy). Through this student's response, we see the notion of antisexism become conditioned through heteropatriarchal values. Here the common trope of "respect for women" is seen as most valued in an imagined future in which boys will be prepared to fulfill the role of benevolent patriarch in a marriage and a family. While it was clear (for the most part) that LMS did not condone misogynistic remarks, I observed these comments habitually chalked up to a "boys will be boys" justification. Overall, an emphasis on building and restoring traditional manhood hindered a critical consciousness around gender justice and substantive engagements with a feminist or queer pedagogy, and led to a very limited, sometimes problematic, definition of Latino male empowerment.

CONCLUSION: THE (NOT SO) HIDDEN CURRICULUM OF NEOLIBERAL MANHOOD

For over half a century, the notion of the "hidden curriculum" has been used by critical educational researchers to describe the implicit and unspoken norms, behaviors, and cultural messages that are communicated to students while they are in school. For Marxists, the hidden curriculum is the everyday school practices that naturalize capitalist sensibilities and create worker subjectivities (Anyon 2006; Giroux and Purpel 1983). These might include raising hands, becoming accustomed to bell schedules, normalizing hierarchical relations between teachers and students, and accepting "merit-based" differences among students. This chapter has shown how the values of neoliberal empowerment entrench themselves into the everyday practices of a program meant to support Latino boys. While these lessons were at times subtle and implicit, it was striking that at LMS, the normalization of professionalism and respectability was a lesson in itself. Whether presented as formal or informal lessons, building a stronger character was the explicit goal of the program, and everyday practices, competitions, and policies were meant to mold boys into upstanding young men. These practices illustrate neoliberal empowerment in action. They underscore how such approaches to empowerment are often counterproductive and reify key social and racial dilemmas.

A common sentiment among programs meant to support boys of color is that boys need spaces on campus to just be themselves. Research has widely documented the ways schools protect whiteness (Leonardo 2009) and are often violent and unwelcoming places for boys of color (Noguera 2009; Rios 2017). However, far from providing a space to simply be themselves, LMS and similar programs of empowerment are ideologically charged spaces in which students are asked to develop or evolve into more productive versions of themselves. At LMS this meant the boys were implicitly as well as explicitly asked to adopt traits or values like meritocracy and individualism, entrepreneurialism and consumerism, and benevolent heteropatriarchy. But by cultivating these kinds of ideal subjects rather than helping the boys escape ideologies that pathologize and blame them for their own marginalization, programs like LMS ultimately reiterated many of the dilemmas that the boys are already facing in their lives by pushing them to embrace heteropatriarchal values that circumscribe the hegemonic qualities of a good racial subject and imposing a deficit orientation from which they are then expected to emerge.

While this chapter demonstrates the ways neoliberal values of empowerment were practiced and adopted by mentors and students, the subsequent chapters highlight the words and perspectives of the students and mentors themselves, who paint a complicated picture of their relationship to dominant notions of empowerment. While some wholeheartedly embraced the values and practices of LMS, others hesitated and were strategic in how they navigated the program.

THREE

NEOLIBERAL SUPERHEROES

*Mentors Negotiating Narratives of Love,
Deficit, and Heteropatriarchy*

One rainy Friday afternoon in late February, I arrived at Mr. Sergio's classroom to find the class preparing for a movie day. The room buzzed with pre-weekend excitement as the students rearranged their chairs. No one even protested when Mr. Sergio passed out a worksheet for the film and reminded the class that note-taking was required. The day's feature was the 2005 MTV Films production *Coach Carter,* a film that tells the real-life story of Ken Carter, a high school basketball coach who, in 1999, made national headlines for suspending his team's undefeated season until players improved their grades (T. Carter 2005). The film exemplifies the popular belief that heroic men of color have a unique and powerful role to play in transforming the lives of troubled boys.

As the movie began, silence quickly fell on the class. Opening to the song "Untouchable," by DMX, the film sets the scene in what is depicted as the dangerous and blighted streets of Richmond, California, in the San Francisco Bay Area. Carter, played by Samuel L. Jackson, attends a preseason basketball game at Richmond High School where he finds the players of his alma mater undisciplined, frustrated, and losing. One Richmond player instigates a brawl with the opposing team, forcing the game to end early. In the locker room, the boys continue to fight and bicker among themselves. They appear to be unruly, disrespectful, and quick to violence. Out of duty to his community, Carter accepts the position of head coach in hopes of having a positive impact on the boys' lives.

Carter's method of coaching is focused on building discipline and respect. Practices are dedicated to physical conditioning and fundamentals. He requires his players to arrive early to practice and normalizes the habit of calling each other "sir" as well as responding "Yes, sir" to the coach (something Carter does in his everyday life). Tardiness and disrespect are met with harsh consequences. As the boys begin to build skills and character, it becomes apparent that Coach Carter is filling a void left by absent and negative male role models. Some players have lost older brothers to gun violence. Others have never met their father or have fathers in prison. Relatedly, a player named Kenyon struggles with the news that his girlfriend is pregnant. The film follows the saga of the couple as Kenyon's inability to commit to fatherhood puts strain on the relationship. At the end of the film, Kenyon eventually takes responsibility and supports his partner.

The player most resistant to Carter's strict, tough-love approach is Timo Cruz, played by Puerto Rican and Dominican American actor Rick Gonzalez. In his first encounter with Carter's discipline, Cruz attempts to punch Carter. Although Carter is wearing a business suit, he easily subdues Cruz, and in doing so, proves a rugged masculinity that had earlier been questioned by the team. "Teachers ain't supposed to touch students," states Cruz, as Carter holds the boy's head pressed against the wall of the gym. "I'm not a teacher, I'm the new basketball coach," Carter responds. Cruz is kicked off the team and immediately gravitates to the care of his older cousin Renny, a drug dealer. He soon begins to carry a gun and sell drugs. At the film's climax, Cruz witnesses Renny gunned down on the street. While holding the limp body of his cousin, Cruz cries out hysterically in Spanish while sitting on the sidewalk. Minutes later he shows up at Carter's house in the middle of the night. He begs to be allowed to rejoin the team as he crumbles into Carter's arms in tears.

The action-packed teen sports drama proved to be captivating for the students. Many groaned loudly as Mr. Sergio turned off the screen. "Hang on to those worksheets and we will finish on Monday," he instructed. "Yes, sir!" responded one boy, exaggeratedly. Chava, an eighth grader who was the smallest in class, weighing no more than eighty pounds, stood up and playfully put up his fists. "Or what, you gonna make me, Mr. S, sir?" he challenged. Everyone laughed.

After class, Mr. Sergio and I reminisced about the many times we had both seen *Coach Carter* in school. "It's a lot different seeing it as the adult," stated the twenty-three-year-old mentor. Mr. Sergio was only in his third week at LMS, having taken over Mr. Antonio's middle school classroom in the middle of the school year. Later, in a formal interview,

Mr. Sergio described the film as reminding him of the "expectations" and "pressure" that come with being a mentor. These expectations came from ASUSD and Pueblo Unido, but also society in general. "People have these specific ideas about what it's like to be a Latino male mentor, you know, in the 'hood, but they don't really know," he explained. Mr. Sergio found these heroic narratives, similar to the one in *Coach Carter,* to be out of touch with reality. They instead put tremendous pressure on mentors to do the impossible, in part by adopting a larger-than-life persona for their students. "We got all these expectations," explained Mr. Sergio, "then, out of all that, you got to decide what am I actually doing here? And what do I got to do for my students?"

In the neoliberal era, the contradictory rhetoric of duty and damage is a difficult terrain to navigate for youth workers interested in social justice (Baldridge 2019). For men of color like Mr. Sergio and the other mentors of LMS, this contradiction was particularly evident. As educational researchers have long described, boys of color are persistently vilified in educational contexts in the United States as a problematic demographic in need of either correction or expulsion. This leads to the widely held belief that mentors like those at LMS can serve as positive role models and help fix the problems that boys of color supposedly represent (Dumas 2016a). This contradictory framing of the boys themselves as problems has been widely adopted by a range of actors and influences the goals of public and philanthropic interventions in schools. As Kimberlé Crenshaw (2014) aptly put it, the topic of "fixing men of color . . . hits a political sweet spot among populations that both love and fear them." Whether acting out of fear of the dangerous bad boy or love for the vulnerable child, a variety of philanthropists, community members, politicians, educators, and even former president Obama himself have made addressing the perceived boy-of-color crisis a top priority. This has resulted in a unique blending of ideological interests that converge on this popular subject. Although this odd union has led to the rapid growth of a vast boy-of-color empowerment industry, a number of critical race scholars have been quick to challenge problematic racial logics that undergird many of these efforts (Baldridge 2017). Neoliberal buzzwords like *grit, resiliency, character development,* and *excellence* are often attached to boy-of-color initiatives. These terms individualize the struggles of students while obscuring and even perpetuating racist and damage-centered approaches to education (Love 2019).

For justice-oriented youth workers like many of the mentors at LMS, everyday negotiations and compromises are often facts of life (Baldridge 2019). This is particularly true for Black and Latino men educators who have the unique experience of navigating what the boys of color are confronting in their lives and are therefore thought to be holding the key to success. In this framing, which Ed Brockenbourgh (2018) describes as a "saviorist discourse," men of color are portrayed as having the ability to dramatically change the educational outcomes of boys of color. Despite being presented as superhero-like role models to save boys, this framing causes mentors at programs like LMS to understand their role and purpose in the program in ways that reimpose narratives of damage and deficit onto their students. For Latino men and boys, I argue that the figure of the *positive Latino male role model* represents the convergence of neoliberal discourses of race, gender, sexuality, and other social categories to construct the epitome of Latino male respectability. This figure can perform the dangerous work of shifting focus from the structural issues of inequality toward the individualist notions of character, grit, and personal responsibility. In this paternalistic intervention, the positive Latino male role model, which is seen as an extreme rarity, transforms the lives and grades of problematic students by embodying a much-needed example of respectable manhood. However, even as it advances (or maintains) problematic racial tropes, the notion of the positive male role model is often couched in a rhetoric of care and concern for "at-risk" boys. This poses numerous complications, particularly for youth workers who are strongly motivated by their love and care for their students and communities.

In this chapter and the next I offer a critical perspective of the notion of the positive Latino male role model and examine the ways racial and heteropatriarchal logics inform this figure. This is not to deny the measurable impacts adults of color can have on the lives of students of color in schools (Bristol and Martin-Fernandez 2019). Rather, in this chapter I explore a neoliberal imaginary that co-opts the image of the role model for its own ideological motivations. By positioning Latino male educators as heroic models of respectability and resilience, attention is deflected from the structural determinants of inequality and instead focused on the individual capacities of role models with characteristics conducive to neoliberal values.

As Mr. Sergio described in the quote above, the mentors at LMS were expected to take on this complicated and problematic role in their students' lives. As I discuss in this chapter, the mentors frequently navigated these expectations and made sense of their role in their classes by drawing on the popular language of damage, deficit, and heteropatriarchal value. Indeed, the very mission of LMS—an organization whose founding was based on the narrative of a perceived Latino male crisis—left mentors with little alternative but to use damage- and deficit-centered language in their work with the students. This was often the case even when mentors described feelings of love and social justice as the primary factors that brought them to the program. But as this chapter shows, discourses of love and deficit intermingle in the mentors' work, underscoring the deep complexity that mentors at LMS and other male educators face as they seek to support Latino boys in schools today.

HOW BOYS AND MEN OF COLOR ARE FRAMED AS DAMAGED AND DEFICIENT

There are numerous ways that narratives of damage and deficit were woven into the curriculum and broader programming at LMS. As discussed in chapters 1 and 2, many of the roots of these narratives can be found in a wave of policies that developed in the 1980s to manage and control populations (Offutt-Chaney 2023). While racial narratives fueled the PIC and the perceived need to remove boys and men of color from the streets, these same narratives of racial deviancy also fueled the NPIC and the need to attend to and reform this demographic. At LMS these deficit narratives are directly integrated into the expectation that mentors themselves will be role models that the students can emulate, helping them escape their supposedly damaged position as Latino boys and become respectable, honorable adults. This can be seen, for example, in the way LMS brochures and fundraising presented the mentors as success stories who had overcome the stereotypes associated with Latinx youth. This chapter will discuss in detail below how this can also be seen in the way the mentors themselves understood their roles as helping the students become "real men."

The use of deficit narratives in an educational support program like LMS poses a number of serious dilemmas for boys of color who are already facing broader social and racial marginalization. In 2009, Eve Tuck, now professor of Critical Race and Indigenous studies at the Ontario Institute for Studies in Education, wrote an open letter to educators and researchers warning of the effects of damage-centered educational research and practice on communities facing racial and colonial oppression. For Tuck, educational research in communities of color has long prioritized documenting the damage inflicted by racism and treated suffering as a spectacle to study. For boys and men of color, one does not have to look hard to find media, movies, and books depicting the suffering and marginalization this group experiences in schools. Popular films sensationalize the run-down and dangerous streets in which boys and young men of color attempt to resist the far-reaching influence of gangs and violence (Yosso and García 2010). Furthermore, statistics depicting deplorable high school dropout rates and low college attendance are pervasive in educational research. Although Tuck acknowledges that at times it is important to document the effects of racial oppression, she calls on researchers to "consider the long-term repercussions of *thinking of ourselves as broken*" (2009, 409; emphasis in the original).

This lens of "thinking of ourselves as broken" is a perspective that boys and men of color like those in LMS must confront every day. They confront it in media representations, films like *Coach Carter*, and in quotidian contexts. Moreover, it is a lens that is fundamentally incorporated into the larger wave of efforts to empower boys of color in schools. This is because, in addition to media and culture, scholars, educators, and policymakers—including well-meaning ones—have also internalized this vision of boys of color, turning to educational ideas that draw on neoliberal rationales and racial ideologies that impose solutions to widespread inequality by trying to "fix" problematic populations. This has led to the proliferation of damage- and deficit-oriented frameworks in education, which hold that a person's lack of positive cultural attributes or skills is a void that must be filled. Similar to "culture of poverty" arguments, focus and attention are placed on the actions of the individual as the primary source of underachievement. Disenfranchised communities are viewed as not possessing qualities that can lead to success. From this perspective, boys of color are seen as a problematic population that holds toxic cultural traits that serve as barriers to reaching their full potential. Deficit ideology is particularly pervasive in educational intervention projects seeking to address inequalities experienced by low-income students and students of color (Valencia 2010).

When educational programs utilize a deficit frame in their approach to working with students, two important things occur. First, the cultural wealth (Yosso 2005) and funds of knowledge (Gonzalez, Moll, and Amanti 2006) found in communities of color are obscured and rendered valueless. This speaks to the systematic devaluation of the cultural knowledge of marginalized groups as a form of social reproduction (Bourdieu and Passeron 1990). Second, when school programs like LMS center the individualized "deficits" of young people, they often do so without mentioning the political and social nature of the problems facing these populations. For example, nearly all of the students at LMS come from working-class households profoundly affected by the rising cost of living and rapid gentrification in Arroyo Seco. Several students in the classrooms I observed had experienced houselessness at one point in their lives or were currently unhoused. While poverty and housing insecurity have a major impact on a child's ability to thrive in school, LMS's apolitical stance led to little discussion on the political nature of racial and economic inequality. However, by focusing on individuals, LMS's framing language shifts to highlight how the students can overcome the (decontextualized) barriers they face. Since the 1970s in the United States, the neoliberal rhetoric of individualism and meritocracy, as well as the ignoring of structural oppression, has opened the floodgates to damage- and deficit-centered discourse that shapes the ways in which educational solutions are imagined for communities of color. Here, there is a heightened focus on individualized traits assigned to specific demographics of children who are viewed as problematic. Neoliberal school reforms have pushed decentralization and privatization, which have forced school districts to serve as managers of a range of privately run programs contracted to address district needs (Burch 2009; Scott and DiMartino 2009). Under this model, districts contract outside programs that advertise their expertise and innovation to address problems. In their efforts to address this problem, school administrators, teachers, and government officials, along with program managers and funders of programs like LMS, focus on "fixing" students to improve gaps in test scores and graduation rates. This has significant consequences for the way young people of color are taught, and, indeed, for the way they understand their own marginalization in their schools as somehow natural or expected.

This deficit approach to boys of color underpins the apparent credibility of neoliberal school intervention programs like LMS and Obama's 2014 MBK initiative. In the case of MBK, Michael Dumas has documented how this rhetoric was fundamental to MBK's approach to change. Instead of seeking to make structural or political change to a school system that produces rampant racial inequality (for students of all genders), Dumas explained, MBK targeted a specific group in hopes of changing its outcome within the existing system. From this perspective, the problem of inequality in schools that underpins the struggles the students face is deemed a technical problem rather than a racial and political one (Spence, 2016). Dumas (2016a) states:

> The rationale for MBK relies on deficit-based representations of Black young men and boys: They lack interest in education, they lack the ability to delay gratification, they are preoccupied with not "acting white," and they are misguided in their pursuit of careers in hip hop and professional sports. (96)

At LMS, an eventual affiliate of MBK, much of this same rhetoric is in place.

One way interventions like LMS and MBK justify their use of deficit- and damage-oriented rhetoric is by pointing to the fact that some men of color do in fact overcome the struggles they face in schools and thrive. Advocates of these kinds of programs consistently frame these exceptions to the rule as supporting the narrative that although many boys of color struggle in schools, some do very well. Success is not impossible. These individuals are the very ones that LMS targets to serve as mentors in their programs. For example, LMS mentors all identify as Latino men from low-income backgrounds. Six of the mentors I spoke with grew up in Arroyo Seco. By celebrating boys and men of color who do well in school, and disparaging those who do not, intervention programs like LMS and MBK idealize the successful male role model to superhero-like proportions. Amid a population widely represented through pathological racial tropes, educators and administrators turn to this positive male role model as a solution to the troubles facing boys and young men of color. But the use of this kind of role model in these programs to show how boys of color can find success is rife with the paradoxes of neoliberalism. Instead of helping to encourage a rethinking and breaking down of the systemic oppression that boys of color are facing, the figure of the positive male role model presents an expectation that young people of color should overcome the stereotypes and structural inequalities imposed on them in the first place.

I want to be clear that while I am critical of the ways a neoliberal multiculturalism has adopted the image of the mentor/role model to aid in its (re)formulation of race and racism, I do not want to diminish the efforts of educators and community members as we work to sustain our communities in difficult times. Furthermore, it is worth reiterating that research shows that students of color have more positive learning experiences and outcomes when working with educators of color (Bristol and Martin-Fernandez 2019; Dee 2004, 2005; Gershenson, Holt, and Papageorge 2016; Villegas and Irvine 2010). This is particularly the case for boys of color and their teachers and mentors of color.[1] Among critical race scholars, however, there is growing concern over how neoliberal school interventions capitalize on damage and deficit discourse surrounding boys of color to offer the extremely limited and individualized notion of the role model as a superhero-like savior to boys of color (Baldridge 2017; Dumas 2016a; Martino 2015; M. V. Singh 2018).

SUPERHEROES AND THE PARADOX OF THE POSITIVE LATINO MALE ROLE MODEL

An increasing amount of educational research has begun to criticize the popular depictions of male educators of color as superhero-like rescuers of boys of color (A. L. Brown 2012; Pabon 2016; M. V. Singh 2018). For Bianca Baldridge, narratives of Black men who have pulled themselves out of the perils of urban poverty to now heroically help mentor troubled youth in similar situations have been particularly exploited for securing funding for educational nonprofits. She explains that "through sustaining narratives of damage and struggle, Black youth in low-income settings are framed as 'broken' and in need of 'fixing.'" In response, Baldridge argues, "Black male educators are then positioned as their 'heroes' and 'saviors.' This positioning of Black males as heroes and the discourse that follow are indicative of the larger political context of neoliberal education reform, which rests on white paternalism" (2017, 781). Embedded in Baldridge's critique of the neoliberal figure of the Black male savior is an intersectional analysis of the ways race and gender converge in the construction of the positive male role model.

Similarly, education scholars of gender and sexuality have criticized the notion of the positive male role model for its role in reproducing confining notions of identity. In their coauthored book *Gender, Race, and the Politics of Role Modelling: The Influence of Male Teachers,* educational researchers Wayne Martino and Goli Rezai-Rashti (2012) found that the idealization of male educators of color is often grounded is reductionist and essentialist notions of racial and gender affiliation. In this critique, the discursive act of defining a positive male role model is inextricably linked to dominant and confining notions of gender, race, and sexual identity (Britzman 1993; Martino 2015). In a more recent study with Black male teacher candidates, Ashley Woodson and Amber Pabon (2016) similarly argue for the necessity to create room for diverse expressions of racial, gendered, and sexual identities among Black men in the teaching profession. In their study of Black men entering the teaching force they found that "heteropatriarchal assumptions" regarding Black men in teacher-recruitment initiatives result in the belief that "the racial identity, gendered identity, and sex category of an individual who is Black and male are naturally cohesive, and result in certain ways of thinking, doing, and being in the social world" (58). As one of their research participants stated, "If cisgender male identity is what Black males need in role models, then I am not an appropriate mentor or teacher. Everyone seems to want a Black male teacher, but they really want a Black cisgender male teacher" (57).

Similarly, LMS's mentors were framed as embodying the superhero who has been able to break through the negative stereotypes of the so-called damaged or at-risk Latino boy, a stereotype that was otherwise imposed on the students in popular culture. This perspective on the mentors at LMS was held not only by the program and school administrators but also by many of the mentors themselves. This was visible, for example, in the "tough love" that the mentors frequently referred to as a method for helping their students. But this tough love—which included the use of discipline and deficit-oriented language—draws heavily on the vision of Latino youth through racial stereotypes, and it also connects with the superhero Latino male that the mentors at LMS were expected to embody.

This archetype of the positive Latino male role model operates at the convergence of neoliberal discourses of race, gender, sexuality, and other social categories to construct the epitome of Latino male respectability in the image of a Latino male role model. While inspiring for things like fundraising events, these representations of respectable Latino manhood are positioned in direct contrast to the deficient and problematic racialized characteristics associated with Latino males discussed in the last chapter. Here, the archetype of the positive Latino male role model challenges toxic patriarchal qualities, which are seen as pervasive among Latino men, with a clean and respectable representation of traditional heteropatriarchal manhood. Embedded in the positive male role model is a politics of respectability that posits positive behaviors and cultural practices of the role model as marking him as deserving and meritocratic.

Additionally, the positive Latino male role model is seen as a hero. If violent schools and problematic behaviors have damaged Latino boys, the role model—who is college-educated, well-dressed, entrepreneurial, culturally relevant, and a masculine classroom patriarch—has the power to intervene. The archetype of the positive Latino male role model is not a fixed or static construction, and no one person can be its ideal embodiment. Instead, shifting intersectional discourses make and remake the image. In this sense, the archetype of the positive Latino male role model is in flux and performative. The solution of the positive Latino male role model puts an extraordinary amount of expectations on the educator, while oversimplifying and at times obscuring the social and political context in which educational inequalities exist. The neoliberal figure of the positive Latino male role model converges with an underlying logic of racialized patriarchy, which then results in the uplifting of the image of the positive Latino male role model as savior for problematic Latino boys. By offering and modeling a respectable Latino manhood, proponents of this discourse believe that they can help Latino boys succeed in the existing schooling system.

LMS mentors frequently discussed their role in the program and with the students in ways that revealed the profound love and passion they bring to their work. These men expressed that they cared deeply about their students as well as the overall mission of helping Latino boys succeed. However, the words the mentors used also demonstrated how much they too had integrated the rhetoric of Latino male deficit into their understanding of the purpose and benefits of LMS. This was the case even for mentors who were cognizant of and sought to resist these kinds of problematic narratives associated with Latino boys. This resulted in an odd and frequently contradictory articulation of the purpose and goals of Latino male mentorship as students and mentors sought to understand the love and camaraderie built in the program amid a neoliberal educational context in which Latino boys are viewed as broken and in need of repair.

BEING A MENTOR FROM THE MENTORS' PERSPECTIVES

Despite all being young Latino men interested in youth work, the mentors of LMS brought a range of worldviews and approaches to working with their students. Some valued the educator aspect of being a mentor and anticipated working in schools throughout their professional careers. Others relished the ability to provide social support and imagined their role as an unofficial social worker and therapist for their boys. Others still saw their ability to discipline and regulate students as the key to success. Multiple mentors expressed interest in a career in law enforcement, and one mentor left LMS during my fieldwork to begin a career as a juvenile probation officer.

Despite this range of perspectives, I believe all the mentors brought love and dedication to their work. This desire to support Latino boys was why they became youth workers. However, interviews with mentors revealed that most perceived their role, in some fashion, as an expert brought into the school to address the perceived deficits of Latino boys. Although several mentors mentioned structural and institutional racism as contributing to the barriers facing Latino boys, these explanations often came second to the cultural factors in which LMS focused its work. These factors included a lack of interest in education among Latino boys, negative attitudes toward teachers, poor study habits, a lack of accountability among families, dishonesty, aggression, and disrespect toward authority. Mentors frequently framed many of these deficits as the result of the individualized trauma that comes with the everyday lives of Latino boys living in impoverished urban neighborhoods. To address these factors, mentors saw themselves as the loving and compassionate role models who could help boys adopt productive and healthy habits to turn their lives around.

Mentors Give (Tough) Love to Latino Boys

The mentors at LMS discussed their belief that schools, as well as society, show Latino men and boys very little love. In making this point, many of them pointed to their own experiences in school. One mentor reflected: "For me, school was a place where I felt unwanted. Like everyone hoped I would just drop out." In response to this lack of love for Latino boys, LMS mentors viewed one of the primary roles of the mentor as providing love and support to Latino male students.

Mr. Samuel is a twenty-four-year-old mentor who had worked at LMS for one year. He grew up in Arroyo Seco, attended college at a local state school in California, and then after graduation, was elated to land a job in his hometown as a Latino male mentor. He has soft eyes and a warm, almost jolly, demeanor that many of the boys in his group respond to. Like all of the mentors at LMS, Mr. Samuel felt strongly that love and compassion were pivotal components in the role of a mentor. In the following quotation, he describes the care and empathy he feels that the mentors of LMS bring to the work of mentorship, and also the way he sees their shared experience of being Latino males as a motivator to show love and care toward their students:

> A big part of being a mentor is showing your students that you love and care about them and that you will be down to support them through whatever they may be going through. You got to show up for them. That's what we try to do. . . . A lot of our mentors come from Arroyo Seco, or from similar neighborhoods, and what we try to do is give them the support that we didn't get, or maybe the support your friend or your cousin needed to be successful. A lot of Latino boys don't have that person, that adult, that really cares about how they're doing.

The other mentors consistently made similar points. As Mr. Anthony, a thirty-year-old mentor who has worked with LMS for three years, stated: "A lot of Latino boys don't have that person on campus, you know? The one that cares about them, the person that knows if they are absent or asks them how they are doing, if they've been OK, how their family is doing. Being that person is essentially why I think I am here."

It was common for mentors to see their love manifesting in a holistic approach to mentoring a student. According to Mr. Iván, "We wear a lot of hats, like, we are mentors, but also a tutor, a coach, a therapist, case worker, family counselor, we do it all . . . whatever it takes." Although Mr. Iván described mentors as happily taking on this heroic role, he also expressed discomfort with how his love for his students is utilized by the larger organization, Pueblo Unido. For Mr. Iván, the assumed love of mentors was exploited by Pueblo Unido, who did not compensate mentors enough for their efforts. When asked if he felt obligated by the organization to take on so many duties in the lives of his students, he responded:

> Well, no, but kind of yes. I'll put it like this: this isn't exactly our "job description" [uses air quotes], but in some ways I do think we are expected to do all these things, because what we actually do as a mentor is unclear. Like, literally doing anything can fall under what we could be doing as a mentor. And we do it sometimes! I can tell

you that I honestly expect mentors to do these things because we
all care about our students. How are you not going to go above and
beyond for them? . . . But what I don't like is that I feel like Pueblo
Unido knows that and takes advantage of it . . . takes advantage
of . . . how much we care. . . . It's stressful.

Moreover, much of the mentors' understanding of their work as being
motivated by love is directly in response to a lack of resources—not
only the lack of resources that students face from growing up in marginalized communities, but also in the LMS program itself. For example, Mr. Iván recounted feeling that a mentor's love for his students is
exploited by Pueblo Unido, who he felt did not give mentors proper resources to help their students succeed. This was a common sentiment of
the mentors, nearly all of whom expressed their unhappiness with how
LMS was valued by Pueblo Unido. This included dissatisfaction with
their salaries as well as the amount of training and resources available.

   In the context of this lack of resources and underfunding, along
with the vast structural discrimination undermining the conditions in
which Latino boys can be successful and thrive in schools, the mentors also knew that compassion alone would be inadequate to overcome
some of the barriers facing their boys. Moreover, LMS and programs
like it have the explicit goal of helping students find "success" within an
educational context that, as discussed in prior chapters, draws heavily on racist and corporate economic ideologies that encourage the use
of discipline against students and ideas of accountability as necessary
tools to help young people of color struggling in the face of such inequality. In this context, and with the lack of training and mentoring
resources at their organization, many mentors found that beyond love,
tough love was the main thing they could immediately offer their students. Nevertheless, this "tough love" was filled with contradictions.

   The notion of tough love describes the process of instilling positive
qualities in students through punitive practices that will be unpleasant
for students. The "love" aspect of tough love derives from educators'
responsibility to do what they believe is best for a student, even when
the student might loathe the method by which they learn. The majority
of mentors directly or indirectly referenced giving their students tough
love in an effort to help their students with the minimal resources available to them. Tough love often became a part of the "whatever it takes"

attitude mentors brought to their work as they tirelessly tried to help students in danger of being pushed out of school.

In the following exchange, Mr. Sergio detailed an account of his initial months as an LMS mentor and the ways love and tough love seemed to be the only thing he was able to give his students:

> MR. SERGIO: I started in the middle of the school year, like around March, when Mr. Antonio left. And for me it was like, crap, what am I doing here? Like, what do I do? I had no training, no curriculum, really. It was just me on my own. The other mentors gave me advice, but I was mostly just winging it for the rest of the year.

> INTERVIEWER: What kind of things did you do in those first months?

> MR. SERGIO: To be honest, we watched a lot of movies [laughter]. But I also tried to just teach them what I know, show them good study habits and discipline, which was hard. That's still what I try to do, because you know, even now that I've been here, it's not like we have a lot of training. So I just try to show them how I have done stuff. How to be a good student.

> INTERVIEWER: Do you think you are successful?

> MR. SERGIO: Um, sometimes with some students. But with others, well, you've seen my classroom. . . . They don't want to listen. Even when you're a Latino man from here, it can be hard to get them to focus and hear what you have to say. So I get on them and show them. I've been working on that, you know, tough love. They get tired of me getting on them and complain when I get mad, but I'm doing this for their own good.

Other mentors also shared how they incorporated tough love into their classrooms. Mr. Iván, a five-year veteran of LMS, believed in the merits of tough love:

> I know I can lose my cool in the classroom but it's not out of anger. . . . Well, sometimes I am angry, but I tell them I'm not doing this to be an asshole. It's because I love them. I need them to calm down and focus. If they can't follow the simple tasks I give them, how can I know they will be following along in like English or geometry? It's the simple things. Man, you got to learn the simple things.

> They need to get that. . . . You see them complain and get mad at me, but they come back every day, you know? Because they know it's tough love. They know I do it because I care about them. . . . I tell them you're gonna learn some discipline from me in one way or another. . . . I won't let you get away with nothing.

For the mentors at LMS, tough love was a means to forcefully shape their boys into ideal students and young men in an effort to give them the best possible chance in school and in life. Despite the emphasis on love and compassion that underpinned this approach for the mentors, this method of teaching and caring for the Latino boys was also steeped in the kind of deficit language ascribed to Latino boys and the Latinx community, and drew firmly on the superhero archetype of the Latino male role model who, having gained credibility as someone who has overcome the same struggles, is presented as able to "repair" the Latino boys in need of fixing.

WHEN MENTORS ARE TASKED WITH CORRECTING INDIVIDUAL AND COMMUNITY DEFICITS

The values of neoliberalism—meritocracy, personal responsibility, and more—that programs like LMS incorporate into their pedagogy directly shape how an educator's love and care is framed. At LMS, the mentors' care for their students was packaged as an individualized solution for their students. In the context of Latino male mentorship, the mentors of LMS found themselves burdened with the tremendous task of guiding their students to academic achievement amid a school and societal context that has never treated Latinx students fairly (Gándara and Contreras 2009). Although they were positioned by LMS as examples of the way some Latino males can and do succeed in schools— and thus could serve as models for the students to emulate—in reality, positioning the mentors in this way presented a narrative of opportunity that obscured the tremendous downward pressure that Latino boys faced in school due to widespread racism and rampant inequalities (Saenz and Ponjuan 2009). Many of the LMS mentors were aware of and concerned about the racial inequality experienced by the Latinx community. Also, many, although by no means all, understood this inequality as a result of structural racism. Indeed, many of the mentors made clear they had an unwavering commitment to helping boys navigate an unfair system that produced inequality. However, through its partnership with the district, LMS was positioned to play a problem-solving role in schools in the face of a Latino male achievement gap. Consequently, LMS and the school district framed the Latino male mentors not as educators providing critical mentoring but rather as outside experts who had come to address a problem in the district. Despite many mentors' broad concern with racism in schools and society, this framing, which drew on basic neoliberal ideas about personal responsibility in the face of economic and structural disenfranchisement—led mentors to understand their work with their students through a deficit- and damage-oriented lens. They consistently described these deficits as existing in the individual students as well as the Latinx community. For example, one mentor, Mr. Juan—who had been working as a mentor at LMS for several years—highlighted poor family structure as the primary problem facing his students: "A lot of Latino parents, for whatever reason, aren't very strict with their kids," he said. "I think about my parents, about how strict they were with me. They were really strict, and it worked. . . . Sometimes parents weren't brought up in the similar environment that we are now, kids are now, so they don't know what to do."

And yet, at the same time mentors mentioned how some families were failing the students at home, they suggested that LMS mentors were able to provide lessons in self-discipline that would help students make better academic choices. In this way, mentors reiterated the idea that tough love and discipline at LMS could address this deficit in the boys—to correct the poor habit brought on by the family's inability to supervise their son. As Mr. Juan stated, "I think we always do a good job of calling them out, and we're like, look, and we explain why we call them out. It's like, we're calling you out because if this is happening in this group, in the class that you supposedly love, imagine what you're doing in class that you really don't like. And this is why you're getting phone calls home, why you are getting sent out. Right? . . . We're checking you [the students] because of the habits that you're creating for yourself, right? You are bringing negativity to yourself by making bad decisions."

By identifying a lack of discipline originating from the family as a pivotal problem facing Latino boys, Mr. Juan is unintentionally providing a powerful example of the way LMS mentors, incorporating neoliberal ideologies, project blame onto the Latino boys and their families for the struggles they had faced at school, even when they were well aware of the larger structural racism and inequality afflicting their communities. Mr. Juan was not the only mentor to suggest the students' families were overly lenient on their children, or even naive and easily manipulated. Furthermore, a number of mentors suggested that this leniency and lack of discipline allowed the Latino boys to give in to problematic habits such as skipping school and playing video games far past their bedtimes. In other instances, however, LMS mentors mentioned numerous factors preventing parents from fulfilling the role of disciplinarian. These included working long hours or holding down more than one job, having too much family to take care of, navigating housing insecurity, and lacking a strong male figure in the household. Mentors also described feeling gratified by the way Latinx families thought of them as disciplinarian saviors to the boys, whom the families and mentors considered desperately in need of avoiding trouble in school. As Mr. Juan stated, "A lot of the parents see how I am with their child, you know, strict, and they're like, 'Gracias a Dios [Thank God]!' . . . because that's what they need most of all."

Although some mentors did on occasion mention structural or cultural racism in schools, nearly all mentors described the primary problem of Latino boys as existing within their actions and bodies. I believe this was largely due to the fact that LMS's programming and curriculum was explicitly framed around mentoring individuals in order to correct problematic qualities assigned to the group (Latino boys). They were quite literally positioned by LMS to mentor boys to develop better character; a more positive Latino manhood was the role they modeled. This led mentors to view their work as directly addressing problematic behavior.

In their descriptions of the central ways problematic boys could be fixed by ideal Latino men, the mentors commonly highlighted three issues: academic self-discipline, emotional self-control, and morality. For example, when asked to highlight the most important ways he supported students, Mr. Oscar, a mentor in his third year with LMS, pointed to his efforts to teach integrity and self-discipline, two qualities he felt have changed the academic trajectory of many of his students: "I think the biggest way is showing them the value of keeping your word," he said, "essentially being a man who his humble and . . . un joven noble [a noble young person]." In drawing this conclusion—and despite being clearly motivated by compassion and love for his students—Mr. Oscar also leaned on some of the same kinds of deficit- and damage-oriented language as Mr. Juan in describing the students:

> You remember how it was to be in middle school. Or maybe, at least I know I was wild'n out sometimes, not caring about consequences. That's how a lot of my kids are, they just don't care, just think everything works out. So that's what we try to do, the mentors, show them, "Hey, you can't, well, this isn't how you want to live your life. There are consequences to your actions." . . . When we set goals with them, they know I'm going to keep them to their word. . . . I hold you accountable to your word. . . . If you say you're going to improve your grades, let's see you put in the effort, keep your word to yourself. So I'm here to hold them accountable to the commitments they make.

Mr. Oscar's descriptions echo a common perception in educational settings in the United States that Latino boys lack self-control and the ability to stay accountable to their academic goals. His words also overlap with common phrases in LMS literature, including "accountability," "keeping your word," and cultivating "joven noble" (noble young person). His positioning as someone who is able to model these positive traits positions him as a fixer of Latino boys who are seen as potentially immoral and whose lack of integrity and self-control contribute to their academic underachievement.

Additionally, Mr. Oscar's statements frame students who are unable to improve their grades as not yet able to reach a level of morality and maturity that has been modeled by their mentor. While it is clearly the case that lessons in truthfulness, accountability, and self-discipline are valuable for all people, across age, race, and gender, in the context of boy-of-color interventions these qualities are not seen as universal skills needed by all students but instead as qualities particularly required by boys of color to help ameliorate the achievement gap.

Other mentors shared similar narratives about their role in the classroom, narratives that underscored how they felt their duty was to be a nearly omnipresent force in the lives of the students if they were going to learn discipline and reach their full potential. Mr. Iván, for example, whose loving yet strict care I had witnessed while participating in his classroom over the course of a school year, also used similar language as Mr. Oscar—language that was strongly present in the LMS program literature:

I try to get across discipline and accountability, discipline and accountability. It's the simple things. So in my class you are quiet, you
follow directions, and if you're not following through, boy I'm gonna
get on you. . . . And they get tired of me being on their ass, but I tell
them, "That's my job! It's my job to be on you." And they know
[laughter], "Oh, Iván is everywhere." I'm chasing you down in the
hallways to get back to class, I'm following up with your teacher to
see if you've been talking in class, I'm calling home if I have to.

Mr. Iván narrated his role in disciplining his student by inserting himself into a variety of aspects of the students' lives. Not only does he instill accountability and control in the classroom, but as a mentor whose
role extends beyond the wall of his room, he positions himself in the
areas in which students are vulnerable to enact problematic behavior
that would get them in trouble. As Mr. Juan stated, "They say they are
going to get focused, but then I catch them walking around in the hallways all day. . . . I tell them, 'You want to be a man? Well, when a grown
man says he's going to do something, he follows through.'" In this response, Mr. Juan connects accountability to another key element in the
mentors' approach to teaching Latino boys: modeling a proper Latino
manhood.

The Role of Mentors in Restoring a Proper Latino Manhood

One of the most notable ways that mentors at LMS illustrated the complicated influence of neoliberal ideologies at LMS, and the contradictions and dilemmas associated with them, was their feeling that their
primary role was to model a proper and traditionally heteropatriarchal
Latino manhood for their students.[2] Many of the mentors described the
Latinx community as having patriarchal absences that disrupted traditional arrangements in which adult men bring security and stability
to the family. The mentors described the absence of a father figure in
two ways, both of which were highlighted as central dilemmas: a literal
absence (in the case of a father not living with their biological children)
or figurative absence (in which a father did not perform the traditional
role of patriarch).

In addition to highlighting how the absence of men performing hegemonic masculinity negatively affected their students, mentors also pointed out a related dilemma that they believed negatively
affected the boy's educational success: the spread of improper and

harmful masculinities in the Latinx community, that is, the prevalence of men performing manhood that was detrimental to themselves and their communities, such as alcoholics, gang members, criminals, high school dropouts, abusers, or simply men struggling to make ends meet financially.

These deviant Latino masculine representations are widely present in popular culture, such as television and the news media (Mirande 1997). Mentors felt that these representations disparaged Latino men through problematic stereotypes and led to anti-Latinx rhetoric in popular culture. In addition to the media, though, mentors also believed that real Latino men in the community of Arroyo Seco offered poor masculine examples for the next generation. But even as mentors sought to critique disparaging stereotypes of Latino men, they leaned on the same kinds of language of personal responsibility, accountability, and deficit narratives that LMS highlighted in its mission and goals of intervention. For example, the mentors frequently suggested that individuals' poor choices would lead to behavior like substance abuse, incarceration, and the abandonment of one's family, which they saw as undermining a proper masculinity. In this sense, mentors were concerned about stereotypical portrayals of bad Latino men in the media as well as what they saw as a very real patriarchal deficit in the Latinx community. This critique, moreover, directly intersected with how they perceived their role as a mentor: fulfilling the image of a *real man* to help the boys in school and life.

Mr. Johnny was one of the newest mentors at LMS, and by the time we met in May 2019 he was getting ready to complete his first year with the program. Like many other mentors, Mr. Johnny felt that one of the most important aspects of his role as a LMS mentor to Latino boys was to offer a positive representation of Latino manhood to counter stereotypes rooted in real life. "Unfortunately, our society does not value Latino males. And our students internalize that," he said. He added: "You turn on the TV and Donald Trump is talking about us being rapists and murderers. . . . We are always the bad guy. Then you look at the community and it's like, well, we are in the 'hood. And sadly, I see a lot of our young men going down a negative road that a lot of young Black and Latino males go down." When asked to elaborate, he said, "I feel like it's me against the 'hood a lot of the time with my guys, in terms of how they understand what it means to be a man. . . . Like, the culture of gangbanging, drugs . . . men having children and not taking care of them. . . . It feels like it's me versus all these things they see all the time. And I am just one person offering an alternative." He described how he felt responsible for providing an alternative for the Latino boys in his classes. When asked what kind of alternative, he pointed to "doing something different, that you don't see Latino males doing." He described how the work of mentors countered a negative masculinity found in the 'hood with a positive masculinity embodied by the mentors of LMS. "LMS shows boys something different: a Latino male who went to college, takes care of his family. . . . I don't have kids, but some of our mentors do. And just for our students to see a Latino man in that role, you know, married, kids, a job like ours that, we don't get paid a ton but it's decent money. That's what this work is all about, showing our students a different life."

Nearly all the LMS mentors I spoke to felt it was their role to serve as an example of Latino men from similar situations who had not only excelled academically but could also provide for their families (or at least had the potential to do so). By demonstrating this ability to perform a traditional heteropatriarchal role, mentors sought to show a clear differentiation between the negative 'hood masculinity and the positive Latino masculinity that they embodied. Mentors, like the LMS administrators, commonly saw the positive patriarchal role as unfulfilled in the Latinx community. Consequently, from their perspective, the temptation that students faced to adopt a negative or deviant masculinity threatened the heteropatriarchal stability of the Latinx community, while also contributing to the disadvantages their students faced in school. Thus, to help their students achieve academic success, mentors saw modeling a positive masculinity connected to a positive patriarchal role fulfillment as key, and many of the mentors in the program highlighted the crucial importance of this. Mr. Nicolás, for example, a mentor in his mid-twenties who was raised in Arroyo Seco, described this as central to his work with the students: "I want my students to know there are men that take care of our families. It is important that that is very visible in a program like this." He noted that this was "an area that we as Latino males have some work to do. . . . We are failing our boys because they don't have good role models of how to be honorable men. And it can be a cycle."

Several mentors stated that preparing boys for fatherhood was an especially important goal in their group, and more than half of them highlighted in their conversations that LMS mentors needed to offer examples of manhood that could help their students prepare to be productive fathers. This was striking, because only two of the thirteen mentors I interviewed over the two years of this study were fathers themselves. Nevertheless, most believed an important role of LMS mentors was to help recuperate a Latino manhood that had been absent in the Latinx community. It was also clear that preparedness for fatherhood did not include the everyday mechanics of being a parent, but that this ideal manhood was inherently connected to fulfilling paternal roles in Latinx families and the community at large. As Mr. Juan describes:

> We aren't talking about changing diapers or anything like that [laughter]. What I mean is, we talk about the values of being a man, a real man. And those apply to being a father when that time comes. Like the four values. Those values are life changing, man. So if a student learns those values with us, you know, being a humble and hardworking man who puts others before himself, those are good things to know as a father. And that's what we are giving. That's why I think, how I am as a mentor, I think I will be as a father.

From this perspective, preparing Latino boys (some as young as sixth grade) for fatherhood meant instilling the values of a proper and productive masculinity, one that was positive and aligned with hegemonic values in a heteropatriarchal society. These values included "accountability," the ability to "provide" for one's family, and "putting others before yourself." This was in direct contrast to what was described as a negative or 'hood masculinity, which led Latino boys to stray from their paternalistic duties. Despite the mentor's well-meaning intentions to help the boys, this framing placed the student's future academic and personal success on the student's own ability to embody this form of masculinity. Moreover, it entirely overlooked the broader dilemmas that many scholars have pointed out with this form of heteropatriarchal ideal (Connell 2005). Instead, the mentors inadvertently saw the Latino boys in Arroyo Seco as beginning to embody, or at risk of embodying, a deviant masculinity. To counter the lack of proper heteropatriarchal representations of Latino maleness in students' homes or in the cultural sphere (movies, news, television), LMS mentors, pushed by the LMS administrators and program literature, sought to fulfill this patriarchal absence and help the boys head off a possible fate of deviant masculinity.

"I'M NOT MAGIC . . . I WISH I WAS, THOUGH":
A BRIEF PORTRAIT OF MR. JOHNNY

Late on a Monday afternoon in May of my second year with LMS, Mr. Johnny and I agreed to meet at an Arroyo Seco coffee shop on the other side of the freeway as Lincoln Middle School. Mr. Johnny had recently taken over the LMS class there after the previous mentor left abruptly. Among the mentors, Lincoln was known as the most difficult middle school to manage, and they saw the school as struggling to maintain organization and structure. In part, this was due to a constant turnover of teachers and administrators. Students at Lincoln were also among the most economically disadvantaged in the district, with nearly 100 percent of them eligible for free or reduced-cost lunch. The student body of the school was roughly half Latinx and half African American.

I arrived at the coffee shop an hour early to do work on my laptop. About ten minutes before our scheduled meeting time, a young Latino man walked into the café. We made eye contact, and since we were the only Latino men in the café, it was clear we had found who we were looking for. Any initial awkwardness that comes with meeting someone for the first time quickly vanished during the early moments of our meeting. Mr. Johnny had a kind face and warm smile. He was large in stature, with a voice that was focused and rhythmic. This heavy voice not only attracted respect and attention, but also offered the same. Although we were both in our late twenties at the time, Mr. Johnny's demeanor led me to feel like I was in the presence of an older man. This was not for lack of humility or a sense of superiority on his part. To the contrary, he was extremely humble and generously praised my upcoming completion of my doctorate. "What you are doing . . . good job, man. I am in awe," he said warmly. I repaid the compliment: "I think your work is more impressive," I stated, genuinely.

I asked Mr. Johnny the same questions I usually asked the mentors about personal background and his journey to becoming an LMS mentor. He described growing up in a predominantly Latinx and Black urban area in California as a small child, which was similar to the Black and Latinx area of North Arroyo Seco in which he now worked. In middle school, his family moved to a neighboring urban suburb where he attended public schools that were almost 100 percent Latinx. He described his schools as "highly underresourced" and "rough places" for a Latino boy to grow up. Despite obstacles, Mr. Johnny had excelled and was placed in honors and AP courses for most of his academic career. During his junior year of high school, though, his father suddenly passed away. This tragic loss led him to stop attending school. "I hit this downward spiral," Mr. Johnny told me. "I stopped going to school. . . . I was affected very negatively, I didn't care. . . . I was depressed." When Mr. Johnny was ready to return to school, he attended adult school to make up credits and graduate. He worked for a year after high school before attending a local community college. There, he began to excel in school once more.

It would be at the community college that Mr. Johnny began to recognize stereotypes associated with Latino men as barriers to his success. These stereotypes even came from other Latino men.

> I didn't know much about transferring so I made an appointment with a counselor. At the time, I really wanted to go to UCLA. But the counselor there was a gatekeeper in a way, now looking back, yeah, he was a gatekeeper. And when I realized that, I was like, "Oh what, a Latino man?" I thought he was going to help me, but no. He pushed me towards Cal State, which isn't bad, but I thought I could go to a higher university. I knew I could.

Mr. Johnny transferred to UC Berkeley, where he majored in sociology and minored in education. As an undergraduate he had made it his mission to help support students of color in ways that he was not supported. This led him to volunteer in local schools and to work part time for the Puente Project, and in the summers with the Upward Bound program. Through these experiences, Mr. Johnny learned that educational outreach programs placed a high value on recruiting academically successful Latino men. "We are in high demand," he noted. "It's something we [LMS mentors] all know about." This realization of his value in the field of education made him a confident applicant.

When a friend from the student group Los Amigos, a university-based social organization for Latino men, emailed him about an open position at LMS, Mr. Johnny admitted that he felt very confident about the position after he saw the application. In particular, his background and identity, coupled with his work experience, compelled him to feel like an obvious match for the program. This would be his first job after finishing his degree.

> When I applied, I thought, man. there's no way I won't get this job . . . because I am that typical, not so typical, Latino success story: from the 'hood, struggled, faced whatever behaviors, lost his role model, went through a downward spiral and then still graduated from a top university . . . first in my family. And this is what I love to do. I would be getting paid to do something that I would have volunteered to do anyway.

Upon starting his position, Mr. Johnny noted the large task ahead of him. "My eighth graders are more like, rough around the edges, they might be bullies . . . at risk, whatever the term might be . . . defiant," he stated. He recognized that these were the students he had been brought in to work with as a fellow Latino male from a similar background. The expectation was that if anyone would be able to turn things around for those students, it would be him. As he stated, "They [the school] had high hopes for me. And I've done my best. I've made some progress with some students but, you know, it can be rough."

Mr. Johnny lamented what felt like an uphill battle with many of his students. Although he demonstrated an awareness of structural issues of racism in North Arroyo Seco, he described his energies as a mentor focusing mostly on changing the habits and values of his students. Mr. Johnny was a big proponent of character development to increase what he described as "respectability in school" for his boys and "accountability toward themselves." He regularly used the phrase "me against the 'hood" to describe his work with his students. This self-framing of the role of an LMS mentor is emblematic of a deficit orientation often embedded in male-of-color programming. Nevertheless, as noted earlier with other mentors, Mr. Johnny approached his work with love and care, and it is important to avoid a reductionist and overly simplistic analysis of his loving and caring work with LMS. While in this chapter I have criticized the archetype of the superhero Latino male role model who corrects the behavior of bad boys, it is also true that Latino male educators do not exist in a binary where their work is either good or bad, deficit- or asset-oriented, neoliberal or not neoliberal. This book's argument, although intended to call out the impact of the integration of neoliberal ideologies in educational programs like LMS, is not in any way intended to obscure the level of care or love that the mentors like Mr. Johnny use in their work.

At the end of our conversation that day, I asked Mr. Johnny if

I could return to the phrase "me against the 'hood." I had written it down in my notepad as something worth revisiting. "Ah . . . that's kind of a bad way of saying it, huh?" he replied. His face slightly cringed as the phrase was repeated out loud. "But that's really how I have to take it sometimes. And me, being from the 'hood . . . I am the one that can reach them." He went on to describe the risky behavior of some of his students. This ranged from habitually skipping school, to getting into fistfights, to drug use. One of his students had expressed an interest in obtaining a firearm for protection. "It is especially sad because, you know, these are middle schoolers. And I see some, just, really going down a dark path because that's all they know. It's what they're surrounded by," he stated. We were both aware that an eighth grade Latino boy from Lincoln Middle School was killed in gang violence the year before. The boy was not involved with LMS, but the tragedy made Mr. Johnny all the more aware of the stakes involved with him reaching his students.

Mr. Johnny identified a few of his boys as being in terrible danger if something did not change in their lives—twelve-year-old children whose fate almost already felt sealed. For these students, he felt that their actions and outlook on life needed to change at all costs:

> I have a student, Lucas, who is, you know, is immersed in that 'hood life . . . all of that. And when he does come to school, sometimes he will come to my class, if he's ditching another class. And I am afraid if I try to take him back [to the class he's ditching], he will just want to leave school for the day. So we talk, you know, and he tries to impress me with talking about drugs and stuff, and that's when I tell him, "Yo, I'm *not* impressed with that. That's not what makes a man. If you look up to me, you got to know, I'm not down with that stuff." I try to say anything I can to reach him and get him out of that cycle. Get him out of that street culture. But it's me, just one person in his life, versus all of that.

Mr. Johnny's voice became heavy with emotion as he said this. We talked more about the "whatever it takes" attitude. For him, it meant doing everything necessary to at least temporarily keep some of his students safe. It was something many mentors brought to their work. Mr. Johnny was a huge proponent of LMS—he believed in the mission of helping Latino boys and knew that a Latino male mentor could make a great impact on a child's life. However, he also knew the odds were stacked against him: "Honestly . . . like honestly, honestly . . . of my students who weren't already on that high-achieving track, I . . . can't say I think many will go to college and graduate. I hope for a few, maybe something can change but . . . yeah it's tough." He then added, "And of course not everyone has to go to college. And I think some might do alright with that." When I asked where he found the most value in his work, he reiterated that it was the "personal connections" he made with his students. He used these connections to try to instill qualities that would help his students in the future. Mr. Johnny hoped that each student could "develop into a person who can successfully participate in society and make a positive contribution."

Although the framing of Latino male interventions poses many problems, I have no intention of minimizing the work of Mr. Johnny. To the contrary, this brief portrait of Mr. Johnny is meant to highlight the extreme circumstances in which Latino male mentorship exists. Despite Mr. Johnny's tremendous efforts, he was fully aware of the uphill battle many of his students faced. A loving mentor could not change their difficult situation. But the mentor would do his best, regardless. During our interview, Mr. Johnny became deeply reflective as he attempted to truthfully answer where he saw many of his students in the next ten years. "My guys, all of them, they have so much potential." In reflecting on his own inability to make up what felt like a massive gap for his students, he shared, "It's just . . . I'm not magic . . . I wish I was, though." Mr. Johnny would go above and beyond to be as magic as possible.

The story of Mr. Johnny demonstrates the complicated and at times contradictory work that Latino male mentors are asked to perform with their students. Like all the mentors I met during my time with LMS, Mr. Johnny was tremendously committed to his students. He had experienced ups and downs throughout his academic career and believed a positive Latino male role model could be highly beneficial. He was also aware that the field of education valued men with stories like his. While Mr. Johnny held a structural critique of race and society, his work as a mentor focused on the individual deficits of his students. Yet in delving deeper into his story, I aim to show that Mr. Johnny's focus on respectability and character development was not necessarily due to a hardline belief in the politics of respectability and neoliberalism's doctrine of individualism. Rather, Mr. Johnny engages with LMS's focus on character development because it is the only thing he has at his disposal to, in his words, "save" his students "from the 'hood." Despite the many problems with the use of the archetype of the positive Latino male role model, it is important to note that Mr. Johnny takes up this image as the best tool available. He feared terrible things for his students and knew that, for some, falling behind now would most likely lead to danger and despair in the future.

CONCLUSION

Mentors at LMS approach their work through profound love and care. This commitment to mentoring and supporting Latino boys led them to adopt, although at times begrudgingly, the prevailing narratives associated with "successful" men of color intervening in the lives of "problematic" boys of color. One result has been an intermingling of discourses of care and love with notions of deficit and damage. Embedded in their understanding of Latino male mentorship is the belief that Latino men may help restore a respectable Latino manhood that is conducive to traditional heteropatriarchal values.

The mentors at LMS also often described the pressure and urgency that come with being positioned as superhero-like educators in the lives of Latino boys. This pressure intersected with the deep love and commitment they felt for their students, and often led mentors to bring a "whatever it takes" attitude to their work. Although an adoption of the archetype of the positive Latino male role model can reify the racial logics undergirding many boy-of-color initiatives, Mr. Johnny's story reminds us of the complicated nature of mentoring Latino boys in the context of a nation's educational and social system that has been constructed to diminish, disenfranchise, and exploit the lives of communities of color. I describe the way Mr. Johnny traverses a rhetoric of deficit, damage, and love as strategy. As educators, we are constantly asked to negotiate the contradictions of our work in the context of schooling systems never meant to help all our students succeed. Although my analysis of the notion of the positive Latino male role model is critical, it is important to avoid operating simplistically in a positive–negative binary when examining the work that communities of color are doing to address their oppression. Throughout my time with LMS, some mentors might have said things that I found egregious and problematic when referring to Latino boys. However, all mentors said things that were deeply meaningful and full of love. Sometimes these statements were made by the *same* mentor. This realization leads me to ask, can there be both?

During the early months of my time at LMS, I enjoyed reading the book *Between the World and Me,* by Ta-Nehisi Coates (2015). Written in the form of a letter to his own son, Coates's book examines the realities of living life as a Black person, and specifically a Black man, in the United States. In the early pages, Coates describes the *fear* Black parents have for their children who must grow up in a country that has always devalued and destroyed Black life. He reflects on the way parents enact strict rules and harsh—at times physical—punishments in an effort to keep children safe. This was the case with Coates's own father, who utilized his belt "with more anxiety than anger" (15) when his son was in trouble. While the experiences of Black and non-Black Latinx people in the United States are historically situated and unique, Coates's words beautifully, and without judgment, illustrate the unjust struggles in which communities of color must seek to keep their children safe amid racial violence. In a neoliberal educational context in which Latino men are lauded as the saviors and disciplinarians of Latino boys, the mentors of LMS similarly grapple with their role in helping to improve the educational lives of their students. Some embraced the role of the positive Latino male role model, while others reluctantly accepted the role as an imperfect survival technique to address a problem not of their students' making.

While acknowledging the complicated terrain in which Latino men do their best to support their students, it is crucial that we continue to search for new ways to intervene in oppression to not just survive, but to demand justice. In the following chapter, I focus on the words and experiences of LMS students as they offer their own perspectives on the purpose and workings of the program. While it was clear that damage- and deficit-based rhetoric deeply influenced how students understood the function of the program, the boys also made clear that what they appreciated most about the program was not necessarily what they saw as its primary goal. Instead, the students found value in the informal moments of mentorship and made the case for a new set of priorities in Latino male programming.

TRAVERSING JOY AND DISCIPLINE

Looking for Fun and Critical Education in a
Program Designed to Fix You

"This program can be cool, but it's also fucked up sometimes," Jasiel shared with me one day during after-school tutoring. Although he was not an after-school regular, Jasiel had stayed late to talk with Mr. Antonio about his behavior. Jasiel was a mature eighth grader who was a strong student, and he was also the school's best soccer player. "This is supposedly a place where we can be ourselves, but then why does Mr. Antonio send me outside for like nothing?" he grumbled, kicking out an empty chair and resting his feet on it. He wore black Adidas soccer warm-ups and brightly colored Kyrie Irving basketball shoes. Earlier that day, a wave of giggles had spread across the class and disrupted Mr. Antonio's opening check-in. Although Jasiel maintained he was not the one whispering jokes, he was the first of several boys whom Mr. Antonio sent out of the room. Jasiel had looked both infuriated and embarrassed as he stormed out into the hallway. "Sometimes we can have fun in here . . . relax and be ourselves . . . and then sometimes Mr. Antonio is all on my ass. So, which one is it?" he complained.

Jasiel had a point. During my time with LMS, I witnessed what felt like two stories running parallel in the program. This made LMS difficult for me to describe and categorize. On the one hand, the program was a loving and caring space. It served students as a refuge in a school environment rife with punishment and surveillance for Latino boys (Rios 2017). On the other hand, however, I had witnessed severe discipline and punishment in the program itself. Beyond individual mentors who enacted these practices, program-wide policies resulted in stern consequences for low GPAs and poor behavior. This led me to view LMS as a program where efforts to spark joy in Latino boys coexisted with efforts to discipline Latino boys. These seemingly contradictory goals were confusing for many of the students. While some boys praised the program for offering a place on campus where they could be themselves and build camaraderie, others criticized the program for being overly punitive and not catering to their needs. In some instances, the very same students both praised *and* highly criticized the program.

Throughout this book, I describe the way LMS existed within an educational landscape influenced by neoliberal multiculturalism. In this era, community goals of social justice have become entangled with philanthropic ventures to fix educational disparities (Baldridge 2019). As a result, deficit- and damage-oriented rhetoric is often espoused to justify programs focused on specific groups of students. This rhetoric shifts focus away from structures of inequality and instead frames students as broken and lacking key qualities needed for success. The mission of these programs is then to repair individuals and fill what is lacking by students. The prior chapter showed how mentors at LMS integrated this rhetoric into their work by embodying an ideal Latino role model, using deficit-oriented language to describe students, and drawing on heteropatriarchal values to critique student behavior. This chapter moves to shed light on how the incorporation of neoliberal logics at LMS affected the students, documenting how Latino boys understand and experience being the targets of a school-based intervention like LMS. I also explore how prevailing narratives of crisis associated with Latino men and boys influence this experience, driving many of the students to incorporate deficit-oriented logics into their own understanding of themselves.

For the most part, research on mentorship programs for Black and Latino boys has highlighted the overwhelmingly positive experiences of students in these programs (Hall 2006). Having a mentor can result in culturally relevant and loving care for boys (Jackson, Sealey-Ruiz, and Watson 2014; Watson, Sealey-Ruiz, and Jackson 2016) and increase the academic performance of students (Sánchez, Esparza, and Colón 2008). A number of scholars have also highlighted how centering the experiential knowledge and cultural wealth of students is a foundational aspect of mentoring Latino boys (Sáenz et al. 2015). This involves accessing the community cultural wealth of the Latinx community (Yosso 2005), as well as building inter-generational and near-peer group mentoring to share knowledge and resources. However, other studies paint a more complicated picture of school-based interventions for boys of color. In his book *Black Boys Apart*, sociologist Freeden Oeur (2018) explores the racial and gender politics of single-sex public high schools for African American boys. Oeur finds that although many school leaders and students in these targeted schools pointed to structural causes of Black male marginalization, the rationale behind Black male academies (and the programming in those academies) overwhelmingly focused on the perceived cultural deficits of Black men and boys. Oeur describes how these "contradictory discourses" (53) were prevalent throughout his ethnographic research. As a result, Black male academies perpetuate an odd mixture of respectability politics and strict discipline, tempered with ideologies of racial uplift and loving care. Despite their dedication to empowering Black boy students, Oeur found that neoliberal racial politics embedded in these schools diverged from the rhetoric and social justice goals of Black feminists and Black radical visions of justice.[1]

At LMS, a similar contradiction to what Oeur observed at single-sex high schools for African American boys was present—the mentors displayed a powerful compassion and dedication to Latino boys, while the program itself employed a rhetoric of personal responsibility and an emphasis on cultural deficits needing to be repaired. In this chapter, I focus on the words and experiences of LMS students as they offer their own perspectives on the purpose and workings of the program. I also highlight their critiques and concerns with LMS and focus on what educational goals they would like to see prioritized in Latino boy programming. It is important to note that many students enthusiastically described LMS as a home place on campus and praised the program as one of their favorite classes. Educational research has suggested that having a place to call home on campus is vital for the academic success of boys of color (Brooms, Clark, and Smith 2018). Nevertheless, while many students reported positive experiences with the program, others reported very negative ones. It was also common for students, regardless of their feelings toward LMS, to draw from deficit- and damage-oriented language when describing the purpose and goals of the program. This led students to describe Latino boys as lost, problematic, and in need of fixing.

While this rhetoric of damage and deficit was pervasive among students, the boys of LMS also reported experiencing fun and joy in the program. They described joy as a secondary or unofficial consequence of the program, but they were clear that fun and pleasure should be a more fixed goal in Latino male empowerment. Students also articulated a desire for more critical race lessons where they learned about race, culture, and society. Indeed, as this chapter outlines, to meaningfully support Latino boys it is essential that LMS and other similar programs move away from damage- and deficit-centered rhetoric, and instead make fun, joy, and critical race pedagogy the primary force supporting their work with students. As Victor, a tenth grader in Mr. Iván's high school group, put it: "[The students] want to talk about what's going on. . . . What's in their mind, what they see every day. That's really important."

MAKING SENSE OF DAMAGE AND DEFICIT NARRATIVES

In 2015, two years before I first visited the program, LMS was featured in a major newspaper in the region. The reporter set the stage for the article by opening with a bleak reality: "The odds are against Latino males in Arroyo Seco schools," reads the opening sentence. It continues by listing an array of damning statistics about Latino boys and compares them to their similarly marginalized Black boy counterparts. It highlights how these boys are more likely to struggle in school, be truant or suspended, and drop out. The term "at risk" is used to describe the students.[2] The article goes on to praise the work of ASUSD in creating targeted programs for Latino boys in the district to help address these problems. It suggests that a powerful aspect of this work is hiring "full-time mentors" who are able to help boys "make positive choices in and out of school." The article also reports that LMS had been successful in "pushing attendance rates up and suspensions down." It closes with the success story of Miguel, one student who—"against all odds"—planned to attend a four-year university. In the article, Miguel explains how LMS has pushed him to believe in himself and ignore negative influences and stereotypes associated with Latino males. In the closing sentences, the article mentions the hardships Miguel has overcome, including the murder of his father in Mexico several years earlier. Overall, the article tries to underscore how Miguel's story reveals the potential of LMS to change the academic and life outcomes of Latino boys in Arroyo Seco.

While the article sought to highlight the success of LMS and its students, it also reproduced common narratives of damage and deficit associated with Latino men and boys. From this perspective, the collective group is seen in peril. Their grades are low, their behavior gets them into trouble, and they lack proper guidance. The article even went out of its way to share that a student's father had been murdered in Mexico. In painting this bleak picture, which is offered with little context, the article framed LMS as a solution to a dire problem. The program offers encouragement, motivation, and discipline to this struggling group in order to change their trajectory. In 2019, Patrick Johnson and David Philoxene coauthored a book chapter where they raise important questions about the impact that damage and deficit discourse can have on students in targeted programs. Based on their research with Oakland Unified School District's Manhood Development Program (MDP), they describe how the pervasive rhetoric of Black male damage and crisis profoundly influences how students understand the rationale and purpose of the MDP (i.e., students are a problem that needs to be fixed). They note, moreover, how it was common for students in the program to adopt this rhetoric even when they simultaneously held strong personal and structural critiques of racism. While praising practitioners and community members, Johnson and Philoxene call on educational leaders and policymakers to "dream outside dominant narratives of Black male damage" (78) by constructing programs that uplift students as critical social thinkers and center Black joy and power in school-based interventions.

The words and experiences of Latino boys in LMS paint a picture similar to Johnson and Philoxene's. This is not to say, however, that the students at Arroyo Seco did not enjoy the LMS program. Most students I spoke with expressed overall satisfaction with LMS and saw their mentor "like family." Nevertheless, while students reported feeling joy and happiness at LMS, they frequently described these feelings as unintended consequences of the program rather than the central goal of the program itself. Indeed, it is important to note that while students generally articulated a positive experience in LMS, when discussing the purpose and objectives of the program they consistently revealed how they viewed LMS as an intervention meant to address the deficits of Latino boys. Students frequently believed that as a group, Latino boys were a problem for schools and society. As a result, they came to understand LMS as existing to *fix* Latino boys. They centered this notion of fixing Latino boys primarily around a lack of responsibility, accountability, and respectfulness. Indeed, as this chapter shows, it was clear that students embraced the pervasive narrative of Latino male brokenness by conceptualizing LMS as an intervention that aimed to fix their problematic tendencies.

Latino Boys Are a Problem

Students who participated in LMS during my time with the program (2017–19) demonstrated a clear awareness of the symbolic connection between their individual existence and the perceived collective short-comings of Latino men and boys. The students astutely understood that their racial and gender affiliation was the reason why they themselves had been the target of LMS. They regularly referenced the notion that Latino men and boys represent a problem for schools and society, and shared their belief that many Latino boys were, as various students put it, "not interested in finishing high school," were tempted to "get into drugs" and "join gangs," and practiced behaviors that would "get them locked up." The students believed that these popular racial storylines associated with Latino boys were the primary reasons why LMS was created.

Pedro is a fifteen-year-old student who was in Mr. Iván's LMS group at Las Palmas High School. With light brown hair and soft eyes, he was a courteous and respectful teenager who was formal and polite when speaking with adults but could be quite the jokester among his friends. His sharp and witty personality sometimes emerged in LMS to troll the stern and serious Mr. Iván. Pedro was also, by chance, Mr. Iván's next-door neighbor. In his conversations with me, Pedro regularly drew on the popular language of individual responsibility and the belief that Latino men and boys easily fall prey to negative behavior and choices that lead to troubled lives.

"I think LMS was started to try to show us a new way," he told me one day while we sat in the reading room of the library. He had finished his homework during study hall and happily agreed to talk with me. "It tries to show us that we don't have to be the stereotype, that we can do something positive with our lives."

"Instead of doing something negative?" I asked.

"Well, that we don't have to join a gang or get involved with drugs. A lot of Latino males get involved in negative things. They make bad choices, and then the consequences for their actions are . . . getting kicked out of school, getting locked up."

Pedro's description of LMS as offering boys a new path away from the negative lives Latino men were seen to commonly lead in his community was a regular theme among students. Many believed that the "problem" of Latino males was the primary motivation for the creation of LMS in the first place. Latino boys were in peril, they noted, and something needed to be done. Students believed that the strategy of LMS was to address this problem by focusing on preventing individual students from taking the route so many had taken before them.

At the end of our conversation, Pedro offered what I describe as an *individual exception perspective* to the "problem" of Latino men and boys. I had asked him if he felt concerned that he himself might become involved in the negative things he had described, such as getting kicked out of school, doing drugs, or getting locked up.

He seemed surprised by the question.

"Me?"

"Yeah," I replied.

He shook his head no, smiling at the question. He was a stellar student. His entry into LMS came at the request of his mother, who had been sold by the benefits described to her by el vecino (the neighbor), Mr. Iván. She insisted Pedro join. Pedro had agreed but did not plan on returning next year.

"I have always been, not into those things. The way my parents raised me, pretty strict, I have always gotten good grades. I am not trying to go down that road."

Pedro was not alone in making this kind of distinction between himself and the larger group, and many other students sought to distance themselves from the problem narrative rather than challenge it. By turning to this sort of individual exception perspective, students like Pedro who were the targets of deficit-oriented programs ended up adopting the belief that their group lacks something but trying to exclude themselves from that problem narrative. For Pedro, this perspective helped him explain his existence in the program. He was clear that Latino men and boys represent a problem. Although he himself was a Latino boy, he understood himself as an exception to this rule. This description was common among particularly high-achieving students (though not exclusively), many of whom directly called out Latino boys as a problem to be solved by LMS while, like Pedro, distancing themselves from the archetype of the bad Latino boy. This reasoning allowed them to differentiate themselves from the perceived norm, placing them on the good side of the good boy–bad boy binary in the Latinx community. To help explain this, many students highlighted things like their positive familial upbringing or what they had learned in LMS. In this way, these students articulated that while bad Latino boys were a problem in their community, they were not one of them.

Alonzo, for example, a ninth grader also in Mr. Iván's LMS group, pointed to LMS as an opportunity for him to escape the problematic paths that Latino boys were prone to follow. In our one-on-one conversations, Alonzo highlighted how many Latino boys struggle with what he considers the academic rigors of high school but that he himself is making a conscious choice to not be one of them.

"I think LMS was created because a lot of Latino males are dropping out of school," he said. "They are lost, you know, they are not understanding this is high school, you have to step up your game. . . . I joined LMS because I am trying to improve myself. I want to be successful, and I am willing to put in the effort for my future."

Although Alonzo and other students in the program felt they did not represent a problem, they still framed their path toward a better future against the common stereotypes about Latino men and boys, describing their intention to put in the effort that they felt was missing from many of their peers.

Many students described stereotypes assigned to Latino men and boys as contributing to "assumptions" about their academic abilities not only from teachers but also from a wider society that they believed was suspicious of their behavior and their right to even exist in the United States. Many students expressed indignation at the way stereotypes were assigned to them as individuals. However, because many students also believed that Latino men and boys did fulfill these common stereotypes, there was a strong emphasis on their own commitment to "break stereotypes" through their actions. Students talked about breaking stereotypes as a personal goal, but this often reified the racial stereotype in question. As Jaime, a tenth grader in LMS, stated: "As a Latino male, sometimes people see you and they stereotype you. . . . They can't tell if you are, like, a gang member or a good kid." Similarly, after expressing common themes of damage and deficit associated with Latino men and boys, Jaime summarized, "My goal is to not be the stereotype." Students continuously described the ways popular racial representations of Latino males informed their own life experiences as Latino boys, and more particularly, as Latino boys in LMS. Although students did describe LMS as "empowering" Latino boys through its work, the language of damage and deficit was pervasive throughout the ways this transformation to empowerment would occur. Students generally understood Latino men and boys in Arroyo Seco to be defined by their problems. They also pointed to—reflecting the mentors' attitudes discussed in the last chapter—the need to embody a proper Latino masculinity to have a promising future. Students regularly suggested that Latino boys struggled, in part, due to their lack of *real* Latino male values that the boys were in the process of learning. This positioned Latino boys as a problem to be fixed.

Latino Boys Need Fixing

While students articulated a clear awareness of how racial stereotypes assigned to Latino men and boys wrongfully described who they were as individuals, they also believed there was some truth behind these stereotypes. Student responses to questions regarding the purpose of LMS revealed that many adopted the readily available language of deficit and damage to describe the problem that Latino boys represented, as well as the belief that LMS could help fix this problem. It is worth reiterating that most LMS mentors resisted the notion that they were "saving" Latino boys and sought to bring an asset-oriented approach to their work. Despite these efforts, the commonsensical logic that a Latino male mentorship program would fix problematic boys as a way to address the Latino male crisis dominated how students understood the function of LMS. In addition to this widely cited societal narrative, the description of LMS as "character development" positions boys as lacking positive characteristics and in need of fixing. Boys particularly focused on the four values of LMS when describing the deficit characteristics of Latino boys that needed fixing: (1) keep your word, (2) don't bring harm to others, (3) take responsibility for your actions, and (4) be a positive example to others.

Abraham, an eleventh grader who was the most senior student I interviewed, had taken an LMS course, off and on, since he was in seventh grade. In his conversation with me, he emphasized LMS's goal of teaching Latino boys to take responsibility. The rationale behind this goal, he made clear, was that Latino boys were frequently irresponsible in his school. He suggested that, by developing responsibility for their academic performance, as well as claiming responsibility for past transgressions, Latino boys would build more positive and productive lives. Abraham reflected:

> LMS is for people who need a second chance . . . who are ready to take responsibility of their actions. I know people who were like troublemakers and then they joined LMS and stuff changed. They got more focused and began to follow through with their goals. . . . For me, back in middle school I would do dumb stuff, and LMS helped me stop that. I used to slack off, not do my homework, and LMS just helped me. I got my backpack clean, you know. I am taking responsibility now.

Abraham connected the notion of taking responsibility to the themes of self-discipline and academic motivation. These were qualities that "troublemakers" were believed to lack. Abraham viewed himself as an example of the power of LMS. He mentioned to me that while he did not feel he necessarily needed LMS anymore, he enjoyed the opportunity to "lead by example" and show younger students that success "is possible." Furthermore, as the oldest student in his group, he had taken a leadership position in his LMS classroom. I had witnessed this on several occasions, noting that when Mr. Iván was out of the room, the class was under Abraham's informal leadership.

In addition to learning personal responsibility, the impact of neoliberal logics on the students and the way that logic encouraged them to internalize deficit-oriented ideas of themselves, can be seen in the way they highlighted the notion of respect as another key quality they were learning at LMS. Many students believed that the program not only taught students how to adopt a respectable way of being, but also to demonstrate respectfulness even when tempted not to. Students focused on how to not be disrespectful or give in to bad behavior. The ability to maintain level-headedness when one was at risk of abandoning respectful behavior was key. One student, for example, who was named Christopher, stated: "In LMS we learn about self-control." Christopher casually described these qualities as "essentially, how to act right." When I asked him about what acting right meant to him, he clarified: "just being respectful, the basics . . . a good kid." Many students understood LMS as helping them to manage their emotions as a way to remedy their poor behavior. The notion that Latino boys must be re-socialized to be more successful in school directly connects to the racial narrative that Latino boys represent behavior problems that create their own underachievement. A lack of respect and accountability were common factors that students offered as to why they felt Latino boys in their school were not academically successful.

While most students displayed an understanding of respect that posited Latino boys as being disrespectful, Abraham, who complicated the narrative, sought to find a more nuanced understanding of the conditions in which Latino boys are read as disrespectful, one which, nevertheless, underscored the same result: that Latino boys have bad tendencies, and LMS was designed to help them with them: "If someone isn't respectful to you," Abraham said, "if they are trying to fight you, just turn the other way. It's not worth it to get caught up in meaningless drama . . . with each other or a teacher. In LMS you learn to act with respect all the time and when that happens you get respect from others."

But in another part of Abraham's description of LMS, when discussing the need to respect teachers, it becomes clear how he too has taken upon himself a very distinct form of respectability politics, and which LMS encouraged. He shared, "Sometimes you might feel like a teacher is acting disrespectful to you, so then, how are you going to give respect back? But guys got to learn it will hurt you more to lose your temper. Even if you are right, what is that going to do? You get sent out? And then you miss the lesson and don't know what's going on. So you would only be hurting yourself to get mad."

In describing the need for self-constraint when dealing with teachers, even when boys believe they are being wrongfully disciplined, Abraham is illustrating how LMS's approach directly intersects with a larger reality for students of color in U.S. education: racial biases lead to disproportionate discipline in schools (Noguera 2012). In this case, the widespread suspicion of Latino boys as dangerous or up to no good (i.e., a problem) places the onus squarely on Latino boys and the programs that support them to respond. While efforts have been made to enhance and expand restorative justice practices in schools (Winn 2018), the words of Abraham demonstrate the ways Latino boys feel pressure, or necessity, to alter their own actions to maintain success in schools. Despite identifying teachers as mistakenly (or intentionally) escalating tension with Latino boys, Abraham is clear that it is the student who must keep calm in an effort to ease tensions.

A consequence of students understanding the work of LMS as correcting problematic qualities possessed by Latino boys is the way it encouraged them to believe that if a student did not improve their academic standing, it was a result of the student's refusal to adopt the positive qualities preached in the program. This resulted in students pointing blame on individuals who were in the program, but continued to struggle academically and socially. It was a common belief that these individuals did not, in good faith, put in the effort needed for success. When I asked students to offer their thoughts on how they saw these kinds of academic struggles, and if they thought there might be other reasons why students, despite being in the program, might still struggle in school, they nearly unanimously replied that it was the students' responsibility. Christopher, for example, suggested that some of these struggles could be due to the fact that some students do not adopt the values of LMS, including those attributed to a proper Latino manhood. He shared, "I think . . . not all students are ready to be a man, so when they hear what Mr. Iván is saying, they just goof off . . . they are still getting there." In other instances, students took the opportunity to call out what they saw as problematic behavior from their classmates. Some focused on personal responsibility. "This is a two-way street," stated one boy, "so if you are not putting in your part, you can't expect the program to do it for you. You have to put in the effort." Others focus on problematic behavior, suggesting that classmates were often "lazy," or not interested in "putting in the work." When I spoke with students, it was understood that I would keep their identities hidden in order to keep our conversations as private as possible. This anonymity led some students to feel at liberty to single out individual peers. Since my questions did not ask for individual examples of other students (and even discouraged it), calling out their fellow classmates like this highlighted how the students gravitated toward an individualistic discourse of blame and personal responsibility. As Gonzalo, an eleventh grader in LMS, elaborated, "For example, there's Bryan, and it's like, 'Bro, why do you come if you're just going to mess around all the time?' It's so annoying. Like, he just wants to wear his headphones and is not interested in doing better. And if you don't want to be here, cool, but just go, so someone else can be here who wants to be here. That's not fair for someone who might be able to benefit from these resources, you know?"[3]

It was common for students to mention by name students they felt had become a nuisance and whom they deemed uninterested in turning around their grades. However, I was struck by the responses of low-performing students who earnestly took responsibility for their low grades. As Giovanni, a student with a GPA below 2.0, told me during our interview, "It's because they don't do the work. Simple as that. That's why I'm failing. I was just being lazy, you know, slacking off, but I'm changing that." Not unexpectedly, in a program focused on personal responsibility, as opposed to critical awareness of the social context, it did not occur to Giovanni that forces beyond individual effort influenced academic achievement. However, research clearly demonstrates that race and class intersect with a myriad of factors that create inequality in educational achievement. For boys of color, these factors include issues such as biased discipline and punishment, but also a range of everyday stresses as well as a scarcity of privileges and resources to make up ground. Meritocracy is a myth in the United States' education system.

As the ideologies of competition, personal responsibility, and meritocracy influence policy and funding for education in the United States, youth programs have become increasingly framed as problem-solving interventions in which the deficit rests on students (Baldridge 2014). The way the students at LMS discussed the program consistently revealed how this framing had a profound impact on how students experienced being targets of this intervention. Their descriptions of being a student in LMS frequently emphasized a central theme: that they understood the core objective of LMS as being able to fix problematic aspects of Latino boys. From their perspective, this fix was primarily focused on behavior issues, such as instilling respectfulness and self-control and motivating a stronger work ethic. Students believed these qualities would have a positive impact on their lives inside and outside of the classroom. Nevertheless, despite having internalized some of the logic underpinning these kinds of neoliberal ideologies, a number of students still expressed misgivings about it—and even yearned to question the program. The following section highlights student perspectives on areas of improvement or critique in LMS. Their voices demonstrate that while students adopted and at times internalized the discourse of damage and deficit, they also brought a critical lens to the program. In contrast to feeling like a problem, students also articulated a need to center joy and critical race education in the work of LMS.

DESIRING A JOYFUL AND CRITICAL PROGRAM

One Monday afternoon in Mr. Sergio's classroom, we had an impromptu conversation on gentrification. The discussion began during opening check-ins when Eric shared that he and his mother had gone to McDonald Park over the weekend. Located several miles south of the boys' middle school, near downtown Arroyo Seco, McDonald Park was a sprawling, scenic park that for many decades had been a popular picnic area for communities of color in the city. While Eric's mom had walked around the path, he explored the park on his skateboard. Eric was struck by the hordes of young white people he encountered in the park, who were drinking alcohol and playing fascinating outdoor games. "It's like a big party!" he had shared. Other students reported similar encounters when their families had gone to the park as well. "Is that gentrification?" asked Chava.

Although we had not talked about gentrification in Mr. Sergio's class, it was clear that students brought a wealth of knowledge to the topic. Many students reported discussing gentrification in other classes or with family members and friends, and it appeared that all students had at least been introduced to the term. At Mr. Sergio's request, I offered a brief definition to the class. However, the majority of the vibrant and informal discussion consisted of personal anecdotes, thoughts, and feelings from students about the changing landscape of Arroyo Seco. Twenty minutes quickly passed, leading Mr. Sergio to decide that we would hold off on the day's formal lesson, the second part of a workshop on résumés, for another day. This announcement was met by a chorus of "Yessss!" from the students. Kevin asked if he could play music. "Go ahead," replied Mr. Sergio, reluctantly, "but we have to continue this discussion." Music played softly in the background as the conversation on gentrification continued. We began making connections between gentrification and related issues such as housing insecurity and policing. Students were very engaged. A lifelong resident of Arroyo Seco, Mr. Sergio also offered his own passionate account of the changes in his home city. Many students nodded in approval. As the conversation came to a close and students began lining up at the door to leave, Chava sought me out. He knew I was doing research on mentorship programs for Latino boys. "This is what LMS is supposed to be all about," he told me. I asked him to elaborate. "More deep conversations. Where we can bond and talk about racism," he emphasized.

Chava's appreciation of critical discussions where students were given space to bond, and even enjoy a little music, was a popular sentiment. While students often espoused damage- and deficit-based rhetoric when describing the purpose and goals of the program, they also made it clear that what they valued most about LMS was not necessarily its main goals. Instead, students articulated a clear appreciation for the fun, bonding, and critical race education that would sometimes occur. They enjoyed these aspects of LMS and believed these qualities should instead be at the fore of Latino male programming.

In their conversations with me, the boys of LMS regularly revealed their belief that there should be more intentional efforts to spark joy and happiness in the program. This was not to say that the program lacked enjoyment. Many students shared that they had experienced happiness and joy in the program and described LMS as a place where you could "be yourself" around other Latino boys. However, sometimes the strictness and rules of LMS could overshadow the happiness. "I like this program, but I hate all the rules," stated Alonzo, a ninth grader in Mr. Iván's class. "We have fun in here, but Mr. Iván can take it [discipline] too far. . . . He won't leave you alone," he complained. While Alonzo admitted he could appreciate Mr. Iván's tenacious effort to get him to improve his grades, he found that these efforts were draining and made him unexcited to come to LMS.[4] Similar to the story of Jasiel that opened this chapter, Alonzo described the coexistence of fun and discipline in LMS. One way students reconciled these contrasting forces was to view joy and happiness as a secondary purpose of LMS. This meant that while LMS's main goal was to instill discipline and respectability in Latino boys, LMS's subsidiary goal was to also offer them a unique and joyful experience at school.

For example, a student named Lalo—after first highlighting the four (deficit-oriented) values discussed above as the primary purpose of the program—also notably mentioned joy and happiness as important needs for Latino men and boys. He recommended LMS focus much more on these things.

"School can be a lot of stress," he shared. He then suggested that "a lot of Latino males struggle, so LMS is also a place where you can have some fun. I like being in here."

I asked him what it was about the program that he found fun.

"How do I say this. . . . It's fun to just be around everyone," he answered. "That's a big one for me. LMS is a place where I have a lot of friends, and we get to talk about things. Sometimes we will talk about our experiences and we can joke around and be ourselves. Yeah. Even Mr. Iván will joke sometimes. We have fun."

His reply prompted me to ask him if he thought that was intentional.

"Do you think that's another purpose of the program?" I asked.

"To be fun?"

"Or, just to offer that space?"

He said he thought it was intentional, that it was part of the purpose of the program.

"They want to give us that. It's not the main thing, but it's part of it. LMS is supposed to give us a place to be ourselves. . . . And when you have that, you begin to build those relationships and support one another. . . . To be honest, I think we should be doing more of that."

While Lalo was sure to point to the academic discipline and character development as the driving forces behind the program, he still affirmed that providing a space to build camaraderie and have fun—having a place to call home—was an important aspect of LMS that should be expanded. But other students went further than Lalo. While Lalo regarded fun as complementing the core goals of LMS like personal responsibility and academic accountability, Hugo considered fun to be the central goal in and of itself. He told me, "I think LMS was created to give Latino males a place at school where we can be around each other, other Latinos, and do fun activities about our culture. That's my favorite part of the program." Although Hugo viewed this as one of the goals of LMS, he also expressed concern that this goal is often forgotten. "Sometimes they [LMS mentors] get so worried about everyone's grades that they forget what this is all about."

LATINO BOYS NEED AND WANT CRITICAL RACE EDUCATION

The majority of the boys I spoke with in the LMS program homed in on LMS's deficit-oriented language when discussing the core goals of the program. But, as the comments from Hugo and Lalo illustrate, there was also an identifiable desire among the boys for joy and happiness to be centered in the program, something that contrasted with the pronounced focus on discipline. But there was also something that several of the boys explicitly discussed that pushed back even more directly: a desire for more critical race education. Although the students did not refer to it as such, they raised points that suggested they were eager for their mentors to lead discussions that interrogate much more directly many of the racial, economic, and carceral structures that define their lives.

Marvin Lynn (1999) describes critical race pedagogy as "an analysis of racial, ethnic, and gender subordination in education that relies mostly on the perceptions, experiences, and counterhegemonic practices of educators of color" (615). Critical race pedagogy is a way educators of color working with young people of color can directly contradict the kinds of neoliberal logics that were so strongly present at LMS. As discussed more below, some students at LMS made clear that, even as they internalized them, they were fed up with the kinds of framing strategies that LMS used when seeking to help Latino boys. Instead of bringing a deficit orientation to working with young people of color, critical race pedagogy builds upon critical race theory, or CRT (Ladson-Billings and Tate 1995; Solorzano and Yosso 2001), to acknowledge the endemic nature of racism and emphasizes the ways in which educators and students of color build upon lived experiences to critically analyze the ways race and racism function in society. Among boys and men of color, critical race pedagogy is an asset that allows them to trace how race and gender affect their lives in schools (Lynn and Jennings 2009).

Political or critical race education was not an official aspect of the LMS's goals or curriculum. However, mentors were generally given the freedom to bring critical race lessons to their groups if they chose. As in the case of Mr. Javier, some mentors were outwardly political with their mentoring and described their mentorship circle as defined by critical race education.[5] Other mentors described their work with LMS as "apolitical." The majority, however, were somewhere in the middle. When asked how to improve and enhance Latino male mentoring, students maintained that LMS should prioritize more critical race education. They described critical race education as something both enjoyable and captivating, as well as something useful in their everyday lives.

Christopher, for example, described critical race education as the most interesting part of LMS. He argued for more of these kinds of lessons in the program to replace such lengthy time dedicated to silent study halls like those in Mr. Iván's class in which two full days a week were allotted for silent homework time in the library. Christopher stated:

> I would like to see more lessons on racism and culture because
> sometimes I'm tired of homework, or, I don't have any. . . . And
> when we do talk about those things, like Cesar Chavez, or we watch
> a movie and talk about it, those are really fun days. You can tell
> everyone is interested. So why don't we do that more often? This is
> supposed to be a class on Latino culture, but it doesn't seem like we
> really get into racism affecting the community.

Christopher told me that his favorite class was his ethnic studies course, and that the class made him "question the world" and learn why things are the way they are. He had thought LMS would be more like that class. Despite being slated as a Chicano studies course on his class schedule, he described LMS as "not really" an ethnic studies class. Christopher felt that by prioritizing critical race lessons, LMS could better engage students while also teaching them important lessons.

Jasiel, the eighth grader whose words opened this chapter, similarly felt that more critical race education could help improve the program. He made the case both for adding new curricular topics that pertain to the students' lives and for reframing existing topics. "We should learn more about stuff going on in the world," he said. "Like, for example, gangs. We talk about them, but not really, [not] the history of them, and how other things affect gangs, like political matters." Jasiel continued to share that while subbing for his mentor, Mr. Javier had discussed the history of gangs in Arroyo Seco. The class had been captivated.

"Mr. Antonio doesn't talk to you about gangs?" I asked.

"Yes, we do sometimes. But not like . . . we don't get into the history and like, police . . . political stuff. Mr. Javier tells us about those things, and things having to do with El Salvador. . . . I learned a lot."

I followed up with Mr. Javier to inquire about his lesson on gangs. He told me that while he was substituting the topic of gangs had come up. He had been involved with organizing anti-gang injunctions as a young person and was knowledgeable on the topic. He had also done personal research on the ways U.S. military interventions in Central America had created the conditions for brutal gang violence in El Salvador. This had led to a multidimensional conversation on gangs, including the ways race, geopolitics, and policing inform the history and evolution of gangs. This perspective broke from what I had generally witnessed in LMS—the topic of gangs had only been broached to warn students of their danger, but in a top-down, noncritical manner. Gang members had been stereotypically portrayed as having diverged from the right path and fulfilling the negative image of the bad hombre. In contrast, Jasiel had been interested in Mr. Javier's critical perspective on gangs. This new perspective did not vilify gang members but instead gave students a sociohistorical context to understand the existence of gangs and their relationship to both global and local notions of race, policing, and politics.

From the perspectives of these students, as well as others, I found that the boys of LMS held high hopes for the program to expand its critical race lessons. These sorts of lessons were appealing to the students and allowed them to build a new understanding of the world. Some students drew connections between the prioritization of discipline and traditional academic improvement and the deprioritization of critical race learning. In the following section I focus on the words and story of Victor, a tenth grader in Mr. Iván's high school class who describes a shift in priorities in the program and discusses why he believes a critical perspective on race will help students better navigate the world.

VICTOR'S COUNTERNARRATIVE

Victor had begun LMS in the eighth grade with Mr. Antonio at Bell Middle School in 2015. Bell was on the far northern end of Arroyo Seco, several miles away from Las Palmas High School, where he was now a student. He explained that his mother had fought for him to go to Las Palmas instead of the local high school. The impetus for the change had been his mother's fear that Victor was becoming involved with the wrong crowd. She had hoped that attending high school in a new area would be a positive change. Victor strongly disagreed with the move.

He was now a tenth grader in Mr. Iván's high school class. By the time I met him in August 2017, Victor had been in the LMS program for three years. Victor was known for his pensive demeanor and impressive art skills. He was also a deep thinker who was drawn to the racial justice themes presented in his ethnic studies and English classes. He described these courses as helping him make sense of the social injustices he frequently witnessed and experienced in his community. On days when the LMS class spent the period in the library for homework hall, it was common for Victor to raise his hand and call me over. Most of the time he did not have a concrete question in mind, but instead wanted to solicit my opinion on a social movement or spark a discussion on a text or theory related to racial justice. Although he was generally soft-spoken in class, he was not shy to talk about things he found important. When he did share, his perspective was always thoughtful and nuanced. I recall that one of Victor's favorite readings was excerpts from the autobiography of Assata Shakur, which had been assigned in his English class. Through this text, he offered profound thoughts on the meaning of law and justice in a racist society. Throughout my time in LMS, Victor and I enjoyed exchanging links to articles and YouTube videos, and we quickly developed a close relationship.

On a brisk Tuesday morning in May 2018, Victor and I excused ourselves from the silent study hall and made our way to an empty room in the back of the library where I had been conducting student interviews over the past month. In our conversation, Victor exemplified the critical perspectives that students bring to their education. Despite often being framed as passive recipients of schooling, students wield power and agency—and utilize it when possible—in order to make their education work for them. Indeed, this was the case with Victor.

Our conversation began with his expectations of LMS and how he understood the goals and mission of the program. Victor described his initial expectations of LMS as influenced by an informal mentoring experience he had in the sixth grade. During his advisory class, a Latino man named José would come in and talk to the Latino boys. This was unrelated to the LMS program, and Victor described José as "not an official mentor" but rather an invited speaker from the community who would come to the school from time to time. "I liked that a lot better," Victor recounted. "He would talk more about things that really happen . . . like, what was really happening in the neighborhood. And he would tell you his experiences." These experiences included poverty and gang violence, as well as his politicization and journey to becoming a community activist. Victor had really enjoyed this informal program for Latino boys, and when LMS started a program at his school in eighth grade he was eager to join. However, after learning more about LMS, he hesitated. "I never saw that first program with José as academics. It wasn't really about school. It was about what's going on. And then when Mr. Antonio was talking about how he wanted to do it academic, I didn't want to join because, that's why—because he said it was academic and I found it boring, so, I didn't join. But in the end, I was like, 'Oh, I guess I want to join.' And he let me in."

Victor reported having just an okay time his first year in the program. "I can't say I liked it, but I won't say I didn't like it either," he told me. However, at the end of eighth grade, Victor described a lot of negativity and uncertainty in his life. This sparked his move to Las Palmas High School, several miles away from his neighborhood. Mr. Iván had approached Victor about joining LMS. "In ninth grade, I just wanted to do good. And Mr. Iván said he could help me. So yeah, it was more support, so I said yes," he recalled.

Although his experiences with José had been nearly four years prior, Victor continued to draw on that experience to narrate how he understood the goals of LMS in relation to what Latino boys in Arroyo Seco need. He shared, "I think the purpose that LMS wants is to get people to achieve success, like, don't go down the wrong path, do good in school. But before [with José], I saw it like talking about experiences, like . . . like a therapist." I followed up by asking if he felt LMS is successful in its goals. "It's like in the middle," Victor shared. He continued, "When people want to do good, I think it's successful. Because they want to work with the teacher . . . like Mr. Iván last year, he helped me a lot. So, yeah, and I think it was really successful. He got my grades up. . . . But for other kids, they don't like to do work, or they're not really into school, so then it doesn't work. Because Mr. Iván is more helpful for work. And then some other students don't want that. They want to talk about what's going on in the community. And Mr. Iván also does that, but he doesn't do it often, like, other teachers, who would talk about it every day or have new conversations."

Although he did not simply criticize and dismiss the program, Victor also does not assign it much credit either. For him, LMS was something that could benefit him if his goals happened to align with those of the program. For example, at the end of eighth grade, at a difficult time in his life, he turned to LMS to get his grades up because he understood the program offered academic support. It was useful. But Victor had also seen the potential of a program like LMS with his informal interactions with José, and remembering the valuable discussion from that time, he noted that many students are not interested in academics. He shared, "Some [students] just mess around, but, most of them, like, people that I knew in my middle school, they just went through a lot and they don't want to do the little things because they don't care. They want to talk about what's going on because they're not thinking about school. They're thinking about . . . what they see every day. That's really important."

He did not fault students for disinterest in school, nor did he see them as squandering the potential of LMS. To the contrary, Victor placed the deficit on the program rather than the student. Students have a lot on their minds, he pointed out. Given their circumstances, he found this understandable. It was the program that was not responsive to the students. Instead of becoming a space for therapeutic reflection and critical awareness, Victor saw grade improvement and discipline as the primary functions of LMS. He believed LMS's culture of discipline needed to change for the program to improve. He continued:

I think they [the LMS program] take strictness too seriously, like, Mr. Iván takes it too seriously. It's not a big deal, you don't need to take it that far. We work a lot, but then there's times that we need to have fun too, we can't be working all day. I feel like sometimes we got to have free time for ourselves. . . . I know people that didn't like LMS last year because Mr. Iván would be on their case a lot, like, too strict. He wouldn't give them a break, so then they decided they didn't want to be in LMS anymore.

Victor's testimony offers a counternarrative to how Latino male programs respond to the needs of students. This book has argued that these programs often bring a deficit orientation to Latino male empowerment. As discussed earlier in this chapter, some of the students are keenly aware of these narratives, even as they are susceptible to adopting perspectives that frame boys as problems to be solved. However, Victor avoids the popular "saving" or "fixing" narratives of LMS and instead describes himself as strategically navigating the program to achieve his own goals. The three-year veteran brings a "better than nothing" attitude to the work of LMS. He was appreciative of Mr. Antonio's and Mr. Iván's energies, but he was sure to give himself the credit.

Furthermore, as opposed to painting the program as the savior of Latino boys, Victor's critique of the narrow and single-minded goals of LMS underscores how some students are also aware of the program's many shortcomings relating to the emotional and psychological impact of the program. Academics were important, but the program failed to prioritize other things that were perhaps even more important to Latino boys. These things included an array of serious issues in the boys' lives, including the symptoms of racism and white supremacy in Arroyo Seco, such as gentrification, housing insecurity, poverty, gang violence, and policing. These issues were on students' minds, and the program needed to focus on helping them unpack and make sense of their experiences. While Victor, like many boys in LMS, appreciated the informal conversations they had on these topics, he felt this should be the primary focus of the program. Instead, the program prioritized academics and discipline. As opposed to approaching students as problems to be solved, Victor argues that the potential of mentorship is found in addressing the students' lived realities. This would make programs responsive to students' needs, rather than simply saving or fixing students.

CONCLUSION: "PROBLEMS" WHO HAVE THEIR OWN SOLUTIONS

Despite learning deficit-oriented ideas about Latino boys, the students at LMS brought a critical perspective to Latino male mentorship. It was evident that the students were well aware of the pervasive rhetoric of damage and deficit associated with Latino male programs. In some cases, they adopted this rhetoric or reified it by distancing themselves from "bad" Latino boys. However, this chapter also uncovers that even when framed as problems to be solved, Latino boys in a program like LMS still find ways to seek out joy and discover critical ways of understanding their circumstances. While the neoliberal imaginary frames mentors as teaching the boys discipline to manage truancy and misbehavior, the boys saw different needs. They wanted fun. They saw LMS as one of the few places on campus where they could be themselves and be happy. This was something to be cherished, and students criticized the program for jeopardizing (or forfeiting) this quality by making academics and discipline the primary focus. They also wanted emotion-filled discussions where they could talk about what was happening in their lives and in their communities. The students articulated that critical framing and context were essential to these discussions. In particular, developing a critical understanding of racism's influence on their lives was paramount. They hoped that LMS could become a place where these discussions could take place.

Educational researchers have made the case that while male educators of color have clear benefits for boys of color in schools, students' voices are often left out of those analyses (Carey 2020). This chapter centers the voices of the students to allow them to (a) articulate how they make sense of Latino male programming and (b) describe what new directions they wish to see. As programs targeting boys and young men of color continue to proliferate, and as the case of LMS shows, it is urgent that schools abandon the pervasive, and at times hidden, deficit narratives associated with this work. Relocating the deficit in youth work requires an intentional rejection of a discourse that locates the problem within young people themselves (Baldridge 2014). Instead, the deficit lies in institutions and structures. A new conceptualization of empowerment must discard discourses of "saving" or "rescuing" students and instead empower young people through listening, honoring their agency, and helping them develop the critical language and tools they are searching for.

At LMS there were two mentors—Mr. Javier and Mr. Agustín—who understood this urgency and sought to disrupt deficit-oriented youth work in their classroom. Their efforts, discussed in the next chapter, help further illuminate the need for justice-centered approaches to mentoring Latino boys.

FIVE

SUBVERSIVE ROLE MODELS

Critical Mentoring and Queer Disruptions

The walls of Mr. Javier's middle school classroom were covered in protest art. Their bold and clear messages spoke directly to ongoing social and political movements affecting the North Arroyo Seco community. Some of the posters read, "Abolish Borders," "Black Lives Matter," and "Arroyo Seco Against Gentrification." A banner hanging above Mr. Javier's desk stated, in graffiti-style letters, "If Capital Can Cross Borders, So Can We." He described this message as a statement "against NAFTA [North American Free Trade Agreement]" and other "neoliberal policies" that lead to forced migration. This type of artwork broke from the common and abstract cultural empowerment images seen in the rooms of most LMS classrooms. Posters provided by LMS's character development curriculum commonly include slogans such as "When you heal, we all heal" as well as an array of inspirational but vague quotes from Cesar Chavez. In the corner of Mr. Javier's classroom was a small bookshelf that included an assortment of zines and books on the topics of Latinx, Black, and Native American life and liberation. A worn copy of Frantz Fanon's *The Wretched of the Earth* sat facing outward. It was one of Mr. Javier's favorite books. The boys were allowed to rummage through the small library and borrow as they wished.

In today's class, Mr. Javier announced he would be doing one of his favorite lessons. This lesson was not an official LMS activity, but Mr. Javier had developed it from a grassroots youth organization that he had been involved with as a teen and young adult. The lesson was titled "Roots of Oppression." Standing at the front of the classroom, Mr. Javier began by asking the students to brainstorm some of the troubles and social ills they saw in their North Arroyo Seco community. As the boys began listing issues, Mr. Javier jotted them down in green marker at the top of the whiteboard. The words and phrases were *robbery, gangs, shootings, police shootings, blocks beefing, trash, houselessness, violence, rape, domestic violence, alcoholism, drug addiction, kids dropping out of school, deportations, depression,* and *retaliation.* Once the brainstorming had finished, Mr. Javier began connecting the words with a brown marker until they resembled green leaves connected by brown branches. He linked the branches to a wide tree trunk and finally six large and intersecting roots. The roots were titled *racism, sexism, classism, ableism, ageism,* and *homophobia.*

As the lesson continued, Mr. Javier and the students discussed the way "systems of oppression" manifest in diverse and sometimes hidden ways in Arroyo Seco. Students conferred about how individual or interpersonal problems were often a symptom of social and historical contexts. Mr. Javier reiterated that it was important to know the root causes of oppression to really understand the circumstances in North Arroyo Seco and later to organize and make "real change." Mr. Javier was a proponent of political organizing and activism. He often shared stories with his students about his own politicization as a young person and his involvement in demanding ethnic studies courses and abolishing police presence in schools. Throughout my time at LMS, I witnessed Mr. Javier's continued political involvement in the Arroyo Seco community.[1]

Toward the end of the lesson, Mr. Javier paused. With a sly grin on his face, he scanned the faces of his students. He then posed the question, "Do you think we are making real change here in LMS?" There was hesitation among the students, followed by deliberation and debate. The general consensus finally emerged: no.

"I agree," stated Mr. Javier.

Some of the boys looked surprised.

He continued, "Don't get me wrong, we do some amazing stuff in this classroom, but a program like this . . . it can't begin to get at those deeper issues." He then continued, more seriously, "And I think in many ways, they don't want us to." The "they" in this accusation was left ambiguous. While reiterating his commitment to the success of his students, Mr. Javier declared, "Me being here is just a Band-Aid . . . I'm a Band-Aid . . . and you all deserve more than a Band-Aid."

In his teaching and mentoring at LMS, Mr. Javier regularly challenged the notion that a mentor and role model was a viable solution for the kinds of racial injustice his students faced. Since the first day I met Mr. Javier, he had been eager to communicate this belief. He had also been upfront about fundamental disagreements he had with what he described as the "conservative" politics of Pueblo Unido. These disagreements led him to bring his own radical lessons to his classroom, as well as openly criticize some LMS practices to his students. In particular, Mr. Javier scrutinized the program's grade competitions, exclusionary punishments for students with low GPAs, and collaborations with the local offices of multinational corporations. Although many mentors expressed frustration with Pueblo Unido leadership (primarily because of a lack of attention to the program), Mr. Javier was one of two mentors, the other being Mr. Agustín, who demonstrated a clear and fervent critique of the politics of Pueblo Unido and their influence on LMS. Both mentors actively sought to resist these politics through their mentoring.

As outlined earlier in chapter 3, youth workers of color exist in a neoliberal context that often posits them as the corrective to the supposed deficits held by problematic children (Baldridge 2014; M. V. Singh 2018, 2021a). In this framing, Latino male mentors are upheld as superhero-like figures who become models of respectability. The figure of the positive Latino male role model is closely shaped by race, gender, class, sexuality, as well as other social categories. This standard of Latino male respectability is implicitly or explicitly positioned in contrast to the deviant or problematic racialized characteristics associated with Latino men and boys. Through its discursive formation and embodied performance, the positive Latino male role model does the work of defining an ideal and proper Latino manhood. Two things occur in this process. First, the hegemonic racial discourse of the moment, which I have described as neoliberal multiculturalism, becomes the natural and commonsense way of understanding "good" Latino maleness that is to be modeled. This positive Latino manhood is infused with traditional heteropatriarchal values that become normalized and reproduced (Melamed 2006). Second, those who exist outside the boundaries of proper Latino manhood are rendered problematic, queer, deviant, and justifiably dispossessed of resources. In an era of U.S. racism that no longer primarily functions in a white–nonwhite binary, the framing and enaction of role modeling can normalize what is deemed an acceptable Latino manhood while simultaneously validating the marginalization of Latino men and other racial subjects. In part, this marginalization is seen as self-inflicted because of poor choices and an unwillingness to accept an invitation to respectability.

In this chapter I focus on the perspectives and strategies of Mr. Javier and Mr. Agustín, two LMS mentors who expressed strong criticism of the LMS program and of their positioning as positive male role models for struggling Latino boys. These two mentors—in their words, actions, and pedagogy—highlight the ways critical awareness among youth workers can lead to agency and resistance. For both mentors, a critical race consciousness led them to disavow what Mr. Agustín described as a "bootstraps ideology" that they found pervasive in the program. They felt this belief overstated the importance of self-discipline and precariously positioned the mentors to be models of an American dream narrative that they found fictional and racist. This mythical role model figure served to deflect attention from the structural determinants of inequality and instead to focus on the individual capacities of positive role models to replace racialized cultural practices among their students with characteristics conducive to neoliberal values. While both mentors describe enacting critical mentoring strategies to challenge the values undergirding LMS (see Weiston-Serdan 2017), they also challenged dominant notions of the positive Latino male role model by rejecting the idea that they themselves embodied a "respectable Latino manhood." Also, as the only LMS mentor who identified as gay, Mr. Agustín's "failure" to perform heteropatriarchal norms associated with Latino male mentorship demonstrates a powerful challenge to the figure of the positive Latino male role model. Through the insights of Mr. Javier and Mr. Agustín, this chapter outlines the ways youth workers may resist and refuse hegemonic notions of role modeling.

MEETING MR. JAVIER AND MR. AGUSTÍN

Mr. Javier identifies as a cisgender man of Salvadoran and Mexican heritage. He was born and raised in North Arroyo Seco and grew up less than two miles from his school site. We first met in the summer of 2017, during my initial meeting with LMS. He was thirty years old at the time and had been working as a mentor for five years. Mr. Javier was one of the three mentors, along with Mr. Antonio and Mr. Iván, who invited me to observe and volunteer in their classroom twice a week. Among the first things one notices when meeting Mr. Javier is his commitment to being his authentic self. This is shown in the way he dresses, speaks, and gives sincere respect to anyone committed to supporting the young people of Arroyo Seco. A progressive Latinx teacher at his school site once described Mr. Javier to me as having a "'hood Chicano" aesthetic that was uniquely Arroyo Seco. They also described him as having "good gender politics" and praised his ability to grab his students' attention with a "warm smile." I agreed.

In my early visits to his middle school classroom, I quickly recognized Mr. Javier as a unique case within the program. Most striking was his tenacious effort to politicize the program's curriculum and his willingness to outwardly critique and resist LMS practices that he felt were complicit with social injustice. Mr. Javier understood his critical consciousness and sense of racial justice as the defining characteristics of his identity as a youth worker and as a human being. He believed that at the root of this quality was his own experiences of racial injustice growing up in North Arroyo Seco. As a teen, guidance from select teachers as well as his involvement in a radical youth organization helped to cultivate his activist identity. He used terms like "decolonial," "intersectional," and "abolitionist" to describe his political views and strove to express these politics in his everyday life. This included his music as an amateur rap artist, his activism, his personal relationships, and his mentoring in LMS.

Mr. Javier shared many commonalities with his students. He was a Spanish speaker, had experienced poverty as a child, and grew up in the predominantly Black and Latinx region of Arroyo Seco where he now worked. Although all youth workers in LMS shared many similar characteristics, Mr. Javier was the sole mentor who did not have a college degree. He believed this exception was permitted because of his good rapport with students and extensive background working with young people in Arroyo Seco. Robert Rivera, the cofounder and former director of LMS, had personally invited him to become a mentor. They had worked with one another on a past youth development project. In the five years Mr. Javier had worked with LMS, the program had never hired another mentor without a bachelor's degree. A bachelor's degree is listed as a requirement on mentor job applications.

Like Mr. Javier, Mr. Agustín was also raised in North Arroyo Seco. He is a cisgender man born in Michoacán, Mexico, and had been raised in North Arroyo Seco since the age of four. I first met Mr. Agustín in the spring of 2018 when he agreed to provide an interview at the end of my first year with LMS. At the time, Mr. Agustín was twenty-three years old and had been working as a mentor for only four months. He had begun in the middle of the school year when a mentor had left LMS for another job. Mr. Agustín had recently graduated from an elite university in California and was happy to be working in his hometown. He had a shy smile that accompanied casual but well-put-together outfits, and a soft voice. Like Mr. Javier, Mr. Agustín brought a political analysis to his work. Although he did not have extensive experience working with young people, he was eager to learn and put into practice some of the theories and concepts he had learned in college.

Also, like Mr. Javier, Mr. Agustín shared many commonalities with his students, such as being a native Spanish speaker, being an immigrant, experiencing poverty as a child, and growing up in the predominantly Black and Latinx region of North Arroyo Seco. Despite being very similar to his fellow youth workers, Mr. Agustín was the only mentor who identified as gay. He found this to be a strong distinction.

After meeting Mr. Javier and Mr. Agustín, I was struck by their insights into the complicated and often contradictory work of Latino male empowerment. It was apparent that both had reflected deeply on the politics of role modeling, and each offered a critical insider's perspective. This approach to their work as mentors ultimately caused Mr. Javier and Mr. Agustín to disrupt homogeneous representations of male Latino educators. Their words and actions highlight the limits and contradictions of role modeling as racial justice work while, on the other hand, illustrate what critical and queer mentoring as resistance can look like.

REJECTING ROLE MODELING AS RACIAL JUSTICE

In our first interview, Mr. Agustín was in his fourth month at LMS. Although he was still learning about the program, he was eager to share some of the striking contradictions he had noticed in his first few months as a mentor. He had entered the job excited to have a positive impact on the lives of his students, but his own analysis of racism in the United States made him hesitant to describe the work of LMS as racial justice. While Mr. Javier viewed his critical perspective as originating from his past involvement in grassroots community organizing, Mr. Agustín believed his critical awareness had been sharpened through his time as a sociology major. In our first interview, he referenced several sociological theories and at times used a Marxist vocabulary to describe his work and experiences as an LMS mentor. From the start, he was eager to offer his unique and well-thought-out perspective on the program. A primary concern of his was that the notion of role modeling in LMS advanced an individualistic solution to what he knew to be a structural problem:

> Unfortunately, I think there's a huge mismatch between what we want to do versus what we're actually doing in LMS. By that I mean, what we want to do is change the outcomes for Latino boys, have them succeed in high school, graduate, and go to college. But I see those issues, or those barriers, as not individually determined. It's not because they [Latino boys] are not working hard enough. The way I see it, it's a lot of outside structural barriers that are shaping their lives. It could be poverty, racism, or any of the other systems of oppression. So by giving them us [mentors/role models], I don't think we're really doing any kind of transformative work. . . . Maybe some of our students will succeed, but not everyone.

By focusing on changing the outcomes of individual boys and his fear that the structural barriers facing his students and community would be forgotten, Mr. Agustín highlights a key quandary that youth workers of color face in their work. As he points out, students' actions will not "solve" the struggles they face when the real source of those struggles is inequality and structural barriers. Moreover, in addition to seeing the limits of this kind of intervention to address racial inequality, Mr. Agustín called out the positive role model discourse as actively contributing to how racism functions:

> It almost feels like deception. It feels like by being this "good role model" [uses air quotes], we are telling them that if you work really hard, if you just focus, if you don't talk during class, you will succeed. It ignores, but also hides, a lot of those barriers that they face, or that their whole community faces.

Here, Mr. Agustín points to one of the fundamental contradictions and dilemmas of role modeling as racial justice: beyond providing an individualistic solution, the positive male role model also resulted in the *individualization* of the problem by shifting focus to the boys themselves. Mr. Agustín's concern here is that a critical outlook on education is replaced by an idea that feels like common sense but that draws on a flawed logic around the ability to succeed in the current system through hard work, or the age-old bootstraps mentality. The presence of a positive role model seemingly proved that success was possible. But as Mr. Agustín points out, this approach poses a number of problems. "That can be dangerous," clarified Mr. Agustín. "It makes students think that maybe something's wrong with them if they aren't turning their grades around."

Mr. Javier shared Mr. Agustín's concern that his position as a positive male role model for Latino boys individualized the problem of racism. However, he found that most people did not share this concern. "People love what this work looks like, visually," he explained, referring to the image of Latino men guiding wayward Latino boys. He was also concerned about the ways the logic behind the mentor/role model intervention placed blame on individual students for their low grades. For Mr. Javier, a central source of this deficit-based framing was Pueblo Unido's "savior complex," a disposition that he saw many educational nonprofits bringing to youth work. Mr. Javier believed that although Pueblo Unido promoted itself aesthetically as a revolutionary Latinx organization, in practice it demonstrated what he felt was a "conservative" form of racial justice. This led Pueblo Unido to do very little to challenge the status quo. For example, during the time of this ethnography, communities of color in Arroyo Seco protested the Arroyo Seco Police Department (ASPD) for corruption, brutality, murder, and a lack of community accountability. In another instance, ASUSD was the target of protests by parents, students, and the teachers' union for the closures of several community schools in the district. Mr. Javier noted that in both instances, Pueblo Unido refused to join these efforts because, as he put it, "ASPD and ASUSD are their partners . . . so they're not here for that kind of change." He continued: "I can't speak for the founders of LMS, but honestly, just how we frame the work that we do makes us seem like a problem, like Latinos are the problem. So, that in its inception is going to only create things that create Band-Aid solutions, including this program. Right?"

Mr. Javier spoke at some length about this issue about how he felt it was important to go beyond just trying to help individual students, how focusing on individual students can undermine an understanding of the bigger picture, and on how nonprofits are part of the problem. "So, yeah," he said, "we're changing individual lives or whatever by giving them a mentor, but we're not changing anything systemic that puts people in this position in the first place. . . . And as far as nonprofits go, I think that's their goal . . . nonprofits were designed by the system itself to placate the movement, if you want it to be real, like people were ready to give their lives for a revolution [during the era of the Chicano Movement] and that's something that is not even in the picture anymore because we have these nonprofits."

Mr. Javier's descriptions of the shifting landscape of racial justice activism show how some youth workers, including those working within educational programs structured around neoliberal logics, feel an urgent need for critical racial justice frameworks in their work. Mr. Javier's observations show a particularly acute grasp of how, in the neoliberal era, corporate philanthropy and nonprofits have come to replace grassroots movements in the struggle for racial justice in schools (Lipman 2011; Scott 2013). This system, which Mr. Javier referred to as the "nonprofit industrial complex,"[2] subdued radical visions of social justice by creating funding structures that narrowly dictated what social justice interventions should look like.

For boys and men of color, private-sector interventions capitalize on a perceived crisis of boys of color and intervene through technocratic and individualized solutions rather than challenging a social and economic order founded upon white supremacy (Dumas 2016a). But this neoliberal reconfiguration of racism accepts the good multicultural subject, defined by its entrepreneurialism and cultural diversity, while justifying the violence experienced by those racialized subjects deemed monocultural, backwards, and unmotivated. Mr. Javier and Mr. Agustín both asserted that their positioning as role models for struggling Latino boys served to reify the notion that Latino boys play a large role in their own "underachievement." Through the intervention of a Latino male mentor and role model, boys would be able to succeed in an inclusive, market-oriented world through learning to shed bad habits and attitudes in the classroom. But as Mr. Javier and Mr. Agustín point out, this risks maintaining inequality rather than combating it. In their work, they rejected this perspective on the Latino male role model and looked for ways to push back. But doing so was not always straightforward, since many of the habits and attitudes were fundamentally encouraged by the core curriculum they were expected to teach.

For example, self-discipline was key in LMS, and learning to be "held accountable" and "keep your word" were top priorities. Mr. Agustín described his reservations about role modeling and instilling accountability in Latino boys as an educational intervention: "I recognize the importance of holding these youth accountable and teaching responsibility, but, for me, it also seems to tread along the line of personal responsibility, pull-yourself-up-by-your-bootstraps ideology that has been particularly harmful to impoverished communities [and] especially communities of color." He also pointed to the false promises this discourse entailed: "You can teach them to be responsible or to take responsibility for their actions but it's hard to pull yourself up by your bootstraps if you have all these structural barriers that are preventing you from succeeding. . . . It seems we are, how can I say this, it seems we're presenting that this American dream does exist."

The way Mr. Agustín challenged the rationale that a lack of responsibility is why Latino boys experience low educational achievement shows how some mentors resisted the ideologies that LMS and its funders encouraged mentors to use in their work with students. They sought to push back against the racist belief that boys of color are prone to disruptive behavior and are uninterested in education (A. A. Ferguson 2001; Rios 2011, 2017). Furthermore, Mr. Agustín rejected the way LMS positioned him as a productive and respectable Latino man, a position he felt reified the notion that bad and undeserving Latino males exist in the world—and that those who did not succeed had just chosen to not be saved. Mr. Javier echoed this sentiment and questioned the role of the Latino male mentor in constructing a proper and deserving Latino boy in the eyes of Pueblo Unido. "We are put in a position to get kids to act a certain way . . . to change them. They [Pueblo Unido] don't want little free-thinking revolutionaries running around. . . . They want a real corporate-looking business kids," shared Mr. Javier, as he pretended to tighten a necktie and scrunched up his face in an exaggerated manner. "That's why they want to take kids to Morgan Stanley," he continued, "so they can learn how to be a part of this system. And so that corporation can give to Pueblo Unido."

Mr. Javier's critique and rejection of this ideal type of Latino boy is another good example of the way some mentors, drawing on their critical race consciousness, actively rejected the pedagogical framing that LMS was pushing for. Here, Mr. Javier postulates that the philanthropic partnership with the investment banking company Morgan Stanley influences this imagined boy, and he laments that an upcoming tour of their local office will hinder a critical awareness of how racial capitalism functions. Despite his bringing up this issue in several staff meetings, his critiques of the partnership would fall on deaf ears. Although this constant pushback on LMS could have had repercussions for his good standing with Pueblo Unido, it was clear that Mr. Javier and Mr. Agustín felt a sense of responsibility to voice their perspectives on these issues in their classrooms.

"I TRY NOT TO BE A GOOD EXAMPLE": CRITICAL MENTORING AND BEING A BAD EXAMPLE

Although Mr. Javier and Mr. Agustín expressed strong disagreement with how Pueblo Unido and LMS approached Latino male mentorship, they also found that very little oversight in the program gave them the freedom to teach how and what they wished. In the case of Mr. Javier, my participant observations in his classroom revealed that generally twice a week he brought in political lessons absent from the other two classrooms I observed. This was made possible by the relative autonomy that mentors had over their day-to-day mentoring. In place of biweekly study halls (Mr. Iván's classroom) or team-building games and outdoor activities (Mr. Antonio and Mr. Sergio's classroom), Mr. Javier taught political education workshops. In these lessons, he connected school problems to decidedly political problems, such as the historic disinvestment and segregation in North Arroyo Seco and the wealth gap between the boys' families and the new, more white and wealthy residents of Arroyo Seco. He did not shy away from words like *racism* and *colonialism*, and he encouraged his students to name and analyze racist practices that they felt they experienced in school. He also taught lessons on the gender wage gap and the rise of Chicana feminism in response to patriarchy in the Chicano Movement. Beyond his role as LMS mentor, Mr. Javier, along with a Latina teacher, facilitated an all-gender Raza Club at lunch. During meetings, the group held activities and dialogues surrounding racism, gentrification, and Black and Latinx solidarity.

Mr. Javier understood that his lessons were "more radical" than the goals of LMS. He also acknowledged that Pueblo Unido administrators, as well as some LMS mentors, would probably be uncomfortable if they ever observed several of his workshops. For example, some of Mr. Javier's lessons were informed by a prison abolition pedagogy (D. Rodríguez 2010) and were intended to get students to think critically about why police and prisons exist. In his classroom, I observed and participated in multiple lessons on the history of policing, community efforts to resist policing, and conversations on imagining a world without prisons (A. Y. Davis 2003). While most if not all LMS mentors and Pueblo Unido staff strongly condemned police brutality, LMS had no set curriculum or guidelines on how to talk to students about police. Disagreements in staff meetings on the topic of policing had laid bare clear ideological differences among the mentors. In contrast to Mr. Javier's abolitionist beliefs, many LMS mentors harbored reformist attitudes to policing and believed that diversifying the police force was a viable step in ending unjust policing practices. In their formal interviews, two LMS mentors shared with me that they aspired to become police officers in the future. During the middle of my second year of research, a third mentor left the program to pursue a career as a juvenile probation officer.

While Mr. Javier knew his "fuck the police" point of view was detested by some of his colleagues, there was a general respect among the mentors for the autonomy of each mentor to run his class as he wished. Furthermore, Pueblo Unido administrators rarely, if ever, observed or inquired about the day-to-day lessons of individual mentors. Mr. Javier reported that while he did not advertise his radical lesson around the Pueblo Unido office, his teaching had never been censored. On the rare occasion that his classroom was visited by administrators, he noted that the trendiness of social justice messaging made the radical politics of his mentoring and classroom artwork less obvious.

"No one really tells me anything," he told me one day. "Teaching with freedom keeps me here. If I couldn't do that, I would be somewhere else." But he also felt that he was teaching in ways that went against the program's values. "It's like sometimes stuff sounds the same, like people don't realize what I'm saying is different . . . it all sounds fluffy social justice to them. That gives me an in, though. . . . We [i.e., radical educators in general] are like the little viruses in the matrix, you know what I'm saying? Hopefully we can taint it."

In her book *Critical Mentoring: A Practical Guide,* Torie Weiston-Serdan (2017) describes how dominant notions of mentoring, as of teaching, are rooted in power. As she notes, many mentorship programs like LMS, even those that acknowledge unjust inequality, "fail to see that the problems are often more nuanced and complex than typical mentoring programs can handle" (9). This leads mentorship programs to instead focus on "more manageable tasks" such as "improving student attendance, increasing grade point averages, and decreasing negative behaviors" (9). To resist hegemonic notions of mentorship, Weiston-Serdan offers the notion of *critical mentoring.* At LMS, Mr. Javier's and Mr. Agustín's method of mentorship can be characterized as this type of mentorship. Critical mentoring is a style of mentorship "rooted in the premise that the mentoring process should be informed by critical theories so that it becomes a strategy capable of addressing the marginalization and minoritization of our young people" (2). Weiston-Serdan states that critical mentoring

> challenges deficit-based notions of protégés, halts the force of protégé adaptation to dominant ideology, and engages in liberatory processes that trigger critical consciousness and an ongoing and joint struggle for transformation. It differs from mentoring as we currently know it, in that it moves beyond the dyadic structure of mentoring. Mentoring becomes much more about interrogating context and acting based on a critical analysis of that context, rather than an immobile relationship reinforced by hierarchies and saviorism. (1–2)

Mr. Javier and Mr. Agustín enacted a critical mentoring approach through critical lessons that shed light on social and historical contexts. In some cases, this meant making intentional adjustments to preexisting lessons. For instance, Mr. Agustín described reservations he had about teaching a financial literacy workshop a fellow mentor had shared with him. While he appreciated the skill-building aspect of the lesson (e.g., budget making, learning about credit), he was concerned that without a critical lesson on capitalism and the historical dispossession of communities of color (Marable 1999), the lesson would lead students to see poverty as a result of poor money management. I had similar concerns while witnessing the workshop taught by another mentor. The workshop ended with a lengthy conversation criticizing the irresponsibility of young men of color in poverty who purchased Air Jordans and other expensive sneakers.[3] Mr. Agustín's critical mentoring challenged (rather than reproduced) the misconception that poverty is a result of individuals' poor choices and financial irresponsibility. While he still taught useful financial skills, he maintained that the focus of the workshop was on the unjust lack of finances in communities of color rather than the lack of financial responsibility. As Mr. Agustín stated, "without teaching about why poverty exists . . . how people's labor gets exploited . . . it seems like people are just poor. But poverty doesn't have to exist. It's not a natural thing."

In addition to the ways subversive curriculum and lessons may spark a critical consciousness in young people, critical mentoring pushes mentors to avoid deficit-based framing of students. For Latino men who mentor Latino boys, I have argued that this entails avoiding an identification with the image of the positive Latino male role model. To resist deficit-based orientations of role modeling, Mr. Javier actively sought to counter the label of "positive role model" in his work as a mentor. This involved disrupting neoliberal notions of human value through his own image. During one of our conversations, in strikingly personal and direct language, Mr. Javier made it clear how he sought to use his own story to help distance his work from these kinds of orientations:

> It's all about how you value human beings. I tell them [the students] I don't see success as who can get the most money or getting the best GPA or going to college. That messaging already exists out there way too much. I don't need to be a part of that narrative. Even the college thing. I didn't go to college. Or, I did, but I didn't finish, right? I would be a hypocrite if I just preached that going to college is the ultimate success, and not going is failure. My students know I don't have a college degree, and I talk about it with them. I'm not like ashamed or anything, I don't say I made a mistake. And maybe I will finish my degree someday. But my students respect me, and I hope they respect everyone like that. Because it's not bad [not having a college degree]. We shouldn't see people as unsuccessful or lesser.

By using his own "bad example," Mr. Javier sought to avoid creating hierarchies of human value. His approach was a means of challenging a good/bad Latino male binary often touted by neoliberal multiculturalism. "I have to tell them, I don't think any lesser of you if you have a 0.0 [GPA]," affirmed Mr. Javier. By being a "bad example" of academic excellence (although a brilliant example of a critical mentor), Mr. Javier sought to redefine what success should look like.

Mr. Agustín also sought to resist identifying with cookie-cutter images of success. Although his journey from poverty to college graduate is a life narrative highly valued in a society rooted in the myth of meritocracy and individualism, Mr. Agustín was critical of the ways this narrative assigned little value to the Black and Latinx community in which he was raised. From his perspective, his community experienced racial oppression. If he allowed his story to promote the myth that individual merit and hard work would lead to success, he felt he would be complicit in a "culture of poverty" explanation for racial inequality. "I try not to be a good example . . . like *that*," elaborated Mr. Agustín. "This system is unfair. . . . I don't want them to see me as someone who 'made it.'" His resistance to being seen as a good example led him to actively remove himself as the image of success. By refusing to identify with the image of the positive Latino male role model, Mr. Javier and Mr. Agustín challenge the values that shape an idealized Latino manhood. In addition to refusing to be seen as the typical good example—which Mr. Agustín and Mr. Javier both felt reinforced racial stereotypes of Latino boys—Mr. Agustín's perspective as a gay man also led him to call out and question the sort of ideal Latino manhood defined by heteropatriarchal values that LMS otherwise sought to inculcate in the students.

QUEERING THE POSITIVE LATINO MALE ROLE MODEL

By many popular measures, Mr. Agustín was an ideal role model for Latino boys in search of an American dream seldom achieved by Latinx students (Gándara and Contreras 2009). Although he resisted this label, he also knew that his life history and background had made him a strong candidate for the position of mentor with LMS. "I am sure who I am played a big role in me getting this job," Mr. Agustín explained. "It's why I am here." In particular, he felt that the "bootstraps" immigrant narrative of his life was highly valued. He was born in Mexico and grew up in an impoverished urban neighborhood in California. He had faced adversity. Despite attending low-performing schools, he was a strong student. During his final years of high school, his father was sent to prison, causing his family great financial and emotional strain. In an effort to overcome this hardship, Mr. Agustín decided to attend community college rather than a four-year university. At community college, he continued to excel and eventually transferred to one of California's top public universities. There, he graduated in two years with a strong GPA. While his against-all-odds story is a narrative widely valued by programs for boys of color that idolize hardworking, self-made men, Mr. Agustín knew that a key aspect of his own identity contrasted starkly with this narrative: he identifies as gay.

The incompatibility of Mr. Agustín's sexuality with what I have described as the archetype of the positive Latino male role model is illuminated through the intellectual tradition commonly referred to as *queer of color critique*. In 2003, Roderick A. Ferguson outlined a series of ideas on Black queer subjectivity in his influential book *Aberrations in Black: Toward a Queer of Color Critique*. In this work, Ferguson defined *queer of color critique* as tracing the ways interconnected discourses of race, gender, sexuality, and capital assign normalcy and value to hegemonic subjectivities (e.g., whiteness, heterosexuality, traditional gender roles) while simultaneously rendering queer-of-color subjects as unproductive, marginal, and deviant. Similar to women-of-color feminisms (Moraga and Anzaldúa 1983), queer-of-color critique situates sexuality as constitutive of gender and race. From this intersectional perspective, queer-of-color critique centers the epistemologies and lived experiences of queer people of color to make space for fluid and liberating ways of being. In doing so, it mounts a powerful challenge to hegemonic logics of capital, race, and heteropatriarchy that govern social hierarchies.

Building from this intellectual tradition, Richard T. Rodríguez brings a queer-of-color critique to the study of Chicano manhood and la familia. In *Next of Kin: The Family in Chicano/a Cultural Politics* (2009), he describes the ways cultural expression emerging from the Chicano Movement promoted Chicano nationalist representations of masculinity that were defined through men's patriarchal role in the idea and institution of the family. The Chicano Movement, which reached its peak in the late 1960s and early 1970s, was a cultural nationalist movement that sought to empower the Chicanx community, in part, by pushing back against prevailing stereotypes in the United States of Mexican American culture, including those that depicted Latino men as lazy and failed patriarchs. But the effort to reject those stereotypes of Latino men largely focused on restoring a vision of Chicano/Latino manhood as one defined by empowered leaders, providers, and protectors. Although this movement sought to push back against racial stereotypes, this move of patriarchal restoration ultimately reproduced the idea that, as Rodríguez writes, "masculinity must always be achieved within a heterosexual and reproductive kinship matrix" (53). Rodríguez condemns cultural nationalist expressions of manhood which he finds subtly or outwardly homophobic and sexist, and instead he argues for approaches that can uplift queer Chicano cultural workers and challenge the heteropatriarchal formations of Chicano/Latino manhood. At LMS, although he never described his work as employing a "queer-of-color critique," Mr. Agustín largely sought to enact this cultural resistance by challenging the presumed heteronormativity of an empowered Latino male subjectivity.

Mr. Agustín told me about how, upon his arrival to the program, he was struck by the uniqueness of the type of Latino masculinity cultivated in LMS. "We are all, like, young Latino guys, so of course we are similar," he recounted, "but . . . there's a certain way manhood is thought about." Most obvious to him was the way heterosexual norms embedded in the culture and values of the program marked his own sexuality as incongruent with LMS. Mr. Agustín quickly noted that this was not because the program was outwardly against homosexuality but because the presentation of the ideal role model for Latino boys was always noticeably straight.

> If we operate from a belief that it's important for these Latino students to have Latino male role models that they look up to, you can't ignore that most of those Latino mentors are also . . . well . . . I'm the only gay one here. Aside from providing a Latino male mentor, it seems infused in that we are also providing a cisgender male mentor, a straight cisgender male mentor. So even though it may not be our intention to reproduce those power structures of male domination, of straight domination, it feels unintentional. It feels like those are also being reproduced.

Reflecting on his days in the office or at staff retreats, he added, "I definitely get microaggressions from some people [fellow LMS mentors]. . . . And I don't think it's intentional, but it is because I am different . . . not your typical Latino male mentor." In these self-reflective words, Mr. Agustín finds his queerness presenting a deviation from the assumed heterosexuality of the positive Latino male role model archetype.

In addition to calling out the presence and problems of this archetype at LMS, Mr. Agustín sought to disrupt confining and limited notions of the Latino manhood by bringing queer Latinx voices to his teaching and mentoring. He did this not only by seeking out new lessons but also by mining his own experience. For example, in one conversation with me, he described how he had gathered an array of teaching resources that challenged dominant narratives of Chicanx history and identity (Blackwell 2011; Quesada, Gomez, and Vidal-Ortiz 2015), only to quickly become aware that his own experience and knowledge was perhaps the most powerful teaching tool. Educational researcher Cindy Cruz (2001, 2012) has written extensively about the epistemological power of the racialized queer body and the ways in which curriculum and knowledge emerge from personal stories as counter-narrative. Similarly, in his work at LMS, Mr. Agustín noted the pedagogical power in his own body and experiences as a queer Latino male mentor from the same neighborhood as his students. As he put it, "I think literally me being me . . . that's something that changes how my students might think about this program and themselves . . . how they define masculinity." Although he found that having a gay Latino male mentor was not what his students imagined when joining LMS, Mr. Agustín felt that, as a mentor, it was important for him to bring all aspects of his life to his classroom.[4]

By directly embracing this aspect of his identity in his work, Mr. Agustín made use of his embodied pedagogical gender performance. He was not interested in signaling hegemonic notions of manhood. In addition, he described himself as "not straight passing," and he felt this contributed to his ability to resist the positive role model image on a day-to-day basis. Not only was he against enacting masculine tough love (something often presumed of male educators of color), but he felt he did not have the ability to enact this particular form of masculine discipline because of his natural demeanor. "I wouldn't want to intimidate my students into doing what I tell them . . . aggressively," he stated, before adding, "but I don't think it would actually be possible." With a smile, he gestured at his smaller build. Mr. Agustín's disinterest in and inability to signal what he described as "stereotypical male behavior" led him to avoid popular areas of male camaraderie—from making hypermasculine gestures to bonding over sports and misogynistic culture—and allowed him to avoid reproducing hegemonic notions of masculinity.[5]

However, on another level, Mr. Agustín's resistance was discursive—he was an openly gay Latino male mentor. "I didn't declare it to my class or anything, but it is known," he recounted. "Like if they ask if I've had girlfriends, I say 'No, but I have had boyfriends.'" In this way, Mr. Agustín challenged the presumed straightness of the positive Latino male mentor. "The benefits of me being the only queer one is that I do get to disrupt the whole straight Latino male narrative and bring more queer voices into the classroom, queer Latino male voices . . . including my own."

One area in which Mr. Agustín's queerness challenged the normalizing politics embedded in Latino male role modeling was the belief that successful Latino men would one day be successful husbands and fathers. "A lot of our lessons on gender are very men/women and male/female," explained Mr. Agustín. "The gender binary is presented as very complementary, very 'This is your role as a man.'" As discussed in detail in chapter 3, one of these roles is heteronormative fatherhood, and like most mentors, Mr. Agustín understood that a sizable part of his work of Latino male mentorship was to cultivate preparedness for respectable fatherhood. This fatherhood was commonly, if not always, assumed to be in a monogamous, heterosexual relationship established through marriage. Consequently, this model of masculinity positioned Mr. Agustín as outside the ideal example for Latino boys. "I always get asked by my students if I want to get married or have children. I am like, 'Not really to the marriage. Maybe to the kids.' Because a lot of the curriculum is like, we're trying to picture this path where you can be that responsible father and husband. And because I have never seen myself in a husband role in the future, it was hard for me to be like, 'Yes, this is what you would do to do that in the future.' Because that's not what I'm doing."

Mr. Agustín's departure from heteropatriarchal notions of successful manhood powerfully disidentifies with the image of the positive Latino male role model expected in the LMS mentor. His disinterest in a heteronormative lifestyle conflicts with the envisioned values that a positive male role model must embody, a conflict that extended beyond his sexuality as a gay man and into other queer departures, such as disinterest in marriage and uncertainty about fatherhood.

In the groundbreaking book *Disidentifications: Queers of Color and the Performance of Politics,* José Esteban Muñoz introduced the notion of disidentification to describe the ways queer people of color strategically negotiate identity in ways that allow them to survive and subvert dominant ideology. For Muñoz, heteronormative and white capitalist values normalize proper subjectivities (heterosexual, cisgender, white, middle class, male) while rendering queer people of color as deviant. Disidentification describes the ways these subjects neither adopt (identify) nor reject (counter-identify) dominant ideology. Instead, disidentification is "a third mode of dealing with dominant ideology, one that neither opts to assimilate within such a structure nor strictly opposes it. . . . A strategy that works on and against dominant ideology" (1999, 11). In the case of Mr. Agustín, he decided to become an LMS mentor because he saw value in supporting Latino boys in his community. However, as a gay man who was uninterested in a heteronormative life, he also fails to embody and perform heteropatriarchal values that are foundational in the figure of the positive Latino male role model. This *queer failure* (Halberstam 2011) works to short-circuit the figure of the role model. Although the ability (and desire) to be a good patriarch in a heteronuclear family is presented as a universally positive quality to be modeled by a successful man, Mr. Agustín's disidentification with the figure of the positive Latino male role model both illuminates and challenges heteropatriarchal values that shape its image. By queering the image of the role model, Mr. Agustín neither rejects nor identifies with being a Latino male role model. In doing so, he challenges essentialist and hegemonic notions of manhood and creates space for new ways of being for Latino men and boys. "My online bio will never say, 'Mr. Agustín is a devoted husband and father of two kids . . . the whole white picket fence thing,'" he joked with me at the end of our interview, "and I think there's value in that."

IMPLICATIONS: SEVEN JUSTICE-ORIENTED PRINCIPLES FOR MEN OF COLOR WORKING WITH BOYS OF COLOR

The perspectives of Mr. Javier and Mr. Agustín on their work in the LMS program highlight the ways some Latino male mentors challenge the neoliberal figure of the positive Latino male role model through pedagogical and embodied disruptions. Both mentors brought a critical perspective to their positioning as role models and scrutinized the notion that Latino boys simply need positive male examples to overcome structural inequalities in schools. Although both mentors found the framing and mission of LMS problematic, they also maintained that their work with students was valuable and important. Their perspectives on how to subvert deficit-oriented mentoring have implications for other male educators of color who find themselves in similar positions. Educational research documents that social justice–oriented youth workers often find themselves in compromising positions within the neoliberal landscape of urban education (Baldridge 2019). In the following sections I outline several of the most effective critical perspectives, mentoring strategies, and queer disruptions that Mr. Javier and Mr. Agustín demonstrated in their work and conversations that helped push back against the harmful neoliberal logics that LMS and other programs like it employ in their work with boys of color. Their strategies highlight key principles of justice-centered approaches to youth work and role modeling and serve as a powerful tool for youth workers in similar positions who hope to subvert their framing as positive male role models within neoliberal narratives of success for boys of color.[6]

Challenge Deficit-Based Perspectives

Male educators of color are frequently seen as the success stories of a demographic at risk of failure. While stories of beating-the-odds success may be inspiring to some students, they also deemphasize the structural nature of inequality and instead highlight individual qualities that have seemingly contributed to individual success (e.g., positive attitude, strong character, self-discipline, grit, etc.). These narratives often rely on racial stereotypes and pathologize "bad" members of a group (e.g., "Mr. Javier chose to avoid falling in with the wrong crowd, like others, and instead worked hard and stayed on the right path."). Rejecting the deficit model means challenging the idea that the problem exists within the students themselves and refusing to view students as the ones in need of repair. It also means challenging the notion that role models have something special that students lack. These educators are often positioned as needing to help build positive character in young men, as if it is the individual student, and not societal structures, who contributes to inequality. Instead, male educators of color should be valued for their skills as educators and their ability to recognize the wealth of knowledge and capabilities that students bring from their own lives and communities (Gonzalez, Moll, and Amanti 2006; Yosso 2005).

Refuse the Roles of Hero and Savior

Male educators of color are often upheld as heroes who have returned to the classroom to save boys similar to themselves. Their biographies are often made into stories of survival and redemption and are neatly packaged and embellished for philanthropists eager to fund their heroism (Baldridge 2017). However, this framing reinforces the narrative that boys of color are at risk, broken, and in constant peril, while also positioning individual educators as unrealistic fixes to racial inequality in education. Racial inequality in schools is rooted in systemic racism. This includes issues of school funding, the school-to-prison pipeline, policy, and curriculum, as well as societal problems such as wealth inequality, mass incarceration, policing, food insecurity, housing segregation, and houselessness. While honoring the impactful role that individuals can play in the lives of young people, male educators of color must refuse to be positioned as heroes and saviors. This unfairly puts the onus of change on individual educators while also obscuring the complexity and deep roots of racial inequality inside and outside of schools.

Disrupt the Heteropatriarchal Imagination of Male Mentorship

Women-of-color feminists have long pointed to the ways visions of racial empowerment frequently reproduce patriarchal and heterosexual norms (García 1997; Lorde 2007; Moraga and Anzaldúa 1983). Today, feminist and queer scholars have approached the movement to empower boys and men of color with hesitation and concern (Lindsay 2018). Kimberlé Crenshaw (2016) describes MBK and similar programs as employing a discourse of *patriarchy enhancement*—extending the notion that racial justice will be achieved by restoring men of color into traditional (heteropatriarchal) roles in the family and community. This framing positions male educators of color as potential models of ideal manhood, as those who will guide their protégés down a similar path. While having a role model is important, educators must actively disrupt, rather than uphold, heteropatriarchal expectations of manhood. This is particularly important for educators who identify as cisgender, heterosexual men and whose everyday behavior may unconsciously normalize hegemonic ways of being a man (i.e., men must be masculine leaders, protectors, athletic, tough, dominant, straight, and aspire to be fathers and husbands in traditional family arrangements). Instead, educators must be conscious of their gender performance—that is, how they signal and embody manhood to those around them—and reflect on how their own expression of manhood influences the ways their students recognize what makes a "successful" man. Intentional efforts must be made to make space for diverse masculinities and queer futures for all students (McCready 2010, 2019). This does not mean ignoring the unique experiences that boys face, but rather acknowledging that their experiences are not monolithic. It also requires an awareness that dominant notions of gender and sexuality inform how society defines "good male role models."

Deconstruct (Not Reconstruct) Manhood

Male educators of color are often touted as models of reformed or nontoxic masculinity (Martino and Rezai-Rashti 2012). However, educators must disrupt the belief that they are guides toward building a better manhood and instead deprioritize the importance of manhood itself.

For example, statements like *Real men don't hit women* or *Real men are able to show emotion* make the error of prioritizing the construction of new and corrected boundaries of manhood as the goal of the statement. This comes at the detriment of the important issues: the public health crisis of intimate partner violence and the importance of learning emotional intelligence. Male educators of color must deemphasize the focus on their ability to be models of a reformed manhood and instead prioritize teaching against ideologies that shape gender inequality and oppression (e.g., patriarchy, misogyny, homophobia, transphobia). While still addressing the unique (and diverse) experiences of boys of color, educators (and programs) must avoid creating new boundaries of what defines a proper man. This inevitably leads to essentialist and exclusionary gender practices. Currently, many school-based programs for boys of color invest in the importance of manhood. This is the case with LMS. I urge educators to approach investments in manhood with caution. Although proclamations of progressive gender politics have become the norm in male-centered programs, research shows that patriarchal narratives of male empowerment often continue to guide program missions. Furthermore, some all-male spaces continue to be spaces in which issues of misogyny, homophobia, and transphobia remain commonplace and unaddressed (Fergus, Noguera, and Martin 2014; Lindsay 2018; Oeur 2018).

Critically Analyze How Cultural Relevancy Is Valued

For decades, the term *culturally relevant pedagogy* (CRP) has been used to describe the ways justice-oriented educators make teaching relevant and responsive to the social realities, cultural practices, and languages of their students (Ladson-Billings 1995). However, in recent years, critical race educators have criticized the ways CRP has become a catch-all phrase for anything remotely relatable to students, arguing that CRP is frequently robbed of its political and emancipatory foundations (Paris and Alim 2017). For example, in schools, male educators of color are often valued for their ability to culturally relate with boys of color. Unfortunately, cultural relevancy can be easily co-opted in ways that uphold liberal multiculturalism and the current status quo. Male educators of color report that they are often thrust into the role of disciplinarian at their school because colleagues perceive them to be best suited to talk to (and punish) boys of color (Brockenbrough 2015). Being the friendly enforcer of school discipline or the relatable and charismatic teacher who upholds problematic curriculum and policy should not be the goal of educator diversity. Instead, male educators of color must conscientiously strive to push beyond superficial expressions of cultural relevancy and instead employ a pedagogy that is decidedly critical, emancipatory, and humanizing.

Challenge Anti-Black Framings of Multiculturalism

Anti-Blackness is interwoven into the fabric of how urban schooling is imagined and materially structured in the United States (Grant, Woodson, and Dumas 2020). While emergent ideologies of multiculturalism have begun to celebrate racial diversity in schools, Blackness continues to exist in tension with liberal expressions of multiculturalism, which have little interest in radically affirming Black life and freedom (Dumas and ross 2016; Shange 2019). Instead, Blackness is often framed as antagonistic to multicultural opportunity—positing Black people as making poor individual choices, lacking determination and hard work, and being unwilling to assimilate in an increasingly "fair" and "inclusive" society. In the national educational discourse, Black boys in particular are imagined to represent a persistent problem (Noguera 2009). Because male educators of color are often framed as models of respectability, they must take great care to disrupt, and not uphold, anti-Blackness in schools. For non-Black male educators of color in particular, there must be an awareness of the ways the imagined figure of the positive male role model can often be articulated in relation to Blackness (M. V. Singh 2021a, 2023). This juxtaposition contrasts "respectable" male educators of color with anti-Black images of a problematic and deviant manhood, which is often articulated through anti-Black language (e.g., thugs, delinquents, gangsters, urban juveniles, ghetto, etc.). It is crucial for non-Black men of color to reject a model minority–like positionality and to disrupt the dichotomy of good male role models and bad boys. This also means refusing to pathologize, and instead honoring, markers of Blackness in our cultures, communities, ourselves, and our students. This includes refusing anti-Black dress codes, disciplinary policies, respectability politics, grading practices, and also being responsive to the larger societal context of anti-Black racism. It also means actively becoming authentic allies and co-conspirators, and helping make space for Black joy, life, and freedom.

Teach and Dream toward Educational Justice

Much of the discourse on male educators of color is that they serve as role models to help boys succeed within the current system. They are framed as proof that resilience and hard work can bring about success. While the previous points outline the ways educators can deconstruct and refuse the compromising discourses that frame their roles in schools, it is also important that men of color become agents of transformational justice. Presently, we are in an era in which almost everything in education is labeled *social justice.* Tuck and Yang (2018) bring a "warm ambivalence" (3) to the term and remind us of the importance of clarity and commitment in how we define justice projects. Beyond reformist iterations of social justice, abolitionist and decolonial movements in education offer compelling visions of how to imagine education beyond its current form (Grant, Woodson, and Dumas 2020; Tuck and Yang 2018). As more male educators of color are recruited into the field of education, moreover, it is imperative that the goal is not simply to help students survive but instead to radically reimagine schooling beyond survival and toward freedom (Love 2019). Male educators of color must be allies and co-conspirators in these movements as they play a part in working toward intersectional racial justice in schools and beyond.

The seven principles I have outlined are points that I continue to reflect on in my own work with young people. As educators, we teach in institutions in which our communities were never meant to succeed. We navigate contradictions and are forced to make compromises. For those of us who are men of color, the neoliberal multicultural moment often assigns value to our work in ways that we may find problematic, even racist. Drawing from my research with LMS, these seven points are meant to help educators recognize and disrupt the ways problematic discourses can frame our work with students. This list is not meant to be exhaustive, and I encourage educators to add to it or reevaluate some of these points. Instead, I aim to contribute to a larger conversation surrounding how men of color may navigate the contradictory politics that praise us as successful role models working in a system not meant for our success. It is my hope that these seven principles will help to support male educators of color as they deconstruct problematic discourses surrounding their presence in schools and continue to work toward more radical and emancipatory visions of justice in education.

CONCLUSION

On a hot and sunny day in July 2019, I met with Mr. Agustín at a coffee shop in North Arroyo Seco. My two years of fieldwork with LMS had officially ended the previous month, but I had sought out Mr. Agustín for one final interview. If he was open to it, I wanted to discuss some troubling news I had heard a couple of months earlier: Mr. Agustín had been fired.

As I walked into the partially open-air café, the aroma of roasting coffee beans blended nicely with the warm summer air and the oily smell of the North Arroyo Seco streets. Although I arrived ten minutes early, I spotted Mr. Agustín already sitting along a brick wall. He smiled as I walked up, and we gave each other a hug.

"Have you been here yet?" asked Mr. Agustín, signaling to the beautiful café. It was a new, Black-owned coffee shop at the edge of the Mariposa District. Its brick walls featured the artwork of an array of local artists.

"No, not yet. I'm glad you suggested this place," I replied.

As we settled into coffee and conversation, Mr. Agustín broached the topic of his termination. He stated that throughout the fall he had struggled with classroom management. "It's always been an issue with me," he shared, "but I think that's the same with a lot of first-year educators." However, without his knowledge, Mrs. Sánchez, the Latina Spanish teacher who shared his classroom, had raised concerns about Mr. Agustín's capabilities to the school principal. Then, during winter break there had been a meeting between the principal and the LMS director. The principal had demanded that LMS assign a new mentor to the school. With few options, LMS informed Mr. Agustín that he would not be returning to his high school site and that Mr. Nicolás would take over after winter break. Mr. Agustín didn't even get a chance to say goodbye to his class.

Although novice teachers often need additional support through their first years of teaching, Mr. Agustín was not a teacher. As the school viewed it, an LMS mentor was an outside expert, a professional contracted to run a circle for Latino boys. If the mentor was unable to manage his group, there was clearly no need to continue to hire out this service.

"It was pretty embarrassing," Mr. Agustín reflected, taking a long sip of coffee.

Pueblo Unido had quickly offered him a new position, outside of LMS, as a youth career coach in a new program the nonprofit was starting. His supervisor assured him that Pueblo Unido valued his capabilities as an employee, but his departure from LMS was bitter, particularly because of such little warning and communication.

"Everything felt so abrupt," he shared, reflecting on the previous winter. For Mr. Agustín, there was little doubt that his gender performance as a gay man had contributed to his removal. It was not that classroom management was not an issue, as he readily accepted, but that perhaps the administration had imagined a more authoritative "father-figure" at the school. For him, his identity as a gay man—who was, as he put it, "not straight passing"—made him undesirable by the school, who actually refused LMS's offer to give Mr. Agustín further training in classroom management.

His transition to his new role was quick. His new co-workers avoided the topic of his old position and his connection with the LMS mentors had begun to feel distant. It was like everyone wanted to forget he had ever been a mentor. On top of everything, the looming issue of his sexuality, which he felt was obviously implicated in his removal, was never addressed. He shared, "In that moment, it definitely felt like my queerness was not addressed, yet it was why there was such a push to get me out of that school."

In this chapter I have focused on the ways some LMS mentors were keenly aware of the politics undergirding their image as mentors and role models for Latino boys in North Arroyo Seco. In particular, Mr. Agustín and Mr. Javier recognized the deficit approach to youth work in LMS, and they described a range of ways they sought to disrupt it. In part, this disruption came from enacting critical mentoring strategies. Critical mentoring, similar to critical pedagogy, recognizes the ways mentoring is an educative act rooted in power. Critical mentoring refuses to focus on managing students' habits and behaviors, and instead sparks a critical consciousness among young people. Critical mentoring does not seek to help students simply navigate oppressive systems, but instead recognizes and seeks to challenge those systems (Weiston-Serdan 2017). The critical lessons and perspectives taught by Mr. Agustín and Mr. Javier exemplify critical mentoring.

However, beyond critical mentoring, I describe Mr. Agustín and Mr. Javier as subversive role models. The notion of the subversive role model disrupts dominant notions of patriarchal role models.

Alternatively, subversive role models perform the role of "bad example" as a means to reflect a critical perspective on what is usually uncritically deemed "good." For both men, this meant disrupting clean-cut narratives of success and respectability assigned to LMS mentors. For Mr. Agustín, part of being a subversive role model was queering the image of the positive Latino male role model. By both intentionally and unintentionally helping to undo the heteronormative and patriarchal ideals of the role model, Mr. Agustín boldly offered a queer disruption to the status quo. Unfortunately, he, as well as I, felt this departure from the norm had cost him his job. I asked if he was thinking about challenging his removal and if I could support him. He was not. Mr. Agustín was planning to apply to graduate school soon and felt that as long as he still had a job, it would not be worth the hassle. Among the most regrettable things about his removal was that Mr. Agustín really loved being a mentor. "I really liked my job," he shared with me, "And I think I have a lot to offer students from this community . . . from my community." I wholeheartedly agreed.

ENGAGING ANTI-BLACKNESS WHILE MENTORING NON-BLACK LATINO BOYS

"I will not say the N-word. I will not say the N-word." Darwin's pen pressed hard against a piece of lined paper as he scribbled this sentence over and over again. He had finished about half of the one hundred lines he needed to fill before going home. "This is some BS," he said to himself in a loud whisper, which was audible across the room. Darwin was an eighth grader in Mr. Antonio's class. He was tall and slim, with dark brown skin, straight black hair, and an athletic build. His parents were from El Salvador, but he was born and raised in North Arroyo Seco—something in which he took great pride.

His punishment came from an incident that occurred earlier that day. It was a sunny afternoon and the class had been outside on the field. He and Jasiel had been chosen to be team captains for a game of football. As Darwin slowly pondered his first draft choice, Jasiel made a loud, humming noise to signal his impatience. "Damn n***a, can you hold up? I'm thinking," shouted Darwin. This caught the attention of a school staff person, a Black woman who looked to be in her mid-forties, who was walking past the field. The boys looked surprised to see that we were not alone. "Oh no, no. We do not use that word. Who is the adult here?" the woman demanded. Mr. Antonio stepped forward and attempted, unconvincingly, to look as if he had not heard what was said. "He needs to know that that word does not belong in this school," the woman said sternly. Although she spoke to Darwin and Mr. Antonio, it felt like we were all in trouble. As an adult present, I felt embarrassed.

After the exchange, Mr. Antonio had been upset with Darwin. "How are you going to say that when there's a Black lady walking right there?" he asked the boy, looking more bothered by the awkward encounter than the transgression. Darwin was benched for the football game and was ordered to stay after school to write lines. He was furious with the punishment.

To be clear, it is my belief that it is not okay for non-Black people to use any iteration of the N-word, ever—a point I shared with LMS.[1] And to the best of my knowledge, no LMS students or mentors identify as Black or Afro-Latinx. However, Darwin's indignation was understandable. During my time in Mr. Antonio's class I had heard the N-word used countless times by students and a handful of times by mentors. That word, similar to curse words, was treated as language generally inappropriate for school but accepted as common vernacular used by Latino boys in Arroyo Seco. In the relaxed environment of Mr. Antonio's LMS circle, a place where boys could simply be themselves, Mr. Antonio looked the other way on this language or simply shushed it. For perhaps this reason, Darwin seemed to feel unfairly punished and the victim of a vague and inconsistently applied rule. He was offered no deeper explanation for his punishment, and the class held no discussion on the N-word or Latinx relationality to Black people in the United States or in Arroyo Seco. Shortly after the incident, the boys returned to their normal banter in the classroom, including the use of the word.

While I never once heard this word spoken with ill intent toward African Americans, this incident demonstrates that there was confusing and inconsistent messaging about Blackness at LMS.

"I don't really get why Mr. Antonio made me write those lines," Darwin told me the next week. "He knows we say it all the time."

From Darwin's perspective, this was everyday language for Latino boys in Arroyo Seco, and in some ways he felt LMS acknowledged this and that it was acceptable (mostly). This incident, among many others, revealed an ambiguity about the way the boys in the program understood their own relation to Blackness, as well as uncertainty among mentors at LMS for how to contend with this ambiguity. But not all mentors dealt with this ambiguity in the same way. Some chose to confront anti-Blackness through their pedagogy and coalition building. Others tried to avoid the issue altogether. And a small handful expressed prejudiced beliefs and used anti-Black rhetoric when speaking about urban schooling and poverty in Arroyo Seco.

In conversations about boys of color—whose commonalities and distinctions are homogenized into the catch-all category—the subject of anti-Blackness is often avoided. In this book I have demonstrated the ways neoliberal multiculturalism shapes how race functions in programs meant to empower Latino boys. In this framing, good and respectable multicultural subjects are created through their juxtaposition to deviant racial others. In this chapter I will show that, in part, this deviant racial other is often marked by a disdain for Blackness. While the United States continues to fashion itself as a proponent of multiculturalism in both rights (granted by the state) and opportunity (granted by the free market), scholars of race and education point to the inherent anti-Blackness in the multicultural project. As Michael Dumas and kihana ross (2016) maintain, "Black people become—or rather, remain—a problem, as the least assimilable to this multicultural imagination" (430). In the national educational discourse, Black boys in particular represent a persistent "problem" and have become the face of "crisis" in urban education (Howard 2013; Noguera 2009).[2]

This sustained focus on both the punishment and the empowerment of Black boys places Latino boys, and in particular non-Black Latino boys, in a unique position. While non-Black Latino boys are frequently situated as the similarly marginalized counterparts to Black boys, a conceptual lens attuned to the politics of anti-Blackness illuminates the specificities of anti-Black racism and the ways in which efforts to empower Latino boys may be rooted in anti-Black beliefs. A deeper engagement with anti-Blackness is paramount when examining how a positive Latino maleness is constructed within the anti-Black landscape of urban education and neoliberal empowerment. This chapter explores how Blackness and anti-Blackness affect the ways mentorship of non-Black Latino boys is understood and practiced in LMS. I argue that an anti-Black imagination of positive multicultural manhood deeply influences how a positive Latino male subjectivity is shaped in schools. As this book shows, rethinking the framing, approach, and pedagogy of mentorship programs for Latino boys is an important part of a larger effort to dismantle liberal and multiculturalist iterations of racism in the United States. A relevant and crucial part of this will be developing strategies to empower non-Black boys of color in ways that help them contend with their own proximity and relationality to anti-Blackness.

ANTI-BLACKNESS AND MULTICULTURALISM IN SCHOOLS

Anti-Blackness is entrenched in the fabric of urban education (Grant, Woodson, and Dumas 2020). It influences how the United States has come to imagine urban schools (Leonardo and Hunter 2007) as well as how urban schools have become underresourced (Anyon 1997) and hyperpoliced (A. A. Ferguson 2001; Nolan 2011). The notion of anti-Blackness refers to the historical and present-day violence inflicted against Black people. This violence is rooted in the fundamental disregard and disdain for Black life and has existed from the era of chattel slavery until the present. According to Dumas and ross (2016), "antiblackness is not simply racism against Black people. Rather, antiblackness refers to a broader antagonistic relationship between blackness and (the possibility of) humanity" (429). Anti-Blackness justifies the continued dehumanization of Black people as individuals and as a collective group in what Saidiya Hartman (1997) refers to as "the afterlife of slavery" (6). It validates not just racial inequality but also the pervasive murder and premature death of human beings because of their embodiment of, or proximity to, Blackness. Anti-Blackness is endemic and central to how the United States understands social, cultural, economic, and historical dimensions of human life (Wilderson 2020).

Scholars of anti-Blackness in education argue that anti-Blackness is the defining quality in which to understand racial violence in schooling (Dumas 2016b). This includes policy efforts surrounding Black and non-Black boys of color. For example, Dumas (2016a) argues that an anti-Black imagination provided the impetus for neoliberal reform efforts found in the 2014 My Brother's Keeper initiative, even while accounting for all boys and men of color.

> Even as MBK is intended to be inclusive of all boys and young men of color, I contend that the imagination of the problem is decidedly and specifically *Black*. My focus on blackness here is not intended to render these other groups of color invisible; rather my analysis proceeds with the understanding that it is the deployment of blackness that most heavily informs the racial-neoliberal logics of MBK. (96–97)

In this framing, the racialized "problems" that non-Black boys of color represent become associated with the "problem" of Blackness, and in particular, an anti-Black fear of Black maleness (A. A. Ferguson 2001). While this close proximity to Blackness reveals avenues of potential solidarity and coalition, liberal and neoliberal multiculturalist goals of urban education frame Blackness as stagnant and a barrier to the multicultural vision of the United States (Dumas and ross 2016). Blackness is posited as something to be avoided and rejected—an abject essence at odds with multiculturalism and diversity. Scholars of anti-Blackness clarify and reassert theses of canonical racial theory, maintaining that notions of the color line and colonialism are marked not by the polarizing forces of whiteness and non-whiteness but rather by *Blackness* (Du Bois 2012; Fanon 2008). In this way, in the United States, scholars of race, and particularly of race and urban education, must contend with anti-Blackness in schools.

Blackness as a Problem for Latinidad

The term *Latinidad* refers to the various cultures, qualities, and shared experiences of people in Latin America as well as their descendants outside of the region. In the United States this term attempts to bring together a large group of diverse people under a common category that is decidedly different from Anglo whites. Despite its popularity, critics of the term point to its sweeping generalizations as well as the ways in which the notion of Latinidad has excluded, erased, and harmed Black and Indigenous people—and continues to do so.[3] This is due in part to Latinidad's long-standing idealization of mestizaje and the enduring narrative that racial mixing in Latin America has allowed Latinx people to transcend race. However, anti-Blackness remains endemic in Latin America, and Afro-Latinx scholars have long documented the ways Latinidad perpetuates a white-supremacist imagination of Latinidad, which marks Blackness as negative and suspect (Hernández 2003, 2022; A. P. Lopez 2020).

In U.S. schools, Afro-Latinx students often receive conflicting messaging surrounding Blackness, and third spaces are often needed to allow students to build positive and affirming Afro-Latinx identities (Salas Pujols 2022). This is a consequence of both anti-Black racism in the United States and pervasive anti-Black beliefs within Latinx communities (Haywood 2017; Román and Flores 2010). Latinidad's contentious relationship to Blackness requires close attention to anti-Blackness when studying Latinx education, even when, as in the case of LMS, few, if any, Latinx students identify as Black or Afro-Latinx.

To be clear, bringing close attention to anti-Black racism in research does not negate the fact that non-Black Latinx students experience racism across many contexts, including schools (Gándara and Contreras 2009; Valenzuela 1999). However, it does require an attention to the strong anti-Black prejudices that continue to shape Latinidad around the globe (García Peña 2022) and in U.S. schools (Gamez 2023).

Furthermore, while it is of the utmost importance to condemn anti-Blackness at all levels, this book is less interested in "calling out" individuals as anti-Black than in tracing the ways neoliberal multiculturalism and anti-Blackness work in tandem. This is particularly important given non-Black Latino boys' proximity to Blackness and the ways anti-Blackness dictates larger conversations surrounding boys and men of color.

Relational Analyses of Race

In her book *Progressive Dystopia: Abolition, Antiblackness, and Schooling in San Francisco*, Savannah Shange explores the ways anti-Blackness infiltrates, and in many ways undergirds, progressive schooling projects aimed at multiracial empowerment and solidarity. Her research uncovers the ways multicultural uplift often comes with caveats and conditions and how it exhumes what she refers to as carceral progressivism—"the paradoxical dynamic in which social reform practices, particularly those that target inequities in communities of color, can perpetuate antiblack racism even as they seek to eliminate it" (2019, 14). In part, her analysis examines the ways carceral progressivism's conditional inclusion of Latinidad can come at the expense of Black students.[4]

Relational theories of race are rare in race research and even rarer in educational ethnographies (see Gamez and Monreal 2021; Museus 2022). For the most part, studies of race and schools take a one-at-a-time approach, in which the experience of a single marginalized group is studied in relation to white supremacy in schools. However, these approaches often encourage conceptualizations of race that exist as independent and isolated constituencies. In other instances, racial groups are coupled to demonstrate the shared experiences of racism, as in the popular study of boys of color, who are often framed as having nearly identical racial experiences in schools. However, racialization is a dynamic and ongoing process (Omi and Winant 2014). Race does not exist in a vacuum, and racial projects uniquely affect malleable racial categories as shifts in policy, politics, and racial discourses occur (Omi and Winant 2014). A relational conception of race takes into account the ways racialization happens not just in relation to whiteness but in relation to other subordinated groups (Molina, HoSang, and Gutiérrez 2019). This approach to race scholarship uncovers the connections among marginalized groups and the racial logics circumscribing inclusion, exclusion, and dispossession. Michael Rodríguez-Muñiz explains that a relational approach "does not presume the existence of independent, already formed groups" but "holds that ethnoracial boundaries, identities, and political affiliations do not precede, but rather are the *effects* of these relations" (quoted in Molina, HoSang, and Gutiérrez 2019, 7).

THE DILEMMAS OF ANTI-BLACKNESS IN MENTORING PROGRAMS FOR LATINO BOYS

Employing a relational approach to race often pushes scholars to enter literature outside their initial scope and expertise (Molina, HoSang, and Gutiérrez 2019). While my central scholarly focus does not center around theorizations of anti-Blackness, my research necessitated that I help start a conversation on the relational politics of race within the larger conversation of boys of color in schools (Davila 2021). After having carried out this research, I believe it makes sense to engage with theories of anti-Blackness to understand Latino male empowerment in a multiracial urban school district. While this study by no means offers a thorough investigation of the relational politics of race among Black and non-Black Latino boys in schools, this chapter engages moments in which it became clear that anti-Blackness had a profound impact on LMS and its conceptualization of Latino male empowerment.

As discussed in previous chapters, the LMS program consistently used deficit-oriented language to frame how Latino boys might improve their lives. In this framing, Latino boys were presented as struggling against an inherent proclivity for "badness" and for following troublesome paths in life. As many of the students themselves noted, LMS itself was, at bottom, created to help Latino boys avoid this troubled route in life. But this framing of Latino boys as fighting against an inherent deviancy is directly tied to a much larger, deeply embedded history of racial designation in the United States, one that defines one's privilege and centrality according to one's distance from or proximity to Blackness. During the era of slavery, the designation of Blackness was used to dehumanize and deprive human beings of humanity and freedom. In the wake of slavery's horror, notions of Blackness continue to be remade through violence—culturally constructed as deviant, criminal, and the natural recipient of racial violence and dispossession (Sharpe 2016). Today, the continuity of anti-Blackness influences how racial and social hierarchies continue to operate—with "good" multicultural subjects recognizably good by their distance from Blackness.

Anti-Blackness has had significant consequences on racialization and structural hierarchies in the United States and on how communities of color have come to understand social improvement.

Part of the "culturally rooted" goals of LMS—which involved redirecting Latino boys down the "right path" and toward what was considered a traditional and noble Latino manhood—was a project of restoration. The character development program was thought to help boys return to their roles as honorable family men—a duty that colonization and racial oppression taught them to neglect. But as we have seen, this construction of manhood was built around a patriarchal, heteronormative understanding of masculinity, one that drew strongly on neoliberal logics and deficit-oriented framings of Latino boys. However, more than that, these articulations of a positive Latino manhood were, in part, also articulated via its distance from cultural pathologizations of Blackness.

In recent years the term "boys of color" has become widely used by education policy makers and researchers to help bring about a more targeted focus on Black and Latino boys as well as Native, Asian, and Pacific Islanders. This is not without reason. Scholars have pointed out that Black and Latino boys share similar experiences of criminalization in schools (Rios 2011), have similar academic struggles (Noguera 2012), and also benefit from similar mentorship-based intervention strategies (Brooms, Clark, and Smith 2018; Hall 2006). Although the term "boys of color" provides a conceptual tool to highlight specific patterns of unequal institutional treatment across groups of young people in the United States, racial and ethnic categories are imperfect social creations that also produce confining and exclusionary boundaries of identity—forcing students to "choose." For example, many Latino boys are also Black boys. While this was generally not the case in LMS, it was clear that racialization in the United States messily intersects with socially constructed racial and ethnic identities. In other instances, for example, some students may identify as Black, Indigenous, and Latinx. Although the blanket category "boys of color" emphasizes the shared experiences and barriers faced by students in this group, the term threatens to forfeit specificity and lacks a relational understanding of racial identities (Molina, HoSang, and Gutiérrez 2019). This chapter seeks to offer a better understanding of racial formation for Latino boys by analyzing the ways notions of anti-Blackness influence how a redeemable and positive Latino manhood was constructed in LMS.

"WHAT TYPE OF CULTURE ARE WE SUPPOSED TO TEACH THEM TO AVOID?": MENTORING LATINO BOYS IN BLACK NEIGHBORHOODS

Like most of his students, Mr. Javier was born and raised in the predominantly Black and Latinx neighborhoods of North Arroyo Seco. "Kids from North Arroyo Seco . . . there's a lot of pride, it's like, you really rep it . . . there's a culture to it," he said. While Mr. Javier had grown up proud of his Mexican and Salvadoran roots, he also acknowledged that as a child of Arroyo Seco, his upbringing was also deeply affected by Black American culture. "In North Arroyo Seco, you are always immersed in Black culture and history," he shared. "It's embedded in the city's culture." While growing up in Arroyo Seco did not make him feel entitled to the Black experience, he did feel it gave him a heightened awareness of anti-Blackness. In part this was because North Arroyo Seco was a geographic signifier of urban Blackness:

> When you say you're from North Arroyo Seco, people think ghetto, they think Black, and they think bad. . . . A lot of Latinos hate on Latinos from Arroyo Seco because they say we act Black, or, that we are too ghetto or whatever. It's racist. What they really mean is, why do you associate yourself with Black people? Why do you talk a certain way? It's not what we are supposed to do.

Critical geographers and social scientists have long recognized the ways racial power comes to define space (McKittrick and Woods 2007). Phenomena such as redlining and legal housing segregation have shaped the ways spaces structurally and physically become racially segregated (Rothstein 2017). However, culturally, space can also signal racial meaning. For example, when former president Donald Trump berated the city of Baltimore or referred to Haiti as a "shithole country," the language of space takes on racial meaning to express anti-Blackness (Holcombe 2019; Vitali, Hunt, and Thorp 2018).

From an early age, Mr. Javier described an awareness of the pervasive disdain of Blackness, Black culture, and Black people. Blackness, he was taught, was something to be rejected, especially for Latinx people navigating the racial landscape of the United States. He felt that embedded in LMS's vision of Latino male empowerment was the belief that successful Latinidad must reject and distance itself from the urban Blackness often associated with Arroyo Seco. Research has documented the ways liberal and even radical spaces of social justice education adopt frameworks that pathologize Blackness (Baldridge 2020a; Brooms 2022; M. V. Singh 2023; Shange 2019). As this book has contended, Pueblo Unido and LMS offered a very specific vision of what social justice should look like. This vision was largely defined by respectability and playing by the rules.

In my conversations with them, many mentors at LMS complained of the middle-class sensibilities of Pueblo Unido administrators and took note that on the rare occasion that administrators visited their LMS classrooms, they were visibly uncomfortable around students. While this sentiment speaks to the politics of respectability embedded in neoliberal multiculturalism, the nuanced critiques of Mr. Javier describe the ways Blackness becomes the polarized opposite of a respectable Latinx identity. "A lot of the staff, the CEO, you can tell they don't feel comfortable around Black folks . . . fearful," he shared. Mr. Javier described Pueblo Unido's underlying anti-Blackness as manifesting in two important ways. The first area was the massive social justice nonprofit's lack of support for Black liberationist politics in the city. These spanned movements to defund the school district and city police, radically challenge gentrification, and elect progressive Black women politicians to local offices.[5] "They're neutral on everything," Mr. Javier explained. "We are the multicultural nonprofit holding back real change." Second, Mr. Javier believed that the life trajectories cultivated in LMS had underlying anti-Black sentiments. The program sought to cultivate a proud and traditional Latinidad while also exposing boys to whiteness that existed beyond their neighborhood. He offered the trip to the corporate office of Morgan Stanley as an example. "On the one hand we are reinforcing traditional Latino values, but on the other we want them to be these corporate kids," he said, highlighting his belief that as a Latino male mentor his role was to cultivate a Latinidad that also aligned with markers of whiteness. "So what are we supposed to be fighting in them? Or teaching them to avoid? . . . Blackness." Simultaneously, mentors were supposed to purge students of abject qualities associated with what was at times referred to as "urban youth"—a term commonly used to signal and pathologize Blackness (Leonardo and Hunter 2007). In this sense, the boys, despite physically occupying the urban center of North Arroyo Seco, could still, through good grades, self-reliance, and accountability, find ways to culturally distance themselves from its pathological markers of Blackness. Positioned as a positive role model himself, Mr. Javier found that this rejection of urban Blackness was most clearly visible in the ways Latino boys were asked how and why to value, or not value, Black male role models.

Bad Black Male Role Models

On March 31, 2019, the rapper and community advocate Nipsey Hussle was shot and killed at his storefront in South Los Angeles. The Grammy-nominated artist had grown up in the area, located near the intersection of West Slauson Avenue and Crenshaw Boulevard, and had been a member of the Rollin' 60s Neighborhood Crips, a local street gang. Nipsey Hussle's musical career had slowly carried him to moderate fame in the rap world, but it was his love for and investment in his local community that made him a beloved and inspiring figure in Los Angeles as well as around the world. Nipsey Hussle was committed to helping resist gentrification in South LA and was unafraid to take political stances that supported Black and Brown communities. News coverage surrounding his death made national headlines for the days to come. The Staples Center in Los Angeles hosted a massive public remembrance eleven days after his death, followed by a twenty-five-mile funeral procession through the city. Murals honoring the slain rapper quickly emerged throughout the city, and a wave of mourning circulated on social media.

Nipsey Hussle's death was a loss for the boys of LMS as well. Although his life and legacy are most directly associated with Black Los Angeles, the rapper had a profound impact on a wide range of people, including Latino boys in North Arroyo Seco. The artist had served as a source of inspiration and political unity across differences. His popular collaboration single with YG, "FDT (Fuck Donald Trump)," reinforced his solidarity with the Latinx community. The song emphasizes the common struggle faced by Black and Latinx people by evoking a longer lineage of Black-Brown unity in the California rap scene as well as by directly challenging racist anti-immigrant rhetoric against Mexican and Latinx people. At LMS, after Nipsey Hussle's death, several boys began playing his music in the hallways or as they entered the classroom. One student bought and wore to school a T-shirt featuring the rapper with angel wings and a gold halo. The topic of his life and death was consistently in their conversations.

After Nipsey Hussle's death, there was talk among the students at LMS about honoring him. Mr. Javier, an amateur rapper himself, was also a fan, and he and the students arranged to have a day dedicated to talking about Nipsey Hussle—someone who he felt should be honored as a hero and role model. However, the politics of honoring the slain rapper were complicated. "Nipsey Hussle is not the type of guy Pueblo Unido thinks is a good role model for our students," Mr. Javier explained to me. In the wake of Nipsey Hussle's death there had been much public debate about how to honor and value the artist and community advocate. Although many viewed him as a loving community advocate and symbol of resilience, others dismissed the artist as simply a gangster or thug—identities frequently seen as disposable. Based on conversations around the Pueblo Unido office, Mr. Javier shared that he was well aware that this lesson would not be sanctioned or embraced by Pueblo Unido.

This tension between how Nipsey Hussle was viewed by members of the LMS community, however, points to a larger dilemma within the empowerment strategies at the heart of the LMS program. Although the rapper was beloved by students and had rightfully received praise for his community advocacy and solidarity work, his direct association with street life made him a precarious role model. Mr. Javier shared:

> I think people right now are barely getting to see who Nipsey Hussle was as a human being. And what's a trip though is because he was a rapper, because he was a Crip, and because he was Black, there's a lot of backlash because of the way people view those things. People are like, "Oh, how are you guys turning this gang member into a hero?" And for me, that was just a perfect example of what this country tries to do. For me, I don't see it that way. . . . Nipsey Hussle, we have to talk about him with our students. He's someone we should admire. But he doesn't fit into how they say we should value someone.

The rejection of Nipsey Hussle by administrative figures at LMS as a proper male role model for students in the program highlights one of the ways that neoliberalism in educational support programs for young people of color can reiterate anti-Black racism. As discussed above, historically, one of the ways that populations racialized as nonwhite in the United States have sought social status has been to distance themselves from "Blackness" via a politics of respectability. While disdain for rappers and street culture is informed by this kind of respectability politics, as Mr. Javier described, Nipsey Hussle's cultural association with urban life and Blackness also marked him as the embodiment of a form of masculinity that programs like LMS sought to keep at a distance, rather than honor. Furthermore, the debates about Nipsey Hussle at LMS underscore how an imagined proper Latino masculinity is placed in opposition to the Blackness that Nipsey Hussle was framed as depicting by those opposed to honoring him.

Despite the tension LMS administrators saw between honoring an individual like Nipsey Hussle and a "proper" role model for the Latino students in the program, many of the students felt personally inspired by Nipsey Hussle's work as an artist and as a community activist. Mr. Javier, who was against the anti-Black ideology he felt was evident in a rejection of Nipsey Hussle, tried to encourage his students to discuss this issue. During this time, for example, in his conversations on Nipsey Hussle with his students, Mr. Javier raised the issues of respectability and anti-Blackness directly, and he asked the students what they thought about these debates surrounding how, or if, the rapper should be honored. Many of the students, likely encouraged by Mr. Javier, openly embraced the rapper's values and work. As one student noted, "That's interesting that people don't want us to look up to him, but he's the one out there doing work for people and not forgetting where he comes from . . . not judging people." Another student suggested that "honoring his legacy is a good way to unite." Through this critical and emotion-filled dialogue, the boys were able to mourn the loss of Nipsey Hussle and appreciate the shared struggle that made them feel so connected to his image and music. The conversation also highlighted how some students in a program for Latino boys confront the kinds of anti-Black ideologies that neoliberal logics can push on them as they seek to get ahead in life, and in the process helped to build a larger awareness of whose deaths matter and are worth mourning (see Cacho 2007).

Black Male President as Role Model

Although Nipsey Hussle was not the type of Black male role model approved of by LMS administration, there was one individual who was held in very high esteem by the administrators: former president Barack Obama. There is nothing surprising about Obama being held up as an important role model for students. However, within the broader context of LMS's respectability politics and approaches to constructing an ideal Latino male role model, it is a comparison that also clarifies how the program integrated a broader vision of racial respectability politics into youth empowerment. Just a month prior to Nipsey Hussle's death, Mr. Javier was notified that LMS had been invited to send several students and mentors to attend the MBK Rising! convening in Oakland, California. Although Mr. Javier would not be attending, he was asked to select one of his students to join the LMS representatives. This selection would be particularly sought-after, because former president Obama would be in attendance and give a speech. The figure of the former president, arguably now one of the most iconic men of color in history, serves as a central image of MBK itself, holding up the nation's first Black president as the ultimate role model for boys of color. This is an image the president has gladly accepted, using his own example, however unique, to counsel large crowds of wide-eyed boys of color, elated to meet the president. Images of the president sharing his story with boys of color have been widely publicized on MBK websites and flyers, reminding the community of the power of positive role models.

On the day Mr. Javier announced the event to the class, a cheer of excitement swept through the students as the former president's name was mentioned. Years earlier, an LMS student had had the opportunity to meet President Obama shortly after LMS had entered the MBK network. It had been a tremendous moment for the program, and the story of this student was frequently told and retold in classrooms, around the office, and particularly during fundraising events. Although the room buzzed with excitement, Mr. Javier approached the front of the classroom ready to lead a critical discussion on the topic. "Before we get too excited, I just want us to think about what it means to meet Obama," he shared. "To be honest, if it was me, I couldn't bring myself to shake his hand." This caused a murmur of discussion. Mr. Javier enjoyed starting critical conversation by abruptly asserting a counter-perspective (in this case, the notion that meeting the former president was not simply an honor one should unquestionably accept).

"To begin with, I want to be clear that I wouldn't shake his hand not because he's a Black president. Are we clear on that? And if you hear anyone criticizing him just because he is a Black man, you know that's not what we are about in here," he added. Anthony raised his hand and asked, "Is it because he supports deportations?" "That's part of it," replied Mr. Javier. This began a critical conversation on the Obama presidency—an era marked by an abysmal number of deportations, drone strikes, and a brutal crackdown on Central American minors making their way to the United States. This led to a deeper discussion of the racial violence inflicted under and by the Obama administration. For many of the boys, Obama's victory in the 2008 election was the earliest presidential election they could remember. The eight years following 2008, however, had not been years of racial harmony in North Arroyo Seco. At the discussion's end, Mr. Javier finally announced that Celso would be the representative of the group. Celso was a small-framed eighth grader who had modest grades and was well liked by the group. Though he was among the smallest students in the classroom, he had a large presence. The class nodded in approval of his selection.

It is worth underscoring the immense representational power of having a Black man as president for communities of color and especially for Black folks. However, few things are more emblematic of the neoliberal multicultural era than having a Black man as president of the United States. The Obama presidency laid bare the ways the United States, a multicultural country, can still reproduce a white-supremacist racial order—through imperialist bombings, mass deportations, and maintaining the racial capitalist world system—with a liberal Black man as head of state. However, beyond the continued racial policies enacted by President Obama, scholars also note the ways his presidency marketed a rejuvenation of racial respectability politics. This was in part due to Obama's general silence on issues of structural racism and systematic poverty. When Obama did make moves to address racial inequality, this focus entailed transforming individuals rather than transforming communities and was littered in neoliberal vocabulary like *opportunity* and the reiterated promise that his solutions would not be government handouts (Harris 2013). This made the use of Obama as a model role model for LMS particularly well suited to the program. However, the same logic upholding Obama similarly positions an individual like Nipsey Hussle—who does not signal racial respectability—as a problematic role model. In this narrative, young men of color who do not disavow street culture (and the imagined social vices associated with it) are marked as embodying a problematic social (racial) designation, no matter the politics and values behind their lives.

I watched a live stream of MBK Rising! from my apartment. The star-studded event featured such names as Steph Curry, John Legend, and Michael B. Jordan. I noted new and progressive shifts made by the organizers of the event that have not always been a part of MBK programming. For example, Corrina Gould, a tribal spokesperson for the Confederated Villages of Lisjan, welcomed the attendees as visitors to the unceded Ohlone territory of Huchiun (Oakland, California). There was also a panel titled "Our Sisters' Keeper: The MBK Responsibility to Sister and the LGBTQ+ Community," which delved beyond surface-level conversations of toxic masculinity and into issues of transphobia, patriarchy, and heteronormativity.[6] However, despite these progressive shifts in programming, the former president's town hall continued to echo its themes of individual responsibility, drawing criticism (Purnell 2019). While the former president did acknowledge systemic racial issues, many critics condemned his "scolding" of boys of color for their imagined poor choices and insecurities (Purnell 2019). Obama, who introduced himself as "Michelle's husband," reminded the attendees, "If you are really confident about your financial situation . . . you are probably not going to be wearing an eight-pound chain around your neck." He also cautioned boys against partaking in frivolous and hypersexual behavior. "If you are very confident about your sexuality, you don't have to have eight women around you twerking," he told them, "Why are you all like, I mean, you seem stressed acting that way. Because I got one woman who I'm very happy with. And she is a strong woman." This final comment reiterated racial scripts of communities of color living in sexual excess. Obama offers his family's "good example" of heteronormativity as part of the racial respectability needed by boys of color.

Despite Obama's finger-wagging, his charisma and banter with the moderator, basketball superstar Steph Curry, resulted in a lively, crowd-pleasing town hall. The week after MBK Rising!, I caught up with Celso and asked about the event. He shrugged, "It was okay." He elaborated that "it was an honor to go . . . but it was kind of boring." He lamented not getting to meet Steph Curry. During Celso's report back to the class, he reiterated his disappointment in the long event, which had a lot of talking that was boring and uninteresting to him and the other LMS boys who attended. After fielding a few questions from his classmates, mostly about if he had met anyone famous, the class moved on from the topic and the MBK Rising! event never came back into discussion for the rest of the year. Both Mr. Javier's and Celso's critical and lackluster take on Obama serves as a counternarrative to the dominant ways in which mentoring programs for boys of color are meant to approach the figure of the former president, who is often held up as the ultimate man-of-color role model in the land. Instead of upholding the figure of the former president as inspiring, motivating, and trailblazing, though, Mr. Javier's and Celso's disinterest and criticisms of the former president reframes the figure of Obama as a hegemonic role model that should be questioned and challenged.

Juxtaposing the figures of President Obama and Nipsey Hussle helps illuminate the way neoliberal logics influence the way non-Black Latino boys might honor and relate to Black male role models. While many students at LMS understood Nipsey Hussle to be a source of relatability and inspiration, many other people in the organization, as well as in the larger public, condemned Nipsey Hussle as a generally negative influence. However, the way the fallen rapper was seen as a negative role model also reveals that despite his popularity and political engagement, it is his association with street life and urban Blackness that made his image deplorable. Mr. Javier's refusal to let his death go unacknowledged and unmourned helped to disrupt the notion that Black men's lives are only of value when embodying a dominant and respectable image of manhood.[7]

On the other hand, unlike Nipsey Hussle, the former president is positioned as a hegemonic role model for boys of color—highlighted by his respectability as a leader and traditional family man. This is not to say that Obama's ascendency to the presidency was not marred with anti-Black criticism and hate for him and his family. However, by holding Obama up as the ultimate positive role model, LMS and other programs aimed at boys of color are also upholding neoliberal multicultural values that depart from (and challenge) other approaches to fighting systemic racism, including those found in the Black radical tradition (Kelley 2003). Their juxtaposition highlights that just because a program or curriculum celebrates (some) Black figures as role models, it does not mean an anti-Black imaginary does not permeate the goals and mission. "It has to do with what brand of racial justice someone is about," Mr. Javier shared with me. "That's why one exception is Obama. Pueblo Unido doesn't mind shouting out Obama one bit."

COLLABORATION AND COMPETITION WITH
BLACK MALE PROGRAMS

In the United States, Black and Latinx communities have, both historically and in the present era, faced state-sanctioned violence, racial terror, and death. In schools, racially charged education policies continue to marginalize Black and Latinx students. This includes the hyperpolicing of Black and Latinx bodies in schools (Nolan 2011; Rios 2017), inequitable school funding (Alemán, Bahena, and Alemán 2019;

Grooms 2019; Kozol 2012), and disproportionate school closures in Black and Latinx communities (Lipman 2011; Stovall 2016; Tieken and Auldridge-Reveles 2019). The experiences of Black and Latino boys are so similar that educational researchers and policy habitually use the category *boys of color* to describe both groups. This is the case with the MBK initiative, which uses the term *boys of color* to describe its work with Black and Latino boys and young men. However, despite facing similar and often interconnected oppression, Black and Latinx communities have not always collaboratively resisted racist educational policy and practice.

For example, in the 1940s and 1950s, Mexican American activists sought to desegregate California and Texas schools, a battle that Thurgood Marshall vehemently supported. However, Mexican litigants undermined Black activists' demands for an end to school segregation by making claims to white citizenship as a means for Mexican children to access white schools (Foley 2017).[8] Today, scholars have documented the ways a lack of resources to support the needs of Black and Latinx students frequently sparks tension and competition, prevents coalition, and leads both groups to feel their needs are being forgotten (Sampson, Demps, and Rodriguez-Martinez 2020). Similarly, an influx of Latinx students to formerly majority-Black districts has led to tension over who has the right to govern Black and Brown schools and allocate the (insufficient) resources available to them (Straus 2009). This sense of competition has become exacerbated by neoliberal policies that stress competition, measurable gains, and notions of deservingness (Lipman 2011; Sampson, Demps, and Rodriguez-Martinez 2020).

From the outside, LMS expressed clear and unwavering solidarity with the Black community and the plight of Black men and boys in particular. Shortly before LMS was established in 2010, ASUSD created a similar school-day mentorship program for African American boys called Black Males Rising (BMR). LMS and BMR were both affiliated with the MBK network, and they were often mentioned in the same breath in Arroyo Seco. Furthermore, district and program leaders frequently praised each other's inspiring work in local newspaper articles and at fundraisers. However, despite their outward support for each other, I found that a subtle yet undeniable sense of competition existed between the two programs. This was powered not only by the clear dislike that some individual mentors had toward BMR but also by a conspicuous absence of collaboration over the years between the two programs. This friction between those seeking to empower Latino boys at LMS and those seeking to empower Black boys at BMR, however, is an expected consequence of the neoliberal shift in urban education, which forces youth programs to market themselves as deserving and compete with one another for the attention of private philanthropic dollars. This strained relationship between LMS and BMR is a devastating consequence of neoliberalism and points to an urgent need for educators to cultivate and grow solidarity between Black and Latinx educational programs.

Competition and Resentment

Despite the importance of collective efforts to address systemic racism and anti-Blackness in educational contexts, LMS mentors rarely collaborated with Black male spaces, even though nearly all LMS schools had sizable African American student populations. This was even more surprising because BMR operated in six of LMS's ten school sites. Although LMS and BMR coexisted in the schools, and on one campus even shared a classroom, the programs remained distant and at times noticeably ambivalent toward one another. Although I spoke with several BMR students and educators during this study, including a formal interview with a BMR mentor, this section does not attempt to describe or generalize the perspectives of BMR or of individuals affiliated with the program. Instead, I limit my analysis to the ways in which LMS mentors made sense of their proximity to BMR and how they viewed their relationship as Latino male mentors to efforts to empower Black men and boys.

I asked all LMS mentors about their program's relationship to BMR, if their school had a BMR class, and if so, what their connection was to the BMR group. I found that for some LMS mentors there was a clear sense of competition and resentment toward BMR. This resentment stemmed from feeling that LMS was in the shadow of BMR in Arroyo Seco. Even the diplomatic Gerald Espinoza, the CEO of Pueblo Unido, had sourly pointed out to me that one local tech giant had chosen to fund BMR but not LMS. Several mentors pointed to BMR's large media attention and big-name funders and explained that they felt African American issues were prioritized over Latinx needs. One high school mentor described a number of notable disagreements he had with the BMR mentor with whom he shared a classroom. He said they had originally talked of collaborating, but in his five years, plans had stalled because of disagreements. "We see eye to eye on how the school treats us poorly," he said, "but for me, things are always put as a Black and white issue, so they [BMR] get more attention and they get more funding. Latinos are always then second-, and well, in this case third- or fourth-class, depending on how you want to see it."

I asked for clarification. Did he feel this was due to favoritism in the district? Or was this in reference to local media? Or the larger national discourse on boys of color? He elaborated:

> It's more political, like I said it's always been a white and Black
> thing. I think there's been an equal amount of oppression among
> Black and Indigenous people, our gente [people] . . . Asians . . .
> equally harsh, but it always becomes a Black and white thing. We
> were talking about *The People v. O. J. Simpson* [the TV show chroni-
> cling the trial of O. J. Simpson] and how Johnny Cochran used the
> race card, and I was like. . . . Sometimes I feel like people use their
> own oppression to still perpetuate . . . like . . . it's always a race
> thing, saying, "We deserve these, these, this, and this."

This mentor's feelings of competition between Latinx and Black communities, however, also went beyond just a sense of unfair distribution of resources within the school-based programs and revealed how this tension pushed him to express broader generalizations and criticism of Black people as a group:

> For them [Black people], I feel like they always use that race card, as
> a way of saying, "We've always been oppressed, we've always been
> oppressed"—but do something about it man, stop perpetuating that
> cycle of violence and poverty. Get educated, kind of like, be hon-
> est with what's going on, awaken these people to be more aware to
> know what's happening to their gente, and how the system works.

While this mentor's perspective was not the perspective of most LMS mentors, multiple mentors also used anti-Black language to describe why they felt resentful of or competitive with BMR.[9] This language echoed anti-Black stereotypes, such as associating Black culture with drug use and welfare dependency. This line of thought also questioned if Black school-based organizations *deserved* more resources. Others criticized the specificity of the phrase Black Lives Matter and complained about receiving pushback if they asserted that Brown or Latino lives matter as well.[10]

The prejudice evident in these comments is directly tied to the kinds of racial hierarchies and anti-Black racism that have long been used in the United States to assert social power. Furthermore, I believe the incorporation of neoliberal ideologies that encourage students and mentors to "buck up" and take control of their lives, even as they face immense racial and social marginalization, also encouraged competition among racial groups. In addition to the aforementioned mentor, other mentors also spoke about BMR in ways that highlighted how anti-Blackness was present in the Latino empowerment discourse— promoting competition and questioning merit. One mentor, in our formal interview session, explicitly described how the tension he felt with the BMR mentor at his school site, as well as other Black staff and educators, was related to larger racial biases on campus and a culture of what he describes as "protecting your own."

"I didn't become more racist until I actually got to this school," he told me. "I'm telling you I wasn't, I wasn't. But being around this school opened my eyes to a lot more things that I never would have thought." When I asked him to elaborate, he explained:

> It's just . . . like the racists; the racism—I tell you, I grew up in Baker Square [a predominantly Black neighborhood in Arroyo Seco]. I kicked it with my cousins in a tagging crew and we hung around with the Black dudes because our beef, which was stupid, right, was with other Latinos. And that was always my mentality [non-racially specific social groups] . . . until I got here. And I'm like, "Fuck, I see it all over the place." You see it from admin to teachers. Yes. I mean if you're—if you're Black you're going to take care of your own kind, that's common sense. And there's no Latinos, so there's nobody to take care of a Latino.

This mentor states that, from his perspective, a culture of racial bias and favoritism existed in his school, and that this is a game he chooses to play himself. He continued, "When I got here, you got this program, you got this program; you're segregated. Fuck it, if it's that way, then let it be. It is what it is." These comments, however, were part of a broader pattern of behavior and comments by several LMS mentors that revealed strong feelings of resentment toward BMR. However, this research did not seek to explore the division of Black and Latinx educators or to determine if favoritism and biases existed. These kinds of divisions within educational or community empowerment programs are often a result of scarce resources and neglecting the role of white supremacy in conflicts between communities of color. However, it was extremely concerning to see the way a small number of mentors openly expressed animosity and competition toward Black male programming. This animosity revealed a lack of awareness of the white-supremacist roots of racism in the United States, and instead focused on differences and competition with Black educational efforts. Often expressed using anti-Black rhetoric, these sentiments hindered cross-racial collaboration.

Despite these examples of animosity and competition toward BMR, I found most LMS mentors sought to diplomatically avoid using the same language of competition and generally tried to stay out of the tension, even though they recognized its presence. One middle school mentor, Mr. Samuel, shared with me that he would like to collaborate with BMR, but in his three years at his school site he lacked a strong relationship with the BMR mentor, whose classroom was on the other end of campus. I asked Mr. Samuel if he felt tension between the two programs. "Ah, so you have noticed too?" he joked with me. He continued, suggesting this tension was the result of a lack of concerted focus on collaboration:

> It's a little like an elephant in the room. Why don't we ever work with one another if we do such similar work? I think, you know, time goes by, you haven't worked together, more times goes by, and then it feels kind of awkward. . . . And I know some mentors maybe feel, some type of way, because they get a lot of attention . . . but for me, I am always open to it, open to working with them. We just need an opportunity.

And yet, despite the presence of tension, there were still some notable efforts to push back against competition. Mr. Javier, for example, was one of the mentors pushing for an approach of solidarity and collaboration, rather than competition and bias.

Love and Solidarity

On a Friday afternoon, Mr. Javier and I loaded popcorn bags into the class microwave, filling the classroom with a buttery aroma. As the 2:30 bell rang, students slowly began rolling into class. Today, Mr. Jalen's Black boy advisory group would be joining us in a joint class on Black-Brown solidarity. Mr. Jalen was a tall Black man in his mid-forties who was popular with many of the students. Unlike most advisory leaders, he was not a classroom teacher, but one of the vice principals at the school. Because there were no Black male teachers on campus, he had agreed to take on an advisory course for Black boys. His advisory course was unaffiliated with BMR, which did not have a program at the middle school. Today's joint meeting had been something Mr. Jalen and Mr. Javier had wanted to do for some time. Both men found it important to underscore that the joint session was not in response to any one event or to address an incident between their groups. Often, educators will use these kinds of solidarity-type events to "heal" divisions after a particular incident. However, there had been no damaging tension or racially charged fights at this school all year. Instead, Mr. Javier and Mr. Jalen had long talked about doing a joint session focused on "love and solidarity" that would bring together both Black and Latino boy advisory groups. Today it finally came to fruition.

As the class began, any initial awkwardness of having boys from separate, racially specific advisory groups quickly gave way to handshakes, laughter, and gossip as friends began to find one another. The boys mingled and ate popcorn as giggling and good-hearted horseplay could be seen around the room. After about ten minutes of settling in, Mr. Jalen and Mr. Javier opened the joint class by underscoring the importance of building solidarity and community among Black and Latino young men in Arroyo Seco. The phrases "common struggle" and "Black and Brown unity" were repeated several times. Mr. Javier shared a brief PowerPoint presentation that highlighted moments of unity. This included a history of the Underground Railroad running south to Mexico, slave revolts in Latin America and their collaboration with Indigenous people, as well as more recent events, such as solidarity in the Chicano and Black Power Movements and contemporary coalitions in the battle against police terror. "Today, we are a part of this legacy," Mr. Javier reminded the students. "It makes me really proud to see all you young men coming together like this," said Mr. Jalen from across the room. The energy of the room was warm and powerful. Many boys shook their heads up and down vigorously at the inspiring words of their mentors, relishing the ability to see and be seen by one another. "It makes me happy to have all of us coming together," shared one student from Mr. Jalen's class, "because there's a lot of racism in the world and it is good to be united with one another." As the students left at the end of the period, Mr. Jalen, Mr. Javier, and I cleaned up and talked about the joint class. We all agreed today's event had been a big success. This event had been a long time coming, and both mentors reiterated the need for more events like it. It just made sense to work together.

Although Mr. Javier made solidarity with Black freedom an intentional part of his work, the collaborative class with Mr. Jalen's group seemed to strengthen and clarify the importance of solidarity. Later in the year, Mr. Javier's class watched the film *Fruitvale Station*, which follows the life of Oscar Grant, a young Black man murdered by police in Oakland, California. Following the film, the boys discussed the ways policing and police terror affected their own lives. This included encounters with the local Arroyo Seco Police Department, police officers in Mexico and El Salvador, and ICE agents in the United States. Although the boys reflected on their own racialized experiences with police, the class also made connections to the uniqueness of anti-Black racism in the film. One student mentioned "stereotypes about Black men" that led to Oscar Grant's murder and the need to support one another. While the boys were able to use the film to reflect on their own experiences with racialized policing, this interaction with the film did not erase the specificity of anti-Black violence. This moment begins to illustrate what Roseann Liu and Savannah Shange (2018) refer to as *thick solidarity*, in which empathy is mobilized "in ways that do not gloss over difference" (190; also see Malone, McAlister, and Perez 2023). I believe having the joint Black-Brown unity class earlier in the year helped students see their struggle as connected to but also distinct from African Americans'—requiring allyship and solidarity with one another.

CONCLUSION

Although they were largely the exception, some mentors at LMS intentionally sought out ways to engage with anti-Blackness through their classroom lessons. For example, Mr. Javier led discussions and workshops on Black culture, history, and revolutionary figures, and he frequently emphasized the overlapping struggles of Black and Latinx people in Arroyo Seco. He was also intentional about naming anti-Blackness as both a founding pillar of U.S. racism and a toxic sentiment often held in the Latinx community. One day, I asked Mr. Javier to elaborate on his approach to engaging anti-Blackness while mentoring non-Black Latino boys.

"I don't think it's a secret that some of our students probably come from homes with very . . . with negative views about Black people," he shared. "You have to be intentional about talking about that . . . you can't pretend that doesn't exist." Despite seeing anti-Blackness as a deeply entrenched sentiment commonly held in the Latinx community, Mr. Javier remained optimistic about the bond and solidarity between Black and Latinx people in Arroyo Seco. "Sometimes you have to do that work . . . [and] acknowledge differences . . . in order to grow. We come from the same blocks, live in the same neighborhoods; our liberation is interconnected."

This look into LMS's distant and at times contentious relationship to BMR, as well as Blackness at large, underscores the need for active solidarity building among programs for Black and Latino boys. History tells us that Black and Latinx communities have built anti-racist alliances with one another that challenge institutional and social repression (G. T. Johnson 2013; Kun and Pulido 2013; J. D. Márquez 2014). However, multiracial solidarity is not easy. While I did encounter individuals who expressed anti-Black sentiments, I want to underscore that during my time with LMS, it was the larger ideological context, rather than individual actions, that were my area of concern. It is also true for issues of anti-Blackness.

Due to its blatant use of neoliberal and corporate ideologies, the goals and curriculum of LMS encouraged its students and mentors to embrace a politics of racial empowerment that emphasized respectability, individual responsibility, and personal gain. By pushing these values on a racialized population designated as "at risk" and likely deviant, this kind of "character building" educational support program pushed the boys to embrace the archetypes of the good racial subject that, at the very least, I argue, had some of its foundation in technologies of anti-Blackness. While the notion of Latinidad itself can be charged for its anti-Black (and anti-Indigenous) undertones, efforts to empower non-Black Latino boys in an urban school district intersect with the United States' long-standing racial violence against Black people, particularly in schools. As policymakers and practitioners continue to work to support Latino men and boys in school, notions of anti-Blackness must not just be acknowledged, but confronted. First, because, of course, many Latino boys *are* Black. Latinx educational spaces must also be spaces of Black empowerment and joy. But second, as this book has contended, Latino male empowerment exists within the contradictory landscape of neoliberal multiculturalism. As this chapter maintains, anti-Black notions of goodness can contribute to how a positive Latino manhood is imagined and constructed in schools. Identifying and shedding light on the problematic discourses of empowerment that seek to shape the good multicultural subject begs the question, then what? What politics should inform our vision of justice for Latino boys? In the conclusion that follows, I describe changes being made to LMS and ask what an abolitionist politics might look like for educational programs working with boys and young men of color.

TOWARD AN ABOLITIONIST APPROACH TO SUPPORTING LATINO MEN AND BOYS

Latino Male Success was a place of love and support. After two years of conducting research with the program, this was indisputable to me. Despite my strong critiques of many of the practices and the framing of the program itself, the everyday joys of being among a caring familia of men and boys felt like a positive thing in the lives of the students, and in all our lives. Students and mentors built lasting relationships with one another. These relationships frequently extended long past the individual school year and allowed students to confidently feel that they had at least one adult on campus truly committed to their well-being.

However, in the larger struggle to end the subjugation and violence experienced by Latino men and boys in schools, it was clear that the program could not do all that it boasted. Advertisements and fundraising literature painted an impossible story. At best, I found the program to be what Mr. Javier once described as a "Band-Aid" solution. The program could make small interventions for a select few students, but it was by no means a fix to the root causes of inequality. At worse, the program was an ideologically charged space that brought a deficit-based perspective to boys and sought to induct them into a world of respectability, individual accountability, and patriarchal norms. These ideologies have come to dominate the national discourse on how to improve the academic achievement of boys and young men of color in schools (Dumas 2016a). Mentors and students were left to navigate these ideologies in LMS, making what they could out of this imperfect, and even problematic, offering. As I have described in this book, the discourses of love and discipline intermingle when it comes to working with boys and young men of color in schools, and this was surely the case in LMS. The contradiction was evident. Students were cared for and supported while also being disciplined and managed to become a very specific image of an upstanding Latino man. However, despite the larger intentions of the program, criticality and subversion manifested, both organically and intentionally, as some students and mentors questioned the politics of LMS and searched for something different. These moments condemned fluffy, superficial images of Latino male empowerment and sought to articulate a more radical politics of liberation. In this section I ruminate on what these radical politics might look like for a program like LMS, and what an abolitionist politics could mean for the larger conversation on boys and young men of color. In this worldview, Latino boys, and all marginalized students, are not taught simply to survive and (potentially) succeed in the current system, but to imagine educational justice beyond the oppressive structures of today.

IN SEARCH OF NEW NARRATIVES

On March 29, 2021, less than two years after I concluded my work with LMS, Adam Toledo, a thirteen-year-old Latino boy, was shot and killed by Chicago police officer Eric Stillman in the Little Village neighborhood on the West Side of Chicago. News of the killing made national headlines. Adam's death came in what feels like a never-ending list of names of boys and men of color who are murdered by the police. I checked in with a few of the LMS mentors via text. We were all emotional and upset. Some posted heartfelt responses to the incident on their social media accounts. Others expressed anger and rage. However, most of all, the mentors, like perhaps many educators and youth workers, shared feelings of fear and terror. They grieved for a child who reminded them so much of their own students. The names of individual students, past and present, immediately came to mind: "This easily could have been him."

From California, we watched as the predominantly Mexican neighborhood of Little Village mourned its loss. Mexican flags littered the several marches that followed the incident, as the community demanded accountability and answers. During the funeral, mariachis serenaded Adam's mother and grandfather as the community mourned the death of another son. Months later, Chicago's National Museum of Mexican Art built an ofrenda (altar) for Adam in its annual Día de los Muertos celebration. Adam's ofrenda was constructed by his mother, Elizabeth Toledo, and his art teacher. It included joyful photos of a smiling Adam as well as some of his favorite things: Chicago Cubs gear, sneakers, a soccer ball, a bag of Cheetos, Legos: the cherished possessions of a middle schooler (Savedra 2021).

In the wake of Adam's death, however, debate emerged as to how his life and death should be understood and remembered. What narrative should we tell? As expected, racist, right-wing media began attempting to assassinate Adam's character, as has happened countless times, to justify the unjustifiable. *He should have done this. He did not do that. He was a threat. He was dangerous. He might have been in a gang.* These racist justifications for the death of an unarmed Latino boy were to be expected. However, also emerging in the aftermath of the shooting was a liberal, deficit-based narrative to understand the life and death of a child in the barrio. *He was a boy we were unable to save from the neighborhood. Shame on us for not saving him,* the storyline went. This narrative paints communities of color as inherently violent places that swallow up their own. It is up to white saviors, and perhaps even respectable multicultural role models, to intervene in these (decontextualized) lives and save troubled boys from falling into the "street life" like so many others. One source of this narrative was national education leader Arne Duncan. Duncan, who served as secretary of education under President Obama (2009–16), was a champion of neoliberal school reform. Before that he had been CEO of Chicago Public Schools. On April 16, 2021, the morning after the video of Adam's murder was released, Duncan tweeted:

> With all children like Adam Toledo who might be struggling, it's up to all of us to mentor them, to guide and nurture them.
> When we don't, the streets will. Every child is looking for their village, their community.
> We decide what they will find. We failed, and the streets won.

An explosion of angry responses began to circulate. Educators and community members alike called out the problematic and racist tweet of a white, liberal leader who had made a grand career as a champion of educational diversity. The tweet echoed news coverage that depicted Adam as a lost youth, failed by his community, whose actions led to an expected outcome.

Amid grief and mourning, the Toledo family was compelled to issue a statement. "We do, however, want to correct the hurtful and false mischaracterization of Adam as a lonely child of the street who had no one to turn to," the family's lawyers shared. The statement continued:

> This is simply not true. Adam was a loved and supported 13-year-old boy. He lived with his mother, his 90-year-old grandfather, and two of his siblings. His father was in his life. They all loved him very much. The Toledo family is a close-knit family. They look after each other. Adam attended Gary Elementary School where he had the support of his teachers and his classmates. Adam was not alone. (Dudek 2021)

The Toledo family's message pushed back against a discourse so common in understanding the loss of Latino boys. This was the same discourse I had heard over and over again to describe the need for programs like LMS. In these storylines, Latino boys are lonely and lost. They are without father figures and male role models. And they are highly susceptible to gravitating to violence and gangs—things widely associated with Latino men and boys. In response, the Toledo family asserted that Adam came from a loving household and community. This statement recognizes the importance of narrative. There is a politics behind making sense of and interpreting this loss. This tragedy was not the doing of Adam, his family, or his community. This had to be made clear.

Refusing deficit-based narratives assigned to young people and their communities means pushing back on the idea that there is something wrong and broken in them. However, this refusal does not deny that culpability and blame exist. It simply means the deficit has been placed in the wrong area (Baldridge 2014). Despite all the debate and reflection on the story of Adam Toledo, it was a police officer's bullet that killed him. This occurred in a country that spends an obscene amount of resources on systems of policing and punishment. This apparatus of control disproportionately targets, punishes, incarcerates, and kills boys and men of color compared to the white population (Gilmore 2007; Rios 2011). This is the same, and at times worse, for women and gender-nonbinary people of color (Morris 2016; Ritchie and Davis 2017). This illogical tendency to focus on and blame individuals for the violence of institutions carrying out their expected functions reveals the great need for an abolitionist approach to supporting boys and young men of color.

ABOLITIONIST APPROACHES TO EDUCATION

The uptake of the notion of abolition emerged in the 1990s to articulate the politics of a growing movement to end the prison-industrial complex (PIC). Taking its name from the long struggle to abolish slavery, this new abolitionist movement finds prisons and policing as an extension of the racist and anti-Black foundations on which the United States was founded. Similar to slavery, the abolitionist movement finds absolutely nothing redeemable or positive about prisons and policing in the United States, and no amount of reform will ever be satisfactory. These institutions are violent, racist, and anti-Black at their core.

While this movement seeks to defund, diminish, and eventually abolish police and prisons, an abolitionist politics extends far beyond simply tearing down oppressive structures. Instead, abolition is about creation; it is about what comes after these institutions are gone. It is about shifting the resources of our society and building a lasting alternative to our current state (see Kaba 2021; Purnell 2021). The PIC both reproduces and maintains inequalities through punishing, hurting, and controlling millions of people. However, it is not an isolated system. Abolition requires rethinking the intersecting forms in which oppression occurs. It extends beyond how a society prioritizes policing and prisons, and into the ways in which we deprioritize healthcare, food, housing, and education. The organization Critical Resistance (2021) states, "An abolitionist vision means that we must build models today that can represent how we want to live in the future. It means developing practical strategies for taking small steps that move us toward making our dreams real and that lead us all to believe that things really could be different."

In recent years, radical educators have embraced the abolitionist perspective to help better understand the role of schooling in a carceral society (Meiners 2011). Indeed, the field of critical education has long pointed to the ways education is deeply embedded in the reproduction of hegemonic power. Abolitionist educator David Stovall (2018) reminds us that in its familiar form, the "ideological and material formation" (52) of traditional schooling has never been connected to any project of liberation in U.S. history. Instead, with relentless fervor, schooling has reproduced the racial hierarchies in which this country was founded. Schools have not just served as pipelines to prisons for young people; they have also functioned as sites of containment themselves (Sojoyner 2016). Taking his cue from prison abolition activism, Stovall asks if, like prisons, there is anything redeemable about schooling in its current form. Why do we still cling to hope that schools will bring about change, when in fact they have taken on a powerful role in keeping things the same? Schooling has always been a culturally and physically violent process for Black, Indigenous, and other people of color in the United States (Dumas 2014; Givens 2021; Marquez 2021; Valenzuela 1999). Is not believing in schools illogical and misguided? Years of reform have changed very little about its systemic outcomes. And today's reforms, led by wealthy philanthropists and increasingly privatized entities, show little sign of making meaningful change (Apple 2006; Lipman 2011). While continuing to support our students in schools today, we must acknowledge that liberatory education will never be the centerpiece of U.S. schooling in its current form. And our organizing and pedagogical strategies must begin to open doors to what comes after schools, as we know them today.

In her book *We Want to Do More Than Survive: Abolitionist Teaching and the Pursuit of Educational Freedom*, Bettina Love (2019) challenges the long-standing belief that educational success for students of color should simply be about enduring racial inequality and trauma. For Love, the current goals of schooling, even those that seek to address inequality, are bent on simply surviving and maintaining traditional forms of schooling. This is expressed in testing company gimmicks that promise higher scores and multinational corporations building "innovative" charter schools. It is programs like Teach for America, which recruit idealistic young college grads to "spend two years in an inner city or rural school with poor and/or dark children and help them survive" (10).

Instead, Love argues that abolitionist education is not about finding ways to have students simply survive schooling, but to help them imagine a just world far beyond the current reality. It requires us to acknowledge that no amount of reform can bring about justice:

> Abolitionist teaching is not a teaching approach: It is a way of life, a way of seeing the world, and a way of taking action against injustice. It seeks to resist, agitate, and tear down the educational survival complex through teachers who work in solidarity with their schools' community to achieve incremental changes in their classrooms and schools for students in the present day, while simultaneously free-

dom dreaming and vigorously creating a vision for what schools will be when the educational survival complex is destroyed. (2019, 89)

As this book has demonstrated, the work of LMS, as a case study of just one of the many programs supporting boys and young men of color, is bent on survival and individual success. It seeks to create extraordinary stories in places of systematic gloom. Mentorship programs for boys and young men of color are often key pieces of Love's notion of the educational survival complex.

COUNTERNARRATIVES THAT DESERVE TO BE WRITTEN

Good Boys, Bad Hombres offers the story of LMS as an up-close look at one school-based mentorship program for Latino boys that emerged among a wave of educational initiatives seeking to improve the life chances and academic outcomes of boys and young men of color in the United States. In chapter 1, I described this wave as part of a larger nonprofit industrial complex (NPIC), which emerged alongside the PIC, to manage and condition problematic populations. The notion of abolition requires us to follow justice-focused scholars, educators, and activists in interrogating the "the rightist ideological foundations of racial-uplift social policies," such as My Brother's Keeper, and "raise critical questions about how the framing of the 'problem' legitimizes interventions that neither disrupt the White supremacist racial hegemony, nor threaten the capitalist economic order" (Dumas 2016a, 108).

As the book has maintained, programs supporting boys and young men of color, like LMS, are often explicitly tailored to help boys navigate and survive schooling in its current form. These programs are less about changing schools and more about changing individual boys into upstanding students and young men. In these programs, male educators of color are framed as the superhero-like saviors of boys of color—creating unreal and unfair expectations for them in the classroom. In chapter 3, I offered the notion of the *positive Latino male role model* to describe the ways neoliberal discourses of respectability and heteropatriarchy work to construct how an ideal role model is imagined and performed. It has also shifted the goals and day-to-day operations of these programs to be less about critical lessons and more about teaching students to adopt values that will help them succeed. This is part of a larger cultural shift that constructs neoliberal subjectivity as necessary and ideal in schools.

While the abolitionist project has no set blueprint, my time spent with LMS, learning from the mentors and students, sparked some ideas. In chapter 5, I synthesized seven justice-oriented principles for men of color working with boys of color:

1. Challenge deficit-based perspectives
2. Refuse the roles of hero and savior
3. Disrupt the heteropatriarchal imagination of male mentorship
4. Deconstruct (not reconstruct) manhood
5. Critically analyze how cultural relevancy is valued
6. Challenge anti-Black framings of multiculturalism
7. Teach and dream toward educational justice

These principles are meant to be helpful to men of color currently working in places that implicitly or explicitly position them as the fixers of problematic boys of color. In continuing with the seventh principle, I ask, What does an abolitionist future look like for those of us who work with boys and men of color? Do our abolitionist dreams include male empowerment programs? Or is this line of programming inherently reformist and problematic?

Over the years, I have met countless men of color working to support boys of color around the country. I have worked alongside these men, and I am always awed by the tireless passion these educators bring to their work. Their goal is always to help enact social justice. However, my research with LMS led me to question the very logic informing why we do this work in the first place. Contradictory and confining visions of Latino manhood and educational justice leave a deep impression on how these programs are framed, funded, and carried out. Despite these contradictions, during my time with LMS I also witnessed counternarratives—stories that challenged the deficit-oriented rationale undergirding the vision of the program. For example, there was Victor, the high school sophomore who saw through the problematic goals of LMS and challenged the idea that Latino boys need changing in the first place. There was also Mr. Agustín, a mentor who queered the image of the positive role model and challenged the heteropatriarchal ideals promoted in LMS. These counternarratives, among many others, reminded me that where there is power, there is always resistance. However, further still, these counternarratives made me question if programs like LMS are the best way to bring about educational justice. Are male-specific empowerment programs worth keeping?

Moments of resistance in my research gave me ideas on how to reform programs targeting boys and men of color, but they also made the case for abolishing them entirely. I am reminded of Kimberlé Crenshaw's critique of MBK—alleging its use of a *discourse of patriarchy enhancement* to justify its intervention (Crenshaw 2016). An abolitionist future surely includes the abolition of hegemonic masculinity. Heteropatriarchy, as a gender expression and organizing principle of society, is toxic and oppressive. Abolitionist visions of educational justice are queer and nonbinary, and they are anticapitalist and intersectional. They abandon deficit frameworks that fix individuals, and they turn toward goals of dismantling systems. Perhaps race-specific male mentorship programs, as we know them, should also be abandoned in our vision of educational justice.

Moving away from male-centered programming does not mean abandoning boys and young men of color. However, it does mean abandoning the neoliberal and heteropatriarchal ideals of manhood that seem to be stubbornly rooted in MBK and similar educational interventions. Instead, our educational abolitionist movement must take its cue from the prison abolition movement, which has long abandoned the narrative of *fixing and redeeming Black and Latino manhood*, for visions of prison abolition that imagine a world where all people, within their unique positionalities in society, get their needs met. This vision of abolition is queer, restorative, and intersectional. How might an abolitionist frame in youth work similarly abandon deficit-oriented and heteropatriarchal language? What would our articulations of justice look like? And how can young people lead these efforts?[1]

As programs for boys and young men of color continue to proliferate, *Good Boys, Bad Hombres* offers a loving critique of how these programs are framed and carried out. It also offers an array of counternarratives: stories of Latino men and boys who identified contradictions in LMS and sought to subvert these issues for an alternative vision of educational justice. As the conversation on boys of color evolves, there must be a conscious engagement with the ways race and racism also continue to change. Furthermore, as the missions of these programs are adapted, reformed, and perhaps abolished, it is important to contemplate what our vision of justice is and if "male empowerment" is a part of it. Are we able to address issues of patriarchy in these programs, or are programs targeting boys and men of color inherently patriarchal and deficit-oriented? And if they are, can we bring what we like about these programs to a new vision of education?

While writing this book, I remained in contact with many of the mentors of LMS, including Mr. Javier. Shortly after I finished my fieldwork in his classroom, he also left the program for a new job. He now works for ASUSD supporting students at Adams High School—the notoriously "bad" school LMS students sought to avoid. In our later conversations we discussed my critiques of LMS, his own critiques, and the growing abolitionist movement in education.

"So, after the revolution, is there a place for LMS?" I asked him.

"Nooo. I would hope not," he laughed. It was not that he saw everything about LMS as negative. He had seen plenty of good, and he had, for the most part, loved his work. But he believed students deserved educational justice, and LMS, in its practice and politics, was not justice.

"So, what would you take with you?" I asked. I wanted to know what, if anything, he found redeemable about LMS. Despite all his critiques, what were the things he thought were clearly positive?

"Oh, the love. Take that love," he responded immediately—thinking of the relationships between mentors and students. "There's so much love in places like LMS. We just need to find new ways to deliver it."

ACKNOWLEDGMENTS

I feel immense gratitude to so many people and communities who supported me during the research and writing of this book. This project began during my dissertation research while I was a graduate student at UC Berkeley. To my doctoral adviser, Zeus Leonardo, your guidance and feedback at all stages of this project were invaluable. I feel blessed to have enjoyed over ten years of your mentorship as well as your friendship. You continue to be such a positive force in my life. I am also immensely grateful to my committee members, Kris Gutiérrez, Juana María Rodríguez, and Michael Dumas. Kris, your methodological coaching pushed me to approach research with rigor and compassion. I hope to pass this on to my own students. Juana, working with you in the Designated Emphasis program in Women, Gender, and Sexuality pushed me to analyze gender and sexuality beyond the confines of my discipline. This intervention has been among the most impactful aspects of my work. Your guidance is so clearly reflected in this book. And Michael, having you arrive at Berkeley while I was in graduate school changed everything. Perhaps no one's research and ideas have been more impactful to this project than yours. Thank you.

Beyond my dissertation committee, so many Berkeley faculty contributed to my training and growth. In the Berkeley School of Education, Na'ilah Nasir, Travis Bristol, Tina Trujillo, Patricia Baquedano-López, and Dan Perlstein played important roles in my training as an educational researcher. I also want to thank the Department of Ethnic Studies at UC Berkeley for its profound impact on both my undergraduate and graduate studies. A special thank-you to Laura Pérez, Keith Feldman, Ramón Grosfoguel, Carlos Muñoz, Pablo Gonzalez, Laura Jimenez-Olvera, and Dewey St. Germaine.

Several scholarly communities at Cal were key in supporting me in my academic, social, and political life during my research for this book. The advisee group of Zeus Leonardo is my original academic community. To Jocyl Sacramento, Ell Lin, Blanca Gamez-Djokic, Gema Cardona, Joy Esboldt, Nicole Rangel, Patrick Johnson, Alice Taylor, and Mali Vafai, I am so grateful for the support and camaraderie felt among us Leonardians. And a special acknowledgment goes to our beloved Hoang Tran, who left this world too soon. Also at Berkeley, the Graduate Fellows Program at the Institute for the Study of Societal Issues provided me with valuable support and feedback during my final two years of dissertation research. I am grateful for the friendship and support of my cohort members, as well as the tireless support provided by the advisers, Christine Trost, Deborah Freedman Lustig, and David Minkus. You three have touched the lives of so many scholars, including mine. The student group Graduate Students de la Raza provided a space for friendships, ideas, and activism to flourish. I am especially grateful to my fellow co-chair, friend, and academic compañera since our first year as graduate students, René Espinoza Kissell, who has offered feedback at all stages of this project. I want to also acknowledge the Multicultural Community Center and the Chicanx Latinx Student Development office for being such homeplaces for me on the UC Berkeley campus. Beyond these groups and spaces, I am immensely grateful to have developed this project among a vibrant intellectual community of graduate students. Our countless discussions, debates, and fun were so impactful to my thinking. A special shout-out to Albert Orozco, Daniel Woo, Caleb Dawson, Rekia Jibrin, Vianney Gavilanes, David Turner, Joanne Tien, Mahasan Offutt-Chaney, Frankie Ramos, and Jesus Camacho. Some of these friendships have blossomed into writing support groups. A heartfelt appreciation goes to Juan Manuel Aldape Muñoz, Marcelo Garzo Montalvo, and the Ánimo writing collective for offering cheerful solidarity throughout the slow and tedious writing process and early years on the tenure track. And of course, a special thank-you to Edward Rivero, whose close friendship existed long before our return to graduate school. Your care and support as a friend and your invaluable feedback as a colleague have meant the world to me.

I am also eternally grateful to the Ronald E. McNair Scholars Program, whose support during my undergraduate years at UC Berkeley helped cultivate my passion for research and made me believe I could one day be a professor and write a book. Thank you to Harold Campbell, Juan Esteva Martínez, Eli Barbosa, and Alex García. Also, a special thank-you to Jordan Beltran Gonzales, who was my graduate student mentor during the McNair program and continues to be among my most trusted editors and academic coaches.

I would also like to acknowledge several institutions that financially supported this project. They include the Center for Race and Gender at UC Berkeley, the Project MALES program at UT Austin, and the Faculty First-Look program at NYU Steinhardt. I also want to thank the National Academy of Education / Spencer Foundation for generously supporting this project at different stages of the work and for connecting me to the invaluable mentorship of Django Paris and Tyrone Howard.

Following graduate school, the support of a UC President's Postdoctoral Fellowship was pivotal in granting me time to grow my dissertation into a book project. I was lucky enough to be hosted by the Department of Chicana/o Studies at UC Santa Barbara. A warm thankyou to Aída Hurtado for mentoring me through this important year. I am also grateful for the camaraderie and friendship of Daina Sanchez, San Juanita García, and Micaela J. Díaz-Sánchez, as well as Dolores Inés Casillas and the Write On Site writing group. Having a welcoming community during my short stay fueled the writing process. Also, thank you to Victor Rios for his encouragement, and Ethan Chang for his friendship and feedback during our short stays at UCSB.

At UC Davis, I have been blessed to be surrounded by a brilliant intellectual community. My colegas in the Department of Chicana/o Studies have been nothing but supportive of this project and have given me so much advice and mentoring through the final stages of the book. Thank you to Carlos Jackson, Sergio de la Mora, Susy Zepeda, Lorena Márquez, Natalia Deeb-Sossa, Maceo Montoya, Ofelia Cuevas, Clarissa Rojas, Yvette Flores, Alan Pelaez Lopez, José Arenas, Monica Torreiro-Casal, Alyssa West, and Alma Martinez. Also at UC Davis, Kimberly Nettles-Barcelón and the CAMPSSAH program offered me valuable support and writing resources as I worked to complete this manuscript. And of course, a heartfelt thank-you to my colleagues in the School of Education at UC Davis, especially Danny Martinez, for always making me a welcome visitor in the SOE, and Yianella Blanco and Alicia Rusoja for their friendship and collaboration.

Beyond Davis, I have countless academic colleagues and interlocutors inside and outside academia. While there are too many to thank, I would like to acknowledge Ed Brockenbrough, Victor Sáenz, and Sofia Villenas. Your supportive letters and professional guidance have been invaluable to my career and to this project. And thank you to Chris Lura, whose sharp editorial eye helped me really begin to think of this project as a book. I also want to thank Bianca Baldridge for her phenomenal feedback on multiple drafts of this manuscript. Beyond your comments and support, your critical scholarship on youth work has had a tremendous impact on this book.

Beyond academia, my foundation through any endeavor I have undertaken in my life has always been my family, and any accomplishment I have achieved is a reflection of their guidance and support. To my sister Elisa, you are my original mentor. Living so close to my big sister during the early years of this project made everything easier. To my parents, Victor and Debbie Singh, I continue to be in awe at the amount of love and encouragement you have blanketed me in throughout my life. You taught me how to be a good student as well as a critical thinker. Thank you for being my foundation. I am so proud to be your son. I would also like to thank my suegros, Moisés Quintero and Ana Tovar, who welcomed me into their loving family while I was working on this book. The care and concern you offer never go unnoticed. And to the rest of my family, the Singh family, the Ramirez family, my grandparents, my great-grandparents, my ancestors, thank you for always being with me. I want to especially acknowledge my maternal grandfather, Albert Ramirez, and my paternal grandmother, Maria Concepción Singh, who continue to be such forces of encouragement in my life. I cannot wait to hand you both a copy of this book. I also want to honor Grandma Hope, Esperanza Ramirez, who transitioned from this world while I was working on the early drafts of my book proposal. I feel your love with me constantly, including while I write.

While conducting fieldwork for this project, I was also falling deeply in love with Lupe Quintero, the love of my life. I feel so blessed to have received your love and support in all stages of this work. From proofreading chapters to editing outlines, you really have done it all. And your smile and warmth are always the best writing fuel. Thank you for cheering me on in every way possible. You are the truest definition of a supportive partner, and I hope to always be the same for you.

Finally, I would like to thank the students and mentors of Latino Male Success. You welcomed a young graduate student into your classroom and into your lives with open arms. From my first email in 2017 until the present, I have never stopped appreciating your generosity and passion. I am especially grateful to the four mentors I shadowed. It truly was an honor to work with you. And a special thank-you to Mr. Javier. Your hope is my hope.

DATA COLLECTION AND RESEARCH METHODOLOGY

This book comes from two years of ethnographic research with Latino Male Success. Fieldwork began in August 2017 and lasted until June 2019. Pseudonyms were assigned to all individuals, organizations, schools, and cities in this study. Over the course of the fieldwork I gathered and analyzed media and documents relating to LMS, spent over five hundred hours of participant observations in LMS classrooms and related sites, and interviewed fifty LMS mentors, students, and administrators. Additionally, I conducted numerous informal interviews with school staff, teachers, parents, non-LMS students, and community members.

Fieldwork began in the summer of 2017 when the program director invited me to attend an LMS staff meeting.[1] There, I introduced myself to the mentors and explained my interest in volunteering and conducting research with the program over the coming school year. The goals of the project were to research Latino male mentoring as well as study the ways Latino male educators and students construct identity through school-based Latino male programming. Three mentors expressed interest in classroom observations and invited me to begin shadowing them and volunteering in their classrooms. Two of these sites were middle schools, and one was a high school. The three mentors whose classrooms I initially began observing were Mr. Javier (middle school), Mr. Antonio (middle school), and Mr. Iván (high school). School site visits began in August 2017 during the beginning of the school year and continued until the end of the following academic year in May 2019. I generally visited each school site twice a week. In April 2018, at the end of the first school year, Mr. Antonio left LMS for another job, and a new mentor, Mr. Sergio, was hired. Mr. Sergio allowed me to continue my volunteering and observations in his classroom for the remainder of the study. Due to time constraints, I could not formally observe Mr. Iván's classroom during the second year of the study.

This project utilizes a qualitative approach to research. Norman Denzin and Yvonna Lincoln (2011) state:

> The word *qualitative* implies an emphasis on the qualities of entities and on processes and meanings that are not experimentally examined or measured (if measured at all) in terms of quantity, amount, intensity, or frequency. Qualitative researchers stress the socially constructed nature of reality, the intimate relationship between the researcher and what is studied. . . . They seek answers to questions that stress *how* social experience is created and given meaning. (8)

I chose a qualitative approach with ethnographic methods to better understand how social and cultural forces inform how those involved with LMS experience, feel, and make sense of school-based Latino male mentorship. Ethnography is characterized by its diverse techniques of qualitative data collection, prolonged time immersed in community, and orientation toward description and interpretation of cultural phenomena (Schram 2005). In ethnographic research, qualitative data take on meaning by being viewed through theoretical or explanatory lenses. They can, therefore, take on different meanings depending on the lens being used by the researcher (LeCompte and Schensul 2012). As a critical ethnographer, it was important to me to take into consideration issues of power and the social context in which school-based Latino male mentorship exists. As Joe Kincheloe and Peter McLaren (2011) state, the *critical* in critical qualitative research pushes researchers to attend to "issues of power and justice" and the ways "the economy, matters of race, class, and gender, ideologies, discourses, education, religion, and other social institutions, and cultural dynamics interact to construct a social system" (288). Furthermore, a critical ethnographic approach attempts to bring about social change by illuminating and problematizing hidden inequalities, contradictions, and oppression. This epistemological orientation was crucial for understanding how social, political, and historical contexts shape the cultural phenomenon of Latino male mentorship.

Ethnography also exists within its own oppressive context and history (Smith 2012). Ethnographic researchers often gain access to the lives and communities of participants to conduct research *on*, rather than alongside or in solidarity *with*, communities. Given this history, I sought to be mindful of how I built authentic and reciprocal relationships throughout this project. I did not take the responsibilities of being a researcher lightly, and I hope all those involved in this work felt the genuine respect and admiration I have for all those who teach in the name of social justice. It was truly an honor to spend two years with LMS.

As a participant observer, I entered the day-to-day routines of Latino men mentoring Latino boys. The majority of my time was spent alongside the four mentors I shadowed across their three school sites. Site visits generally occurred twice a week in each classroom during the mentor's LMS period. My role in the classroom initially began as a volunteer, tutor, and participant in class discussions and activities. As the months passed, mentors asked me to have a bigger role in their classroom, including facilitating group work and sports activities, as well as infrequently teaching lessons. In one instance, Mr. Iván needed to unexpectedly miss class. Rather than call for a last-minute substitute, he asked me to fill in for his period, which I was able to do with ease. It was also common for me to attend additional school-day or after-school activities at each school site. One mentor held an after-school homework hall that I attended on a weekly basis. Another mentor helped facilitate a lunchtime Raza Club at his school which I periodically attended as well.

Beyond the classroom, I sought to immerse myself in the atmosphere in which LMS was embedded. This led me to Pueblo Unido events like LMS fundraisers as well as other community events sponsored by Pueblo Unido in order to familiarize myself with their projects. Throughout this study, I also frequented ASUSD events that seemed relevant or related to LMS. These events included several district board meetings as well as district-led forums on topics ranging from Latinx community engagement to Black male empowerment. By the end of the project I had compiled several hundred pages of field notes from many hundreds of school-site visits. In addition, twenty field notes document outside events, fundraisers, office visits, and district events that I attended.

RESEARCHER POSITIONALITY

A range of identities affected my positionality as a researcher and the ways I entered the field as an ethnographer. I am a cisgender, heterosexual, Latino man (Mexican American/Chicano). During the time of data collection, I was in my late twenties and a graduate student at UC Berkeley. These identities no doubt helped grant me entry into such an intimate and identity-specific space. As a Latino man who fit the profile of an LMS youth worker, students and school staff often viewed me as an unofficial LMS mentor during my two years of participant observations. Despite sharing so many commonalities with my participants, my positionality as a university researcher was a key difference that I sought to acknowledge and interrogate in this work.

My connection to youth work also led me to add a self-reflexive component to my research. Before returning to graduate school, I had previously worked as a school-based mentor in my hometown of Woodland, California. My time with LMS allowed me to remember what it feels like to be positioned as a "good role model" for Latino boys in schools. In addition to the copious field notes documenting my site visits, I also wrote auto-ethnographic memos analyzing my thoughts, feelings, and at times discomfort as I negotiated my own unique positionality as a Latino male doctoral student. I continue to navigate the contradictory image of the positive Latino male role model as an assistant professor in the neoliberal multicultural landscape of higher education.

ACCOUNTABILITY AND RESEARCH IMPACT

As an educational activist and student of critical theory, I approached this research with a commitment to attending to issues of power and injustice. I was also interested in learning alongside research participants and being in solidarity with the goals of the community I was working with. At times this was difficult because, as my research shows, Latino men and boys are not a homogeneous group. The youth workers and students who shared their perspectives and stories in this book all have their own unique perspectives, politics, and vision of Latino male empowerment. My critical race and gender politics as well as critiques of neoliberal school reform most closely aligned my analysis with the perspectives of Mr. Javier, Mr. Agustín, and other educators at my school sites who often critiqued Pueblo Unido's approach to youth work. For these participants, it was important that my research offer a critical account of the contradictions and compromises embedded in Latino male programming. I believe this has been the main contribution of this research. Relatedly, the students of LMS hoped that my work could shed light on unnecessarily rigid disciplinary practices in the program and on the need to center more joyful and community-focused activities and lessons. This was well documented in my research reports to LMS.

Finally, all LMS mentors asked that my work reach practitioners and support Latino male youth workers. This request led me to publish the majority of my findings in a book format, as opposed to academic journal articles. Shortly after finishing this project, I also published a practice brief with the Project MALES program that sought to inform the practice of men of color educators (M. V. Singh 2021b). The publication is titled "Seven Justice-Oriented Principles for Men of Color Working with Boys of Color" and has been well circulated among men-of-color educational spaces. Furthermore, while this research has been presented at academic conferences, the majority of my presentations from this research have been in the form of practitioner workshops, which have taken place around the country.

During the data-collection phase of this research, I sought to establish a reciprocal relationship with LMS classrooms in which I was a visitor. This included dedicating myself to being an active participant in the space by showing up for the students and mentors in whatever way was needed. This led me to plan lessons, substitute-teach, tutor, give rides, pick up class materials, attend soccer games, and even edit personal statements when some mentors sought to return to graduate school. Additionally, with the help of grant funding, I was also able to modestly compensate students and mentors for their time through gift cards.

Lastly, I presented my research findings in LMS staff meetings after each year I was with the program. I also helped to incorporate these findings into efforts to build new LMS curricula. This included a workshop addressing the use of body-shaming language, which Mr. Sergio and I presented to his middle school class. Since the end of the research project, I have returned for semiannual workshops with the program. This has given me an opportunity to meet and support new mentors who have begun working for LMS. Although no LMS mentors or students who participated in my project are currently with LMS, I continue to be in contact with many of these young men—both students and mentors—who welcomed me into their lives. I remain ever grateful for their trust and friendship during this work.

NOTES

INTRODUCTION

1. Pseudonyms have been assigned to all people, organizations, schools, and cities in this study.

2. Heteropatriarchy describes the way patriarchy intersects with hetero-sexism. It is a social system in which cisgender, heterosexual men hold primary power and occupy dominant roles in political, social, and family life. Culturally, heteropatriarchy normalizes specific gender relations and social arrangements. For example, value is ascribed to hetero-monogamous marriage and nuclear familial arrangements, while non-heteronormative and queer lives are thought to be unnatural, undesirable, or unsuccessful. The ability to embody and naturalize heteropatriarchal norms is often implicitly or explicitly expected from male educators of color. For example, qualities like being a "loving husband and father" are seen as professionally important and are frequently added to professional biographies.

3. "Pushout" is the notion that students leave school because they are forced out by repressive school practices, as opposed to simply leaving of their own accord. This is sometimes problematically called a "dropout."

4. I describe the notion of the bad boy as a complex assemblage of racialized deviant masculine practices. In urban education, the strongest discourse associatd with the bad boy is the anti-Black fear and hate projected at Black men and boys specifically, and Blackness generally. In chapter 6, I further explore the ways anti-Blackness influences how a positive Latino maleness is constructed under neoliberal multiculturalism.

5. Neoliberalism is both an economic theory and a social discourse that views economies and human beings as most efficient when detached from governmental regulation and left to self-manage the potential to earn and accumulate capital (Friedman 2002; Hayek 1996). Pauline Lipman (2011) describes neoliberalism as an assemblage of "economic and social policies, forms of governance, and discourses and ideologies that promote individual self-interest, unrestricted flows of capital, deep reductions in the cost of labor, and sharp retrenchment of the public sphere" (6). Since the 1970s, neoliberalism has transformed the organization of the world as governments, led by the United States, promote private enterprise while diminishing and privatizing public services (Harvey 2007).

6. The four high schools served by the LMS mentorship program had an overall student population range of 850 to 1,750 students, and the six middle

schools had 250 to 550 students. The program employed 10 mentors, each assigned to a single classroom at each school site.

7. There is no uniform student admittance process across LMS, and each class composition varied by school site. All classrooms had a variety of students ranging in grade level as well as academic achievement. It was common to have both high- and low-achieving students, with GPAs at times ranging from 4.0 to below 1.0. Generally, student recruitment would be done through both teacher referral and students' interest in the opportunity to get mentorship and participate in an all–Latino male space. In some school sites class size was low due to competition with other elective courses, but in most cases there was a long wait list because of lack of space in the class.

8. For more on my identity and positionality as a researcher, see appendix.

9. For more on my ethnographic methods and data collection in the classroom, see appendix.

10. While this study focuses specifically on Latino men and boys, this research is located within a larger push to address the often ambiguous grouping of "boys of color." The literature's use of "boys of color" generally encapsulates students who are marginalized in the education system due to their gender and racial identities. This category typically includes Black, Latino, Native American, and Southeast Asian boys. While I use the category "boys of color" when drawing from the literature, I note that despite commonalities across these groups, racialization and racism are often experienced uniquely and relationally among racial groups. Furthermore, it must be stated that the composition of racial groups is unstable and malleable. For example, many Latino boys are also Black and/or Indigenous. In chapters 2 and 6, I engage with the ways anti-Blackness influences the ways a successful Latino manhood is envisioned in LMS.

11. Although state policies have powerful roles to play in facilitating the neoliberalization of society—deregulation, selling of public assets, providing a military and police force dedicated to protecting private goods, and securing global and domestic markets—neoliberalism is also a rationality and values system, and it functions as a form of governmentality. Foucault's (2011) notion of governmentality describes the ways the behavior and conduct of a population are managed through self-governance. Here, populations are not simply controlled by oppressive policies and laws; instead, prevailing discourse and rationality shape the social norms and self-awareness of populations who, in turn, regulate themselves. Governmentality posits power as affirming, positive, and horizontal (Dean 2009). *Neoliberal governmentality* refers to the ways neoliberal economic and social discourse inspire and necessitate new understandings of self and humanity, *Homo economicus*. Under neoliberal governmentality, populations adopt a moral responsibility to act through economic

self-interest and market principles that override or blend with other ethical or moral values. This entrepreneurial spirit aims to amass the most "human capital" by adopting market principles in all facets of life.

12. It is important to note that multiculturalism has a long and contested history. This is particularly true regarding schooling and curriculum in the United States. I am critical of what is referred to as liberal and neoliberal multiculturalism, but it should be stated that multiculturalism initially emerged as a radical challenge to Eurocentrism in U.S. textbooks and curriculum (Banks and Banks 2016; Nieto 1999). Although it is safe to say multiculturalism was victorious in the culture wars of the 1990s (Symcox 2001), multicultural education has come to signify a variety of racial politics (Leonardo 2013). This includes what Buras (2008) refers to as "Rightist Multiculturalism."

13. The Moynihan Report refers to a 1965 policy brief titled "The Negro Family: A Case for National Action." In this now infamous report, then Secretary of Labor Patrick Moynihan identifies the roots of Black poverty as located in the cultural dysfunction of the Black family, which he found to be abundantly headed by single-mother households and in disarray. This framing of Black poverty has been widely critiqued by Black feminists (Collins 2008).

14. While the notion of racial respectability politics precedes the rise of neoliberalism, the neoliberal turn exploits the notion of respectability to justify further government retreat from social welfare and the need for free-market incentivization of the individual.

1. MANAGING THE "CRISIS" OF LATINO MEN AND BOYS

1. Note that the CEO differentiates between Black *men* and Latino *boys.* This differentiation speaks to the dehumanizing and anti-Black tendency to see Black males as inherent threats. This notion hinders the ability to even perceive Black boys as children (Dumas and Nelson 2016).

2. In 2001, my California elementary school enrolled me and my classmates in the DARE program. My DARE police officer was a white man named Officer Bennett. He impressed us with his motorcycle and warned us of the fast-approaching time when we would be asked to do drugs and join a gang. Students shared that they knew of friends or family members who might be in gangs or do drugs. We were also asked to sign a pledge stating we vowed to remain drug free and not join a gang for the rest of our lives. DARE culminated in a closing essay contest. My essay won, and I proudly read it aloud at a school assembly. These acts interpellated me as a "good boy" who was on the "right path." However, it also helped define those of my classmates, some of whom were my best friends, as "at-risk" and potentially "bad boys." However, they were not bad boys. Bad boys do not exist.

3. Rodríguez (2017) defines the NPIC as the set of symbiotic relationships that link together political and financial technologies of state and owning-class proctorship and surveillance over public political intercourse, including and especially emergent progressive and leftist social movement, since about the mid-1970s.

4. In describing the evolution of the program from its early days until the beginning of my field work in 2017, I want to take caution to not paint the program as initially health-focused (good) and later academic and deficit-oriented (bad). In fact, research shows that trauma-informed youth work can also bring a deficit model into the classroom by treating students as traumatized and broken (Khasnabis and Goldin 2020). Relatedly, mentors received little to no training as counselors or mental health professionals. While they were positioned as therapist-like mentors, I suspect a lack of training at times led to deficit orientations to counseling and support.

5. This experience of staying out of trouble and putting forth honest academic effort only to see low academic improvement was a common experience among the boys. I will expand on this in chapter 4.

6. During this study I did encounter and, in some cases, build relationships with students who were interested in joining gangs or who had been suspended for fighting on multiple occasions. These children were similar to their peers. They were complex individuals who desired a supportive and rigorous learning environment in school. They were not bad boys.

7. These quotations were gathered from Pueblo Unido documents. The students quoted in this literature were from previous years and are separate from the in-person interviews that I collected.

8. While the notion of racial respectability politics precedes the rise of neoliberalism, the neoliberal turn exploits the notion of respectability to justify further government retreat from social welfare and the need for market-based incentivization.

9. The Códice Florentino, or Florentine Codex, is an encyclopedic work about the people and culture of central Mexico. It was compiled in the sixteenth century by the Spanish Franciscan friar Bernardino de Sahagún. With the help of local Nahua people, Sahagún compiled twelve books documenting Indigenous life, cosmology, language, and culture. Book 6 is titled *Rhetoric and Moral Philosophy*.

2. CULTIVATING HUMAN CAPITAL

1. Several weeks earlier I had sat in on a staff meeting where the decision was made to include the máscaras in the auction. Claire, an energetic white woman from the Pueblo Unido central office, had spearheaded the fundraiser and encouraged the addition as a great accent to the auction items. Although

a small handful of the mentors opposed the inclusion of such a personal item, the majority had approved, and the decision had been made.

2. This orientation of the problem draws from the controversial "acting white" thesis in educational debates—the notion that students of color do not strive to succeed in school in part because they see academic success as synonymous with acting white and will be shamed by their peers. This argument has consistently been challenged by studies which find that students of color aspire to success in school similar to white students (see P. L. Carter 2006; O'Connor 1997).

3. Only two mentors reported an aversion to this practice. Their perspectives are outlined in chapter 5.

4. For more on neoliberalism, masculinity, and education see Stahl, Nelson, and Wallace (2017).

5. This shirt was only given to boys who were overall a success in the program and signaled the embodiment of the "real man" LMS sought to create. Having this shirt was also a privilege at the two middle schools I observed because both campuses allowed LMS students to break dress code on Fridays to wear their program T-shirts. This was a privilege highly valued by the boys.

6. The study reports that "the impact of financial incentives on student achievement is statistically 0, in each city" (Fryer 2011, 1755). It adds that, due to "a lack of power," it cannot be ruled out that "the possibility of effect sizes that would have positive returns on investment. The only statistically significant effect is on English-speaking students in Dallas" (1755).

7. No-excuses charter schools seek to meet their goal of increasing the educational achievement of mostly low-income students of color through high expectations and heavily structured discipline and control. The strict codes of behavior at no-excuses charter schools have been widely criticized for creating environments of intense regulation, anxiety, and pushout. In recent years, even large charter school networks such as KIPP and Noble have acknowledged the wrongfulness of their disciplinary approaches and condemned the no-excuses approach (Golann 2021).

8. I would be remiss if I did not mention that David was excited and hopeful about attending Adams High. His grandmother had assured him that it was a good school, and his best friend, Shondra, would also be attending. Having made no close friends in LMS, he was not concerned that he was the only one attending Adams.

9. My focus in this book is primarily on neoliberal power and how Latino men and boys engage with and resist this power. I believe this point can be argued without sharing the intimate stories of individual participants in sharing circles. Academia has often been quick to consume stories of pain and damage, particularly of boys and young men of color in school. I felt a deep

responsibility when invited to a space in which students shared their most vulnerable and even traumatic moments. In line with Tuck and Yang's (2014) methodological interventions, there are some stories that the academy does not deserve, and research should refuse to offer them for publication. These stories will remain within the sharing circle.

10. I have reserved these data for the sole purpose of helping LMS work toward its goal of improving its engagement with gender and sexuality.

3. NEOLIBERAL SUPERHEROES

1. Research with individual educators as well as programs document how love and caring among men and boys of color create spaces of refuge and empowerment within an educational environment often hostile toward boys and men of color (Brooms, Clark, and Smith 2018; Brown 2009; Fergus, Noguera, and Martin 2014; Lynn 2006a, 2006b; Nasir, Givens, and Chatmon 2018).

2. This finding is consistent with research documenting that men of color educators are pushed to fulfill a perceived lack of hegemonic manhood in communities of color (Woodson and Pabon 2016).

4. TRAVERSING JOY AND DISCIPLINE

1. For more on the racial and gender politics of single-sex schools, see Williams (2016) and Lindsay (2018).

2. The label "at risk" has long been criticized for the way it constructs individual students as problems, while avoiding a critical analysis of poverty and discriminatory educational practices (Swadener and Lubeck 1995). The term "at promise" has become popular to counter the deficit-oriented rhetoric that comes with describing students as "at risk" (Rios and Rios-Mireles 2019).

3. Bryan was not interviewed in this study. He would leave the program before the end of the semester.

4. Alonzo's largest discomfort with Mr. Iván's mentoring style was "yelling." Recently, Mr. Iván had caught Alonzo roaming the hallways during a prolonged bathroom break in a different class. Alonzo described Mr. Iván shouting at him in the otherwise quiet hallway before walking him back to his English class. Then, Mr. Iván had promised he would call Alonzo's home if he found Alonzo outside of class again.

5. Mr. Javier's critical mentoring strategies are highlighted in chapter 5.

5. SUBVERSIVE ROLE MODELS

1. After first meeting Mr. Javier through my research with LMS, we began to cross paths at political and cultural events in the Arroyo Seco community. He was an organizer of events, such as the local Chicano Moratorium commemoration. On May 1, International Worker's Day, he was a speaker and

performer at the city's rally. His words and politically charged rap lyrics spoke to the intersection of racial justice and labor justice.

2. Dylan Rodríguez (2017) defines the nonprofit industrial complex as "the set of symbiotic relationships that link together political and financial technologies of state and owning-class proctorship and surveillance over public political intercourse, including and especially emergent progressive and leftist social movement, since about the mid-1970s" (21–22).

3. In this example, the mentor was himself a shoe aficionado who enjoyed purchasing expensive Jordans from time to time. This example demonstrates the way culturally relatable Latino men, who are in touch with, for example, sneaker culture, can still perpetuate ideas that place individualized blame on disenfranchised communities of color.

4. Whether to disclose one's sexuality is a difficult decision for queer teachers to make. Although schools and districts have widely included sexual orientation into antidiscriminatory policies, school contexts continue to be homophobic and unsupportive of queer teachers. In celebrating and highlighting Mr. Agustín, I also want to be clear that the onus to make queer-inclusive change should be placed on institutions rather than on individual educators. This cannot be overstated. In a study with queer Black men teachers, Brockenbrough (2012) finds that prevailing narratives of Black masculinity among teachers especially contributes to presumed heterosexuality and a hypersurveillance of Black men's gendered and sexual performances in schools. Brockenbrough calls upon schools to "complement policy-level protections with genuine ground-level initiatives that directly target the homophobic dynamics of teacher-student encounters and other aspects of everyday school culture" (758).

5. I want to note that of course gay men can still perpetuate toxic and misogynistic notions of manhood. Beyond Mr. Agustín's sexual orientation, I am attempting to describe the way his queer politics and gender performance work to subvert hegemonic notions of manhood.

6. These principles were first published in a practice brief by the Project MALES program at the University of Texas, Austin. The title of the brief is "Seven Justice-Oriented Principles for Men of Color Working with Boys of Color" (M. V. Singh 2021b).

6. ENGAGING ANTI-BLACKNESS WHILE MENTORING NON-BLACK LATINO BOYS

1. In my research report-backs to LMS, I shared my concern that (a) many LMS students frequently used the N-word with little understanding of its history and impact and that (b) LMS offered mixed messaging regarding Latino boys' relationship to that word. I also offered a brief explanation of why, as

non-Black people, it was harmful for us to use and appropriate the N-word. This led to a discussion and debate among the mentors.

2. I do not want to diminish the extreme racial marginalization experienced by Black women and girls and especially by trans Black women, who are particularly targeted by intersecting forms of racial and gender violence. I make this claim only to point to the ways the racial imaginary in urban education often focuses on Black boys (Noguera 2009).

3. I want to acknowledge that settler and anti-Indigenous ideologies similarly shape the ways an ideal Latino manhood is understood. While a thorough investigation of the ways anti-Indigenous beliefs affect Latino male mentoring was outside the scope of this research project, I want to encourage future research on boys and men of color to explore the ways settler colonialism affects this discussion. In Arroyo Seco, an Indigenous Maya population was growing in schools. I want to emphasize that Chicanx/Latinx empowerment programs can unintentionally promote anti-Indigenous pedagogies. This is even (and perhaps especially) the case when programs use vague "Aztec" imagery and mythology from the era of the Chicano Movement.

4. Shange's work masterfully confronts anti-Blackness in a multiracial context without passing criticism or judgment on non-Black students and families who also navigate institutional racism. She highlights critical Latinx voices in the ethnography. *Progressive Dystopia* is a wonderful example of research that employs a relational analysis of race to trace anti-Blackness while still working in solidarity with other racial and ethnic groups.

5. In recent years Arroyo Seco had seen an upsurge in efforts to protest and dismantle racial injustice. At the fore of these movements was often Black liberationist ideologies of prison abolition and critiques of racial capitalism. The massive Latinx nonprofit had historically avoided joining radical political actions, and the years surrounding this research were no different. During my research, I monitored the social media and newsletters of Pueblo Unido. While the large nonprofit denounced Trumpism and verbalized its support of Black Lives Matter movement, concrete political action and positions were avoided.

6. This panel featured prominent women-of-color activists Alicia Garza (cofounder of Black Lives Matter), Ericka Huggins (activist and former Black Panther Party leader), Aja Brown (mayor of Compton), and M. J. Rodriguez (actress and activist). https://www.youtube.com/watch?v=7yeiFF5yG9k&ab_channel=ObamaFoundation

7. I juxtapose the images of Nipsey Hussle and Obama because they represent contrasting images of Black manhood. However, it must be noted that transcending dominant notions of respectable role models for boys of color also means honoring women of color as role models. Mr. Javier upheld critical

women of color like Angela Davis and Dolores Huerta as heroes and role models to be looked up to in his class.

8. This is just one of the many examples in U.S. history in which non-Black people of color have sought to garner rights by asserting their deservingness on the fact that they were not Black.

9. Anti-Black rhetoric is language that dehumanizes Black people and positions Blackness as backwards and an inherent problem.

10. It is worth reiterating that many Latinx people are Black.

CONCLUSION

1. For more on youth-led visions of justice, see Serrano et al. (2022) and Turner (2021).

APPENDIX

1. Although I made contact with LMS in the spring of 2017, this study's human subjects research protocol did not receive institutional review board (IRB) approval until July 2017. This project was classified as nonexempt of review; however, because it represented no more than minimal risk to human subjects, it required subcommittee approval rather than full IRB review.

BIBLIOGRAPHY

Alemán, Sonya M., Sofia Bahena, and Enrique Alemán. 2019. "Remapping the Latina/o and Chicana/o Pipeline: A Critical Race Analysis of Educational Inequity in Texas." *Journal of Hispanic Higher Education* 21 (1): 17–32. https://doi.org/10.1177/1538192719892878.

Alexander, Michelle. 2012. *The New Jim Crow: Mass Incarceration in the Age of Colorblindness.* New York: The New Press.

Anyon, Jean. 1997. *Ghetto Schooling: A Political Economy of Urban Educational Reform.* New York: Teachers College Press.

Anyon, Jean. 2006. "Social Class, School Knowledge, and the Hidden Curriculum." In *Ideology, Curriculum, and the New Sociology of Education: Revisiting the Work of Michael Apple,* edited by Lois Weis, Greg Dimitriadis, and Cameron McCarthy, 37–45. New York: Routledge.

Apple, Michael W. 2004. *Ideology and Curriculum.* 3rd ed. New York: Routledge.

Apple, Michael W. 2006. *Educating the "Right" Way: Markets, Standards, God, and Inequality.* New York: Taylor & Francis.

Baldridge, Bianca J. 2014. "Relocating the Deficit Reimagining Black Youth in Neoliberal Times." *American Educational Research Journal* 20 (10): 1–33. https://doi.org/10.3102/0002831214532514.

Baldridge, Bianca J. 2017. "'It's Like This Myth of the Supernegro': Resisting Narratives of Damage and Struggle in the Neoliberal Educational Policy Context." *Race Ethnicity and Education* 20 (6): 781–95. https://doi.org/10.1080/13613324.2016.1248819.

Baldridge, Bianca J. 2019. *Reclaiming Community: Race and the Uncertain Future of Youth Work.* Stanford, Calif.: Stanford University Press.

Baldridge, Bianca J. 2020a. "Negotiating Anti-Black Racism in 'Liberal' Contexts: The Experiences of Black Youth Workers in Community-Based Educational Spaces." *Race Ethnicity and Education* 23 (6): 747–66. https://doi.org/10.1080/13613324.2020 .1753682.

Baldridge, Bianca J. 2020b. "The Youthwork Paradox: A Case for Studying the Complexity of Community-Based Youth Work in

Education Research." *Educational Researcher* 49 (8): 618–25. https://doi.org/10.3102/0013189X20937300.

Ball, Stephen J., and Antonio Olmedo. 2013. "Care of the Self, Resistance, and Subjectivity under Neoliberal Governmentalities." *Critical Studies in Education* 54 (1): 85–96. https://doi.org/10.1080/1750 8487.2013.740678.

Banks, James A., and Cherry A. McGee Banks. 2016. *Multicultural Education: Issues and Perspectives.* Hoboken, N.J.: Wiley.

Bell, Courtney A. 2009. "All Choices Created Equal? The Role of Choice Sets in the Selection of Schools." *Peabody Journal of Education* 84 (2): 191–208. https://doi.org/10.1080/01619560902810146.

Blackwell, Maylei. 2011. *¡Chicana Power! Contested Histories of Feminism in the Chicano Movement.* Austin: University of Texas Press.

Bloom, Joshua, and Waldo E. Martin Jr. 2016. *Black against Empire: The History and Politics of the Black Panther Party.* Oakland: University of California Press.

Bourdieu, Pierre, and Jean-Claude Passeron. 1990. *Reproduction in Education, Society, and Culture.* Translated by Richard Nice. 2nd ed. London: Sage.

Bristol, Travis J., and Javier Martin-Fernandez. 2019. "The Added Value of Latinx and Black Teachers for Latinx and Black Students: Implications for Policy." *Policy Insights from the Behavioral and Brain Sciences* 6 (2): 147–53. https://doi.org/10.1177/2372732219862573.

Bristol, Travis J., and Marcelle Mentor. 2018. "Policing and Teaching: The Positioning of Black Male Teachers as Agents in the Universal Carceral Apparatus." *The Urban Review* 50 (2): 218–34.

Britzman, Deborah. 1993. "Beyond Rolling Models: Gender and Multicultural Education." In *Gender and Education,* edited by S. K. Biklen and D. Pollard, 25–42. Chicago: University of Chicago Press.

Brockenbrough, Edward. 2012. "Agency and Abjection in the Closet: The Voices (and Silences) of Black Queer Male Teachers." *International Journal of Qualitative Studies in Education* 25 (6): 741–65. https://doi.org/10.1080/09518398.2011.590157.

Brockenbrough, Edward. 2013. "Introduction to the Special Issue: Queers of Color and Anti-Oppressive Knowledge Production." *Curriculum Inquiry* 43 (4): 426–40. https://doi.org/10.1111/curi.12023.

Brockenbrough, Edward. 2015. "'The Discipline Stop': Black Male Teachers and the Politics of Urban School Discipline." *Education and Urban Society* 47 (5): 499–522. https://doi.org/10.1177 /0013124514530154.

Brockenbrough, Edward. 2018. *Black Men Teaching in Urban Schools: Reassessing Black Masculinity.* New York: Routledge.

Brooms, Derrick R. 2016. *Being Black, Being Male on Campus: Understanding and Confronting Black Male Collegiate Experiences.* New York: SUNY Press.

Brooms, Derrick R. 2022. "What's Going on Here? Black Men and Gendered-Antiblackness at a Hispanic-Serving Institution." *Race Ethnicity and Education.* https://doi.org/10.1080/13613324.2022.21 54371.

Brooms, Derrick R., Jelisa Clark, and Matthew Smith. 2018. *Empowering Men of Color on Campus: Building Student Community in Higher Education.* New Brunswick, N.J.: Rutgers University Press.

Brown, Anthony L. 2009. "'Brothers Gonna Work It Out': Understanding the Pedagogic Performance of African American Male Teachers Working with African American Male Students." *Urban Review* 41 (5): 416–35. https://doi.org/10.1007/s11256-008-0116-8.

Brown, Anthony L. 2011. "'Same Old Stories': The Black Male in Social Science and Educational Literature, 1930s to the Present." *Teachers College Record* 113 (9): 2047–79.

Brown, Anthony L. 2012. "On Human Kinds and Role Models: A Critical Discussion about the African American Male Teacher." *Educational Studies* 48 (3): 296–315. https://doi.org/10.1080/001319 46.2012.660666.

Brown, Anthony L., and Jamel K. Donnor. 2011. "Toward a New Narrative on Black Males, Education, and Public Policy." *Race Ethnicity and Education* 14 (1): 17–32. https://doi.org/10.1080/13613324.2011 .531978.

Brown, Wendy. 2015. *Undoing the Demos: Neoliberalism's Stealth Revolution.* New York: Zone Books.

Buelna, Enrique M. 2019. *Chicano Communists and the Struggle for Social Justice.* Tucson: University of Arizona Press.

Bulkley, Katrina E., and Jeffrey R. Henig. 2015. "Local Politics and Portfolio Management Models: National Reform Ideas and Local Control." *Peabody Journal of Education* 90 (1): 53–83. https://doi.org /10.1080/0161956X.2015.988528.

Bulkley, Katrina E., Jeffrey R. Henig, and Henry M. Levin. 2010. *Between Public and Private: Politics, Governance, and the New Portfolio*

Models for Urban School Reform. Cambridge: Harvard Education Press.

Buras, Kristen L. 2008. *Rightist Multiculturalism*. New York: Routledge.

Buras, Kristen L., and Michael W. Apple. 2005. "School Choice, Neoliberal Promises, and Unpromising Evidence." *Educational Policy* 19 (3): 550–64. https://doi.org/10.1177/0895904805276146.

Burch, Patricia. 2009. *Hidden Markets: The New Education Privatization*. New York: Routledge.

Butler, Judith. 1990. "Performative Acts and Gender Constitution: An Essay in Phenomenology and Feminist Theory." In *Performing Feminisms: Feminist Critical Theory and Theatre*, edited by Sue-Ellen Case, 270–82. Baltimore: Johns Hopkins University Press.

Cabrera, Nolan L., Alex K. Karaman, Tracy Arámbula Ballysingh, Yadira G. Oregon, Eliaquin A. Gonell, Jameson D. Lopez, and Regina Deil-Amen. 2022. "Race without Gender? Trends and Limitations in the Higher Education Scholarship Regarding Men of Color." *Review of Educational Research* 92 (3): 331–69. https://doi.org/10.3102/00346543211054577.

Cacho, Lisa Marie. 2007. "'You Just Don't Know How Much He Meant': Deviancy, Death, and Devaluation." *Latino Studies* 5 (2): 182–208. https://doi.org/10.1057/palgrave.lst.8600246.

Carey, Roderick L. 2020. "Missing Misters: Uncovering the Pedagogies and Positionalities of Male Teachers of Color in the School Lives of Black and Latino Adolescent Boys." *Race Ethnicity and Education* 23 (3): 392–413. https://doi.org/10.1080/13613324.2019.1663991.

Carter, Prudence L. 2006. "Straddling Boundaries: Identity, Culture, and School." *Sociology of Education* 79 (4): 304–28. https://doi.org/10.1177/003804070607900402.

Carter, Thomas. 2005. *Coach Carter*. Los Angeles: Paramount Pictures.

Cervantes, Diana, Jorge Burmicky, and Guillermo Martinez III. 2022. "Latino Men and Men of Color Programs: Research-Based Recommendations for Community College Practitioners." *Journal of Diversity in Higher Education* 15: 537–41. https://doi.org/10.1037/dhe0000423.

Clay, Kevin L. 2019. "'Despite the Odds': Unpacking the Politics of Black Resilience Neoliberalism." *American Educational Research Journal* 56 (1): 75–110. https://doi.org/10.3102/0002831218790214.

Coates, Ta-Nehisi. 2015. *Between the World and Me.* New York: One World.

Collins, Patricia Hill. 2005. *Black Sexual Politics: African Americans, Gender, and the New Racism.* New York: Routledge.

Collins, Patricia Hill. 2008. *Black Feminist Thought: Knowledge, Consciousness, and the Politics of Empowerment.* 2nd ed. New York: Routledge.

Connell, R. W. 2005. *Masculinities.* 2nd ed. Berkeley: University of California Press.

Crenshaw, Kimberle. 2014. "The Girls Obama Forgot." *New York Times,* July 30, 2014, sec. Opinions.

Crenshaw, Kimberle. 2016. "Intersectionality: Kimberle Crenshaw on Race, Gender, Identity and Activism [Live at the Women of the World Festival]." Presented at the Women of the World Festival, London, March 8. https://www.youtube.com/watch?v=-DW4HL gYPlA.

Critical Resistance. 2021. "What Is the PIC? What Is Abolition?— Critical Resistance." http://criticalresistance.org/about/not-so -common-language/.

Cruz, Cindy. 2001. "Toward an Epistemology of a Brown Body." *International Journal of Qualitative Studies in Education* 14 (5): 657–69. https://doi.org/10.1080/09518390110059874.

Cruz, Cindy. 2012. "Making Curriculum from Scratch: Testimonio in an Urban Classroom." *Equity & Excellence in Education* 45 (3): 460–71. https://doi.org/10.1080/10665684.2012.698185.

Dávila, Arlene M. 2004. *Barrio Dreams: Puerto Ricans, Latinos, and the Neoliberal City.* Berkeley: University of California Press.

Davila, Omar. 2021. "The Broken Lens: Equating Badness with Blackness Renders Latino Males Absent." *Journal of Latinos and Education* 20 (4): 334–45. https://doi.org/10.1080/15348431.2019.1589474.

Davis, Angela Y. 2000. "Masked Racism: Reflections on the Prison Industrial Complex." *Indigenous Law Bulletin* 4 (27): 4.

Davis, Angela Y. 2003. *Are Prisons Obsolete?* New York: Seven Stories Press.

Davis, Tomeka M. 2014. "School Choice and Segregation: 'Tracking' Racial Equity in Magnet Schools." *Education and Urban Society* 46 (4): 399–433. https://doi.org/10.1177/0013124512448672.

Dean, Mitchell M. 2009. *Governmentality: Power and Rule in Modern Society.* 2nd ed. London: Sage.

Dee, Thomas S. 2004. "Teachers, Race, and Student Achievement in a Randomized Experiment." *Review of Economics and Statistics* 86 (1): 195–210. https://doi.org/10.1162/003465304323023750.

Dee, Thomas S. 2005. "A Teacher Like Me: Does Race, Ethnicity, or Gender Matter?" *American Economic Review* 95 (2): 158–65.

Delgado Bernal, Dolores. 1998. "Grassroots Leadership Reconceptualized: Chicana Oral Histories and the 1968 East Los Angeles School Blowouts." *Frontiers: A Journal of Women Studies* 19 (2): 113–42. https://doi.org/10.2307/3347162.

Denne, Karen. 2008. "New Education R&D Lab Aims to Advance Innovations in Public Education." *Business Wire*, September 25, 2008. https://www.businesswire.com/news/home/20080925005934/en/New-Education-Lab-Aims-Advance-Innovations-Public.

Denzin, Norman K., and Yvonna S. Lincoln. 2011. "Introduction: The Discipline and Practice of Qualitative Research." In *The SAGE Handbook of Qualitative Research*, 4th ed., 1–20. Thousand Oaks, Calif.: Sage.

Du Bois, W. E. B. 2012. *The Souls of Black Folk*. The Original Classic Edition. Emereo Pty Limited.

Duckworth, Angela Lee, Heidi Grant, Benjamin Loew, Gabriele Oettingen, and Peter M. Gollwitzer. 2011. "Self-Regulation Strategies Improve Self-Discipline in Adolescents: Benefits of Mental Contrasting and Implementation Intentions." *Educational Psychology* 31 (1): 17–26. https://doi.org/10.1080/01443410.2010.506003.

Dudek, Mitch. 2021. "Adam Toledo Remembered as Kid with 'Big Imagination' and an Affinity for Shows about Zombies." *Chicago Sun-Times*, April 5, 2021. https://chicago.suntimes.com/2021/4/5/22369082/adam-toledo-remembered-as-kid-big-imagination-affinity-shows-zombies.

Dumas, Michael J. 2013. "'Waiting for Superman' to Save Black People: Racial Representation and the Official Antiracism of Neoliberal School Reform." *Discourse: Studies in the Cultural Politics of Education* 34 (4): 531–47. https://doi.org/10.1080/01596306.2013.822621.

Dumas, Michael J. 2014. "'Losing an Arm': Schooling as a Site of Black Suffering." *Race Ethnicity and Education* 17 (1): 1–29. https://doi.org/10.1080/13613324.2013.850412.

Dumas, Michael J. 2016a. "My Brother as 'Problem': Neoliberal Governmentality and Interventions for Black Young Men and Boys."

Educational Policy 30 (1): 94–113. https://doi.org/10.1177/08959 04815616487.

Dumas, Michael J. 2016b. "Against the Dark: Antiblackness in Education Policy and Discourse." *Theory Into Practice* 55 (1): 11–19. https://doi.org/10.1080/00405841.2016.1116852.

Dumas, Michael J., and Joseph Derrick Nelson. 2016. "(Re)Imagining Black Boyhood: Toward a Critical Framework for Educational Research." *Harvard Educational Review* 86 (1): 27–47. https://doi .org/10.17763/0017-8055.86.1.27.

Dumas, Michael J., and kihana miraya ross. 2016. "'Be Real Black for Me': Imagining Blackcrit in Education." *Urban Education* 51 (4): 415–42. https://doi.org/10.1177/0042085916628611.

Endo, Rachel. 2019. "Male of Color Refugee Teachers on Being Un/ Desirable Bodies of Difference in Education." *Equity & Excellence in Education* 52 (4): 448–64. https://doi.org/10.1080/10665684.2019 .1684220.

Ewing, Eve L. 2018. *Ghosts in the Schoolyard: Racism and School Closings on Chicago's South Side.* Chicago: University of Chicago Press.

Fanon, Frantz. 2008. *Black Skin, White Masks.* Translated by Richard Philcox. New York: Grove Press.

Fergus, Edward, Pedro Noguera, and Margary Martin. 2014. *Schooling for Resilience: Improving the Life Trajectory of Black and Latino Boys.* Cambridge: Harvard Education Press.

Ferguson, Ann Arnett. 2001. *Bad Boys: Public Schools in the Making of Black Masculinity.* Ann Arbor: University of Michigan Press.

Ferguson, Roderick. 2003. *Aberrations in Black: Toward a Queer of Color Critique.* Minneapolis: University of Minnesota Press.

Fine, Michelle. 1991. *Framing Dropouts: Notes on the Politics of an Urban High School.* Albany: SUNY Press.

Foley, Neil. 2017. *Mexicans in the Making of America.* Cambridge: Belknap Press, An Imprint of Harvard University Press.

Foucault, Michel. 2010. *The Birth of Biopolitics: Lectures at the Collège de France, 1978–1979.* Reprint ed. New York: Picador.

Foucault, Michel. 2011. *The Government of Self and Others: Lectures at the Collège de France, 1982–1983.* Edited by Frédéric Gros, Alessandro Fontana, and François Ewald. Translated by Graham Burchell. New York: Picador.

Freire, Paulo. 2000. *Pedagogy of the Oppressed.* 30th Anniversary ed. New York: Continuum.

Friedman, Milton. 2002. *Capitalism and Freedom.* 40th Anniversary ed. Chicago: University of Chicago Press.

Fryer, Roland G. 2011. "Financial Incentives and Student Achievement: Evidence from Randomized Trials." *Quarterly Journal of Economics* 126 (4): 1755–98.

Gamez, Rebeca. 2023. "Constructing Latinidad as a Constrained Credential: Anti-Blackness and Racialized Inequities in a Majority Latinx Middle School." *Anthropology & Education Quarterly.* https://doi.org/10.1111/aeq.12477.

Gamez, Rebeca, and Timothy Monreal. 2021. "'We Have That Opportunity Now': Black and Latinx Geographies, (Latinx) Racialization, and 'New Latinx South.'" *Journal of Leadership, Equity, and Research* 7 (2). https://eric.ed.gov/?id=EJ1301072.

Gándara, Patricia, and Frances Contreras. 2009. *The Latino Education Crisis: The Consequences of Failed Social Policies.* Cambridge: Harvard University Press.

García, Alma M. 1989. "The Development of Chicana Feminist Discourse, 1970–1980." *Gender & Society* 3 (2): 217–38.

García, Alma M., ed. 1997. *Chicana Feminist Thought: The Basic Historical Writings.* New York: Routledge.

García Peña, Lorgia. 2022. *Translating Blackness: Latinx Colonialities in Global Perspective.* Durham: Duke University Press.

Gershenson, Seth, Stephen B. Holt, and Nicholas W. Papageorge. 2016. "Who Believes in Me? The Effect of Student–Teacher Demographic Match on Teacher Expectations." *Economics of Education Review* 52 (June): 209–24. https://doi.org/10.1016/j.econedurev.2016.03.002.

Gilmore, Ruth Wilson. 2002. "Fatal Couplings of Power and Difference: Notes on Racism and Geography." *Professional Geographer* 54 (1): 15–24. https://doi.org/10.1111/0033-0124.00310.

Gilmore, Ruth Wilson. 2007. *Golden Gulag: Prisons, Surplus, Crisis, and Opposition in Globalizing California.* Berkeley: University of California Press.

Giroux, Henry A., and David E. Purpel. 1983. *The Hidden Curriculum and Moral Education: Deception or Discovery?* Berkeley, Calif.: McCutchan.

Givens, Jarvis R. 2021. *Fugitive Pedagogy: Carter G. Woodson and the Art of Black Teaching.* Cambridge: Harvard University Press.

Golann, Joanne W. 2015. "The Paradox of Success at a No-Excuses

School." *Sociology of Education* 88 (2): 103–19. https://doi.org/10.1177/0038040714567866.

Golann, Joanne W. 2021. *Scripting the Moves: Culture and Control in a "No-Excuses" Charter School.* Princeton, N.J.: Princeton University Press.

Golann, Joanne W., and A. Chris Torres. 2020. "Do No-Excuses Disciplinary Practices Promote Success?" *Journal of Urban Affairs* 42 (4): 617–33. https://doi.org/10.1080/07352166.2018.1427506.

Gonzalez, Norma, Luis C. Moll, and Cathy Amanti. 2006. *Funds of Knowledge: Theorizing Practices in Households, Communities, and Classrooms.* New York: Routledge.

Grant, Carl A., Ashley N. Woodson, and Michael J. Dumas, eds. 2020. *The Future Is Black.* New York: Routledge.

Grooms, Ain. 2019. "Turbulence in St. Louis County: School Transfers, Opportunity Hoarding, and the Legacy of *Brown.*" *Peabody Journal of Education* 94 (4): 403–19. https://doi.org/10.1080/0161956X.2019.1648952.

Halberstam, Jack. 2011. *The Queer Art of Failure.* Durham: Duke University Press.

Hall, Horace R. 2006. *Mentoring Young Men of Color: Meeting the Needs of African American and Latino Students.* Lanham, Md.: Rowman & Littlefield.

Harper, Shaun R. 2015. "Success in These Schools? Visual Counternarratives of Young Men of Color and Urban High Schools They Attend." *Urban Education* 50 (2): 139–69. https://doi.org/10.1177/0042085915569738.

Harris, Fredrick C. 2013. "The Rise of Respectability Politics." *Dissent* 61 (1): 33–37. https://doi.org/10.1353/dss.2014.0010.

Hartman, Saidiya. 1997. *Scenes of Subjection: Terror, Slavery, and Self-Making in Nineteenth-Century America.* New York: Oxford University Press.

Harvey, David. 2007. *A Brief History of Neoliberalism.* New York: Oxford University Press.

Hayek, F. A. 1996. *Individualism and Economic Order.* Reissue ed. Chicago: University of Chicago Press.

Haywood, Jasmine M. 2017. "Anti-Black Latino Racism in an Era of Trumpismo." *International Journal of Qualitative Studies in Education* 30 (10): 957–64. https://doi.org/10.1080/09518398.2017.1312613.

Hernández, Tanya Katerí. 2003. "Too Black to Be Latino/a: Blackness and Blacks as Foreigners in Latino Studies." *Latino Studies* 1 (March): 152–59. https://doi.org/10.1057/palgrave.lst.8600011.

Hernández, Tanya Katerí. 2022. *Racial Innocence: Unmasking Latino Anti-Black Bias and the Struggle for Equality*. Boston: Beacon Press.

Higginbotham, Evelyn Brooks. 1994. *Righteous Discontent: The Women's Movement in the Black Baptist Church, 1880–1920*. Rev. ed. Cambridge: Harvard University Press.

Holcombe, Madeline. 2019. "Baltimore Stands Up for Its City after Trump Tweets 'No Human Being Would Want to Live There' | CNN Politics." CNN, July 28, 2019. https://www.cnn.com/2019 /07/28/politics/baltimore-response-trump-tweets/index.html.

Hong, Grace Kyungwon. 2015. "Neoliberalism." *Critical Ethnic Studies* 1 (1): 56–67. https://doi.org/10.5749/jcritethnstud.1.1.0056.

Hong, Grace Kyungwon, and Roderick A. Ferguson. 2011. *Strange Affinities: The Gender and Sexual Politics of Comparative Racialization*. Durham: Duke University Press.

hooks, bell. 1994. *Teaching to Transgress: Education as the Practice of Freedom*. New York: Routledge.

Howard, Tyrone C. 2013. *Black Male(d): Peril and Promise in the Education of African American Males*. New York: Teachers College Press.

Huber, Lindsay Perez, Ofelia Huidor, Maria C. Malagon, Gloria Sanchez, and Daniel G. Solorzano. 2006. *Falling through the Cracks: Critical Transitions in the Latina/o Educational Pipeline. 2006 Latina/o Education Summit Report. CSRC Research Report. Number 7*. UCLA Chicano Studies Research Center. http://eric .ed.gov/?id=ED493397.

Huerta, Adrian H. 2018. "Educational Persistence in the Face of Violence: Narratives of Resilient Latino Male Youth." *Boyhood Studies* 11 (2): 94–113. https://doi.org/10.3167/bhs.2018.110206.

Huerta, Adrian H., Tyrone C. Howard, and Bianca N. Haro. 2020. "Supporting Black and Latino Boys in School: A Call to Action." *Phi Delta Kappan* 102 (1): 29–33. https://doi.org/10.1177/0031721 720956846.

Hutchings, Quortne R. 2023. "Blackness Preferred, Queerness Deferred: Navigating Sense of Belonging in Black Male Initiative and Men of Color Mentorship Programs." *International Journal of Quali-*

tative Studies in Education. https://doi.org/10.1080/09518398 .2023.2181457.

INCITE! 2017. *The Revolution Will Not Be Funded: Beyond the Non-Profit Industrial Complex.* Reprint ed. Durham: Duke University Press.

Jackson, Iesha, Yolanda Sealey-Ruiz, and Wanda Watson. 2014. "Reciprocal Love: Mentoring Black and Latino Males through an Ethos of Care." *Urban Education* 49 (4): 394–417. https://doi.org/10.1177 /0042085913519336.

Johnson, Gaye Theresa. 2013. *Spaces of Conflict, Sounds of Solidarity: Music, Race, and Spatial Entitlement in Los Angeles.* Berkeley: University of California Press.

Johnson, Patrick, and David Philoxene. 2019. "It Makes Me *Feel* Like I'm a Monster: Navigating Notions of Damage in This Work." In *"We Dare Say Love": Supporting Achievement in the Educational Life of Black Boys,* edited by Na'ilah Suad Nasir, Jarvis R. Givens, and Christopher P. Chatmon, 68–80. New York: Teachers College Press.

Kaba, Mariame. 2021. *We Do This 'Til We Free Us: Abolitionist Organizing and Transforming Justice.* Chicago: Haymarket Books.

Kelley, Robin D. G. 2003. *Freedom Dreams: The Black Radical Imagination.* Boston: Beacon Press.

Khasnabis, Debi, and Simona Goldin. 2020. "Don't Be Fooled, Trauma Is a Systemic Problem: Trauma as a Case of Weaponized Educational Innovation." *Occasional Paper Series* 2020 (43). https:// educate.bankstreet.edu/occasional-paper-series/vol2020/iss43/5.

Kim, Catherine Y., Daniel J. Losen, and Damon T. Hewitt. 2010. *The School-to-Prison Pipeline: Structuring Legal Reform.* New York: NYU Press.

Kincheloe, Joe L., and Peter McLaren. 2011. "Rethinking Critical Theory and Qualitative Research." In *Key Works in Critical Pedagogy,* edited by Kecia Hayes, Shirley R. Steinberg, and Kenneth Tobin, 285–326. Bold Visions in Educational Research 32. Lanham, Md.: SensePublishers. https://doi.org/10.1007/978-94-6091-397-6_23.

Klein, Naomi. 2008. *The Shock Doctrine: The Rise of Disaster Capitalism.* Picador.

Kohl-Arenas, Erica. 2015. *The Self-Help Myth: How Philanthropy Fails to Alleviate Poverty.* Oakland: University of California Press.

Kozol, Jonathan. 2012. *Savage Inequalities: Children in America's Schools.* Reprint ed. New York: Broadway Books.

Kugiya, Jase, Jorge Burmicky, and Victor B. Sáenz. 2020. "High-Achieving Latino Men and Men of Color Programs: Perspectives from Community College Program Staff." *Journal of Minority Achievement, Creativity, and Leadership* 1 (2): 188–217. https://doi.org/10.5325/minoachicrealead.1.2.0188.

Kun, Josh, and Laura Pulido, eds. 2013. *Black and Brown in Los Angeles: Beyond Conflict and Coalition.* Berkeley: University of California Press.

Kwon, Soo Ah. 2013. *Uncivil Youth: Race, Activism, and Affirmative Governmentality.* Durham: Duke University Press.

Ladson-Billings, Gloria. 1995. "Toward a Theory of Culturally Relevant Pedagogy." *American Educational Research Journal* 32 (3): 465–91. https://doi.org/10.3102/00028312032003465.

Ladson-Billings, Gloria, and William Tate. 1995. "Toward a Critical Race Theory of Education." *Teachers College Record* 97 (January): 47–68.

Lara, Gilberto P., and María E. Fránquiz. 2015. "Latino Bilingual Teachers: Negotiating the Figured World of Masculinity." *Bilingual Research Journal* 38 (2): 207–27. https://doi.org/10.1080/15235882.2015.1066720.

LeCompte, Margaret D., and Jean J. Schensul. 2012. *Analysis and Interpretation of Ethnographic Data: A Mixed Methods Approach.* 2nd ed. Lanham, Md.: AltaMira Press.

Leonardo, Zeus. 2007. "The War on Schools: NCLB, Nation Creation, and the Educational Construction of Whiteness." *Race Ethnicity and Education* 10 (3): 261–78. https://doi.org/10.1080/13613320701503249.

Leonardo, Zeus. 2009. *Race, Whiteness, and Education.* New York: Routledge.

Leonardo, Zeus. 2013. *Race Frameworks: A Multidimensional Theory of Racism and Education.* New York: Teachers College Press.

Leonardo, Zeus, and Margaret Hunter. 2007. "Imagining the Urban: The Politics of Race, Class, and Schooling." In *International Handbook of Urban Education,* edited by W. T. Pink and G. W. Noblit, 779–801. Dordrecht: Springer. https://doi.org/10.1007/978-1-4020-5199-9_41.

Lewis, Oscar. 2011. *The Children of Sanchez: Autobiography of a Mexican Family*. 50th Anniversary ed. New York: Vintage.

Lindsay, Keisha. 2018. *In a Classroom of Their Own: The Intersection of Race and Feminist Politics in All-Black Male Schools*. Urbana: University of Illinois Press.

Lipman, Pauline. 2011. *The New Political Economy of Urban Education: Neoliberalism, Race, and the Right to the City*. New York: Taylor & Francis.

Liu, Roseann, and Savannah Shange. 2018. "Toward Thick Solidarity: Theorizing Empathy in Social Justice Movements." *Radical History Review* 2018 (131): 189–98. https://doi.org/10.1215/01636545-435 5341.

Lopez, Alan Pelaez. 2020. *Intergalactic Travels: Poems from a Fugitive Alien*. Brooklyn: Operating System Kin.

López, Ian Haney. 1996. *White by Law: The Legal Construction of Race*. New York: New York University Press.

López, Ian F. Haney. 2004. *Racism on Trial: The Chicano Fight for Justice*. Cambridge: Belknap Press, An Imprint of Harvard University Press.

Lopez, Nancy. 2002. *Hopeful Girls, Troubled Boys: Race and Gender Disparity in Urban Education*. New York: Routledge.

Lorde, Audre. 2007. *Sister Outsider: Essays and Speeches*. Berkeley, Calif.: Crossing Press.

Love, Bettina L. 2019. *We Want to Do More Than Survive: Abolitionist Teaching and the Pursuit of Educational Freedom*. Boston: Beacon Press.

Lynn, Marvin. 1999. "Toward a Critical Race Pedagogy: A Research Note." *Urban Education* 33 (5): 606–26. https://doi.org/10.1177/0042085999335004.

Lynn, Marvin. 2006a. "Dancing between Two Worlds: A Portrait of the Life of a Black Male Teacher in South Central LA." *International Journal of Qualitative Studies in Education* 19 (2): 221–42. https://doi.org/10.1080/09518390600576111.

Lynn, Marvin. 2006b. "Education for the Community: Exploring the Culturally Relevant Practices of Black Male Teachers." *Teachers College Record* 108 (12): 2497–2522. https://doi.org/10.1111/j.1467-9620.2006.00792.x.

Lynn, Marvin, and Michael E. Jennings. 2009. "Power, Politics, and

Critical Race Pedagogy: A Critical Race Analysis of Black Male Teachers' Pedagogy." *Race Ethnicity and Education* 12 (2): 173–96. https://doi.org/10.1080/13613320902995467.

Malagon, Maria C. 2010. "All the Losers Go There: Challenging the Deficit Educational Discourse of Chicano Racialized Masculinity in a Continuation High School." *Educational Foundations* 24: 59–76.

Males, Mike A. 1996. *The Scapegoat Generation: America's War on Adolescents*. Monroe, Me: Common Courage Press.

Malone, Hui-Ling S., Sara McAlister, and Wendy Y. Perez. 2023. "Navigating Intersectionality and Positionality within Black and Latinx Youth Organizing Spaces." *Youth & Society*, https://doi.org/10.1177/0044118X231159710.

Marable, Manning. 1999. *How Capitalism Underdeveloped Black America: Problems in Race, Political Economy, and Society*. Cambridge, Mass.: South End Press.

Marquez, Bayley J. 2021. "'No Women Involved': Settler Colonial Racial Grammars in Black and Indigenous Education." *Feminist Formations* 33 (3): 116–39. https://doi.org/10.1353/ff.2021.0042.

Márquez, John D. 2014. *Black-Brown Solidarity: Racial Politics in the New Gulf South*. Austin: University of Texas Press.

Márquez, Lorena V. 2020. *La Gente: Struggles for Empowerment and Community Self-Determination in Sacramento*. Tucson: University of Arizona Press.

Martino, Wayne. 2015. "The Limits of Role Modeling as a Basis for Critical Multicultural Education: The Case of Black Male Teachers in Urban Schools." *Multicultural Education Review* 7 (1–2): 59–84. https://doi.org/10.1080/2005615X.2015.1061929.

Martino, Wayne, and Blye Frank. 2006. "The Tyranny of Surveillance: Male Teachers and the Policing of Masculinities in a Single Sex School." *Gender and Education* 18 (1): 17–33. https://doi.org/10.1080/09540250500194914.

Martino, Wayne, and Goli Rezai-Rashti. 2012. *Gender, Race, and the Politics of Role Modelling: The Influence of Male Teachers*. New York: Routledge.

McCready, Lance T. 2010. *Making Space for Diverse Masculinities: Difference, Intersectionality, and Engagement in an Urban High School*. New York: Peter Lang.

McCready, Lance T. 2019. "Queeruptions, Queer of Color Analysis, Radical Action, and Education Reform: An Introduction." *Equity &*

Excellence in Education 52 (4): 370–72. https://doi.org/10.1080/1066 5684.2019.1705206.

McKittrick, Katherine, and Clyde Woods, eds. 2007. *Black Geographies and the Politics of Place.* Toronto: Between the Lines.

Meiners, Erica R. 2011. "Ending the School-to-Prison Pipeline/Building Abolition Futures." *Urban Review* 43 (4): 547–65. https://doi .org/10.1007/s11256-011-0187-9.

Melamed, Jodi. 2006. "The Spirit of Neoliberalism: From Racial Liberalism to Neoliberal Multiculturalism." *Social Text* 24 (4 [89]): 1–24. https://doi.org/10.1215/01642472-2006-009.

Melamed, Jodi. 2011. *Represent and Destroy: Rationalizing Violence in the New Racial Capitalism.* Minneapolis: University of Minnesota Press.

Mirande, Alfredo. 1997. *Hombres y Machos: Masculinity and Latino Culture.* Boulder: Westview Press.

Molina, Natalia, Daniel Martinez HoSang, and Ramón A. Gutiérrez, eds. 2019. *Relational Formations of Race: Theory, Method, and Practice.* Oakland: University of California Press.

Moraga, Cherríe, and Gloria Anzaldúa, eds. 1983. *This Bridge Called My Back: Writings by Radical Women of Color.* 2nd ed. Kitchen Table, Women of Color Press.

Morales, Paolo Zitlali, Tina M. Trujillo, and René Espinoza Kissell. 2016. "Educational Policy and Latin@ Youth." In *Educational Policy and Youth in the 21st Century: Problems, Potential, and Progress,* edited by Sharon L Nichols, 3–22. Charlotte, N.C.: Information Age Publishing.

Morris, Monique W. 2016. *Pushout: The Criminalization of Black Girls in Schools.* New York: The New Press.

Muñoz, Carlos. 2007. *Youth, Identity, Power: The Chicano Movement.* Rev. and exp. ed. London: Verso.

Muñoz, José Esteban. 1999. *Disidentifications: Queers of Color and the Performance of Politics.* Minneapolis: University of Minnesota Press.

Museus, Samuel D. 2022. "Relative Racialization and Asian American College Student Activism." *Harvard Educational Review* 92 (2): 182–205. https://doi.org/10.17763/1943-5045-92.2.182.

Nasir, Na'ilah Suad, Jarvis R. Givens, and Christopher P. Chatmon, eds. 2018. *"We Dare Say Love": Supporting Achievement in the Educational Life of Black Boys.* New York: Teachers College Press.

Nieto, Sonia. 1999. *The Light in Their Eyes: Creating Multicultural Learning Communities*. New York: Teachers College Press.

Noguera, Pedro A. 1996. "Responding to the Crisis Confronting California's Black Male Youth: Providing Support without Furthering Marginalization." *Journal of Negro Education* 65 (2): 219–36. https://doi.org/10.2307/2967315.

Noguera, Pedro A. 2003. "The Trouble with Black Boys: The Role and Influence of Environmental and Cultural Factors on the Academic Performance of African American Males." *Urban Education* 38 (4): 431–59. https://doi.org/10.1177/0042085903038004005.

Noguera, Pedro A. 2009. *The Trouble with Black Boys: . . . And Other Reflections on Race, Equity, and the Future of Public Education*. San Francisco: Jossey-Bass.

Noguera, Pedro A. 2012. "Saving Black and Latino Boys: What Schools Can Do to Make a Difference." *Phi Delta Kappan* 93 (5): 8–12. https://doi.org/10.1177/003172171209300503.

Noguera, Pedro, Aída Hurtado, and Edward Fergus, eds. 2011. *Invisible No More: Understanding the Disenfranchisement of Latino Men and Boys*. New York: Routledge.

Nolan, Kathleen. 2011. *Police in the Hallways: Discipline in an Urban High School*. Minneapolis: University of Minnesota Press.

Obama, Barack. 2014a. "Remarks by the President on 'My Brother's Keeper' Initiative." Whitehouse.Gov. February 27, 2014. https:// obamawhitehouse.archives.gov/the-press-office/2014/02/27/ remarks-president-my-brothers-keeper-initiative.

Obama, Barack. 2014b. "Remarks by the President at My Brother's Keeper Town Hall." Whitehouse.Gov. July 21, 2014. https:// obamawhitehouse.archives.gov/the-press-office/2014/07/21/ remarks-president-my-brothers-keeper-town-hall.

O'Connor, Carla. 1997. "Dispositions toward (Collective) Struggle and Educational Resilience in the Inner City: A Case Analysis of Six African-American High School Students." *American Educational Research Journal* 34 (4): 593–629. https://doi.org/10.3102/0002 8312034004593.

Odih, Pamela. 2002. "Mentors and Role Models: Masculinity and the Educational 'Underachievement' of Young Afro-Caribbean Males." *Race Ethnicity and Education* 5 (1): 91–105. https://doi.org/10.1080/ 13613320120117216.

Oeur, Freeden Blume. 2018. *Black Boys Apart: Racial Uplift and Respectability in All-Male Public Schools.* Minneapolis: University of Minnesota Press.

Offutt-Chaney, Mahasan. 2023. "Disciplining Our Own: Politicizing the Image of the Strict Black Principals, 1970–1985." *Journal of Urban History*, January. https://doi.org/10.1177/0096144222 1142061.

Okihiro, Gary Y. 2016. *Third World Studies: Theorizing Liberation.* Durham: Duke University Press.

Omi, Michael, and Howard Winant. 2014. *Racial Formation in the United States.* 3rd ed. New York: Routledge.

Pabon, Amber. 2016. "Waiting for Black Superman: A Look at a Problematic Assumption." *Urban Education* 51 (8): 915–39. https://doi .org/10.1177/0042085914553673.

Paris, Django, and H. Samy Alim. 2017. *Culturally Sustaining Pedagogies: Teaching and Learning for Justice in a Changing World.* New York: Teachers College Press.

Patrón, Oscar E., and Jorge Burmicky. 2023. "It Is 'Just as Personal as It Is Academic': Mobilizing an Intersectional Lens for the Study of Latino Men." *Journal of Diversity in Higher Education,* https://doi .org/10.1037/dhe0000473.

Pedroni, Thomas, and Michael W. Apple. 2005. "Conservative Alliance Building and African American Support of Vouchers: The End of *Brown's* Promise or a New Beginning?" *Teachers College Record* 107 (9): 2068–2105.

Purnell, Derecka. 2019. "Opinion | Why Does Obama Scold Black Boys?" *New York Times,* February 23, 2019, sec. Opinion. https:// www.nytimes.com/2019/02/23/opinion/my-brothers-keeper -obama.html.

Purnell, Derecka. 2021. *Becoming Abolitionists: Police, Protests, and the Pursuit of Freedom.* New York: Astra House.

Quesada, Uriel, Letitia Gomez, and Salvador Vidal-Ortiz, eds. 2015. *Queer Brown Voices: Personal Narratives of Latina/o LGBT Activism.* Austin: University of Texas Press.

Rezai-Rashti, Goli M., and Wayne J. Martino. 2010. "Black Male Teachers as Role Models: Resisting the Homogenizing Impulse of Gender and Racial Affiliation." *American Educational Research Journal* 47 (1): 37–64. https://doi.org/10.3102/0002831209351563.

Rios, Victor M. 2011. *Punished: Policing the Lives of Black and Latino Boys.* New York: NYU Press.

Rios, Victor M. 2017. *Human Targets: Schools, Police, and the Criminalization of Latino Youth.* Chicago: University of Chicago Press.

Rios, Victor, and Rebeca Mireles-Rios. 2019. *My Teacher Believes in Me! The Educator's Guide to At-Promise Students.* CreateSpace Independent Publishing Platform.

Ritchie, Andrea, and Angela Y. Davis. 2017. *Invisible No More: Police Violence against Black Women and Women of Color.* Boston: Beacon Press.

Robinson, Cedric J. 2000. *Black Marxism: The Making of the Black Radical Tradition.* 2nd ed. Chapel Hill: University of North Carolina Press.

Rodríguez, Dylan. 2010. "The Disorientation of the Teaching Act: Abolition as Pedagogical Position." *Radical Teacher* 88 (1): 7–19. https://doi.org/10.1353/rdt.2010.0006.

Rodríguez, Dylan. 2017. "The Political Logic of the Non-profit Industrial Complex." In *The Revolution Will Not Be Funded: Beyond the Non-profit Industrial Complex,* edited by Incite!, 21–40. Durham: Duke University Press.

Rodríguez, Richard T. 2009. *Next of Kin: The Family in Chicano/a Cultural Politics.* Durham: Duke University Press.

Román, Miriam Jiménez, and Juan Flores, eds. 2010. *The Afro-Latin@ Reader: History and Culture in the United States.* Durham: Duke University Press.

Rosales, F. Arturo, and Francisco A. Rosales. 1997. *Chicano! The History of the Mexican American Civil Rights Movement.* 2nd rev. ed. Houston: Arte Publico Press.

Rothstein, Richard. 2017. *The Color of Law: A Forgotten History of How Our Government Segregated America.* New York: Liveright.

Saenz, Victor B., and Luis Ponjuan. 2009. "The Vanishing Latino Male in Higher Education." *Journal of Hispanic Higher Education* 8 (1): 54–89. https://doi.org/10.1177/1538192708326995.

Sáenz, Victor B., and Luis Ponjuan. 2011. *Men of Color: Ensuring the Academic Success of Latino Males in Higher Education.* Institute for Higher Education Policy. https://eric.ed.gov/?id=ED527060.

Sáenz, Victor B., Luis Ponjuán, and Julie López Figueroa. 2016. *Ensuring the Success of Latino Males in Higher Education: A National Imperative.* Sterling, Va.: Stylus Publishing.

Sáenz, Victor B., Luis Ponjuan, Jorge Segovia, and José Del Real Vi-ramontes. 2015. "Developing a Latino Mentoring Program: Project MALES (Mentoring to Achieve Latino Educational Success)." *New Directions for Higher Education* 2015 (171): 75–85. https://doi .org/10.1002/he.20144.

Salas Pujols, Jomaira. 2022. "'It's About the Way I'm Treated': Afro-Latina Black Identity Development in the Third Space." *Youth & Society* 54 (4): 593–610. https://doi.org/10.1177/0044118X20982314.

Sampson, Carrie, Dawn Demps, and Sara Rodriguez-Martinez. 2020. "Engaging (or Not) in Coalition Politics: A Case Study of Black and Latinx Community Advocacy toward Educational Equity." *Race Ethnicity and Education*. https://doi.org/10.1080/13613324.2020.18 42346.

Sánchez, Bernadette, Patricia Esparza, and Yarí Colón. 2008. "Natural Mentoring under the Microscope: An Investigation of Mentoring Relationships and Latino Adolescents' Academic Performance." *Journal of Community Psychology* 36 (4): 468–82. https://doi.org/ 10.1002/jcop.20250.

Santa Ana, Otto. 2002. *Brown Tide Rising: Metaphors of Latinos in Contemporary American Public Discourse*. Austin: University of Texas Press.

Savedra, Madison. 2021. "Adam Toledo, Boy Killed by Chicago Cop, Remembered by National Museum of Mexican Art." *Block Club Chicago*, September 23, 2021. https://blockclubchicago.org/ 2021/09/23/adam-toledo-boy-killed-by-chicago-cop-honored-by -national-museum-of-mexican-art/.

Schott. 2010. "Yes, We Can: The 2010 Schott 50-State Report on Public Education of Black Males." Cambridge, Mass.: Schott Foundation. www.blackboysreport.org.

Schram, Thomas H. 2005. *Conceptualizing and Proposing Qualitative Research*. 2nd ed. Upper Saddle River, N.J.: Pearson.

Scott, Janelle. 2009. "The Politics of Venture Philanthropy in Charter School Policy and Advocacy." *Educational Policy* 23 (1): 106–36. https://doi.org/10.1177/0895904808328531.

Scott, Janelle T. 2013. "A Rosa Parks Moment? School Choice and the Marketization of Civil Rights." *Critical Studies in Education* 54 (1): 5–18. https://doi.org/10.1080/17508487.2013.739570.

Scott, Janelle, and Catherine DiMartino. 2009. "Public Education under New Management: A Typology of Educational Privatization

Applied to New York City's Restructuring." *Peabody Journal of Education* 84 (3): 432–52. https://doi.org/10.1080/01619560902973647.

Serrano, Uriel, David C. Turner, Gabriel Regalado, and Alejandro Banuelos. 2022. "Towards Community Rooted Research and Praxis: Reflections on the BSS Safety and Youth Justice Project." *Social Sciences* 11 (5): 195. https://doi.org/10.3390/socsci11050195.

Shange, Savannah. 2019. *Progressive Dystopia: Abolition, Antiblackness, and Schooling in San Francisco*. Durham: Duke University Press.

Sharpe, Christina. 2016. *In the Wake: On Blackness and Being*. Durham: Duke University Press.

Shiekh, Irum, dir. 1999. *On Strike! Ethnic Studies, 1969–1999*. Fifth Floor Productions.

Singh, Michael V. 2018. "Role Models without Guarantees: Corrective Representations and the Cultural Politics of a Latino Male Teacher in the Borderlands." *Race Ethnicity and Education* 21 (3): 288–305. https://doi.org/10.1080/13613324.2017.1395330.

Singh, Michael V. 2019. "Refusing the Performance: Disrupting Popular Discourses Surrounding Latino Male Teachers and the Possibility of Disidentification." *Educational Studies* 55 (1): 28–45. https://doi.org/10.1080/00131946.2018.1545654.

Singh, Michael V. 2021a. "Resisting the Neoliberal Role Model: Latino Male Mentors' Perspectives on the Intersectional Politics of Role Modeling." *American Educational Research Journal* 58 (2): 283–314. https://doi.org/10.3102/0002831220954861.

Singh, Michael V. 2021b. "Seven Justice-Oriented Principles for Men of Color Working with Boys of Color." *Project MALES Practice Brief*, no. 1 (September): 1–10.

Singh, Michael V. 2023. "Negotiating Antiblackness as Non-Black Latino Men Teachers: Relational Race Politics in the Discourse on Men of Color Teachers." *Urban Education*. https://doi.org/10.1177/00420859231162901.

Singh, Nikhil Pal. 2004. *Black Is a Country: Race and the Unfinished Struggle for Democracy*. Cambridge: Harvard University Press.

Smith, Linda Tuhiwai. 2012. *Decolonizing Methodologies: Research and Indigenous Peoples*. 2nd. ed. London: Zed Books.

Sojoyner, Damien M. 2016. *First Strike: Educational Enclosures in Black Los Angeles*. Minneapolis: University of Minnesota Press.

Solorzano, Daniel G., and Tara J. Yosso. 2001. "Critical Race and LatCrit Theory and Method: Counter-Storytelling." *International*

Journal of Qualitative Studies in Education 14 (4): 471–95. https://doi.org/10.1080/09518390110063365.

Spence, Lester K. 2012. "The Neoliberal Turn in Black Politics." *Souls* 14 (3–4): 139–59. https://doi.org/10.1080/10999949.2012.763682.

Spence, Lester K. 2016. *Knocking the Hustle: Against the Neoliberal Turn in Black Politics.* Brooklyn: Punctum Books.

Stahl, Garth, Joseph Nelson, and Derron Wallace, eds. 2017. *Masculinity and Aspiration in an Era of Neoliberal Education: International Perspectives.* New York: Routledge.

Stovall, David Omotoso. 2016. *Born Out of Struggle: Critical Race Theory, School Creation, and the Politics of Interruption.* Albany: SUNY Press.

Stovall, David. 2018. "Are We Ready for 'School' Abolition? Thoughts and Practices of Radical Imaginary in Education." *Taboo: The Journal of Culture and Education* 17 (1). https://doi.org/10.31390/taboo.17.1.06.

Straus, Emily E. 2009. "Unequal Pieces of a Shrinking Pie: The Struggle between African Americans and Latinos over Education, Employment, and Empowerment in Compton, California." *History of Education Quarterly* 49 (4): 507–29.

Swadener, Beth Blue, and Sally Lubeck, eds. 1995. *Children and Families "at Promise": Deconstructing the Discourse of Risk.* Albany: SUNY Press.

Symcox, Linda. 2001. *Whose History? The Struggle for National Standards in American Classrooms.* New York: Teachers College Press.

Takaki, Ronald. 2008. *A Different Mirror: A History of Multicultural America.* Rev. ed. New York: Back Bay Books.

Tieken, Mara Casey, and Trevor Ray Auldridge-Reveles. 2019. "Rethinking the School Closure Research: School Closure as Spatial Injustice." *Review of Educational Research* 89 (6): 917–53. https://doi.org/10.3102/0034654319877151.

Torres, Mellie. 2017. "'Without My Education, I Can't Be Somebody': Latino Masculinity, School Contexts, and Aspiration." In *Masculinity and Aspiration in an Era of Neoliberal Education: International Perspectives,* edited by Garth Stahl, Joseph Nelson, and Derron Wallace, 126–44. New York: Routledge.

Tuck, Eve. 2009. "Suspending Damage: A Letter to Communities." *Harvard Educational Review* 79 (3): 409–28.

Tuck, Eve, and K. Wayne Yang. 2014. "R-Words: Refusing Research."

In *Humanizing Research: Decolonizing Qualitative Inquiry with Youth and Communities*, edited by Django Paris and Maisha T. Winn, 223–47. Thousand Oaks, Calif.: Sage.

Tuck, Eve, and K. Wayne Yang, eds. 2018. *Toward What Justice? Describing Diverse Dreams of Justice in Education*. New York: Routledge.

Turner, David C. 2021. "The (Good) Trouble with Black Boys: Organizing with Black Boys and Young Men in George Floyd's America." *Theory Into Practice* 60 (4): 422–33. https://doi.org/10.1080/0 0405841.2021.1983317.

Valencia, Richard R. 2010. *Dismantling Contemporary Deficit Thinking*. New York: Routledge.

Valenzuela, Angela. 1999. *Subtractive Schooling: U.S.-Mexican Youth and the Politics of Caring*. Albany: SUNY Press.

Villavicencio, Adriana. 2021. *Am I My Brother's Keeper? Educational Opportunities and Outcomes for Black and Brown Boys*. Cambridge: Harvard Education Press.

Villegas, Ana María, and Jacqueline Jordan Irvine. 2010. "Diversifying the Teaching Force: An Examination of Major Arguments." *Urban Review* 42 (3): 175–92. https://doi.org/10.1007/s11256-010-0150-1.

Vitali, Ali, Kassie Hunt, and Frank Thorp V. 2018. "Trump Referred to Haiti and African Nations as 'Shithole' Countries." NBC News, January 12, 2018. https://www.nbcnews.com/politics/white-house/trump-referred-haiti-african-countries-shithole-nations-n836946.

Wacquant, Loïc. 2009. *Punishing the Poor: The Neoliberal Government of Social Insecurity*. Durham: Duke University Press.

Warren, Chezare A. 2020. "Meeting Myself: Race-Gender Oppression and a Genre Study of Black Men Teachers' Interactions with Black Boys." *Race Ethnicity and Education* 23 (3): 367–91. https://doi.org/10.1080/13613324.2019.1663982.

Watkins, William H. 2001. *The White Architects of Black Education: Ideology and Power in America, 1865–1954*. 2nd ed. New York: Teachers College Press.

Watson, Wanda, Yolanda Sealey-Ruiz, and Iesha Jackson. 2016. "Daring to Care: The Role of Culturally Relevant Care in Mentoring Black and Latino Male High School Students." *Race Ethnicity and Education* 19 (5): 980–1002. https://doi.org/10.1080/13613324.2014.911169.

Weiner, L., and M. Compton, eds. 2008. *The Global Assault on Teaching, Teachers, and Their Unions: Stories for Resistance.* New York: Palgrave Macmillan.

Weiston-Serdan, Torie. 2017. *Critical Mentoring: A Practical Guide.* Sterling, Va.: Stylus.

Wilderson, Frank. 2020. *Afropessimism.* New York: Liveright.

Williams, Juliet A. 2016. *The Separation Solution? Single-Sex Education and the New Politics of Gender Equality.* Oakland: University of California Press.

Winant, Howard. 2002. *The World Is a Ghetto: Race and Democracy since World War II.* New York: Basic Books.

Winn, Maisha T. 2018. *Justice on Both Sides: Transforming Education through Restorative Justice.* Cambridge: Harvard Education Press.

Woodson, Ashley N., and Amber Pabon. 2016. "'I'm None of the Above': Exploring Themes of Heteropatriarchy in the Life Histories of Black Male Educators." *Equity & Excellence in Education* 49 (1): 57–71. https://doi.org/10.1080/10665684.2015.1121456.

Yosso, Tara J. 2005. "Whose Culture Has Capital? A Critical Race Theory Discussion of Community Cultural Wealth." *Race Ethnicity and Education* 8 (1): 69–91. https://doi.org/10.1080/136133205200 0341006.

Yosso, Tara J., and David Gumaro García. 2010. "From Ms. J. to Ms. G.: Analyzing Racial Microaggressions in Hollywood's Urban School Genre." In *Hollywood's Exploited: Education, Politics, and Public Life,* edited by Benjamin Frymer, Tony Kashani, Anthony J. Nocella II, and Rich Van Heertum, 85–103. New York: Palgrave Macmillan.

BIBLIOGRAPHY

Michael V. Singh is assistant professor in the Department of Chicana/o Studies at the University of California, Davis.

Printed and bound by CPI Group (UK) Ltd, Croydon, CR0 4YY

09/05/2024

14500138-0002